Shiva Purana

The Great Hindu Epic of the Indestructible Destroyer

Swami Divyananda

GRAPEVINE INDIA

Published by

GRAPEVINE INDIA PUBLISHERS PVT LTD

www.grapevineindia.com
Delhi | Mumbai
email: grapevineindiapublishers@gmail.com

Ordering Information:
Quantity sales: Special discounts are available on quantity
purchases by corporations, associations, and others.
For details, reach out to the publisher.

First published by Grapevine India 2023

Please note that the focus of this book is to
bring back the forgotten stories about Lord Siva.
This is why the book is written
keeping in mind only the stories.

The Doubt of the Sages

Vyasa said: —

Sages of edified souls, engaged in truthful rites, powerful and blessed, performed a great sacrifice at the confluence of Gaṅga and Kalindi (Yamuna) in the most sacred city of Prayaga, a great holy centre, the path that leads to Brahmaloka. On hearing that a sacrifice was being performed there, the disciple of Vyasa, the great sage Suta, an excellent scholar in the Puranas, arrived there to see the sages. The sages were delighted on seeing him and received him with due hospitality and adoration.

The due adoration being completed, the noble sages, being highly pleased, addressed him in all humility with their palms joined in reverence.

'O Romaharsana, the omniscient, by thy weighty fortune, the entire Puranic lore, pregnant in its meaningful content, has been secured by thee from Vyasa. Hence thou art the receptacle of wonder-inspiring stories, even as the vast ocean is the storehouse of gems of great worth. There is nothing in the three worlds that is not known to thee, of the past, present and future.

It is our great fortune that thou thyself hast come to pay a visit to us. Hence it is not proper on thy part to return without doing us a favour. Indeed, we have already listened to the explanation of the auspicious and the inauspicious. But we are not content. We yearn to hear more and more.

Now, O Suta of good mentality, we have only one point to be clarified. If thou dost desire to bless us, please explain the same, though it is the secret of secrets.'

At the advent of the terrible age of Kali men have become devoid of merits. They are engaged in evil ways of life. They have turned their faces from truthful avocations. They are engaged in calumniating others. They covet other men's wealth. Their attention is diverted to other men's wives. Injuring others has become their chief aim.

They view the physical body as the soul, deluded as they are; they are atheists of mere brutish sense; they hate their parents; their wives are goddesses unto them; they are slaves to lust.

Brahmins are in the clutches of greed, they sell Vedas for livelihood; they acquire learning as a means of earning money; they are deluded by their false pride. They have forsaken the duties of their own castes; they have almost become swindlers of others; they do not offer Sandhya prayers thrice a day; they are deprived of Vedic enlightenment. They are ruthless; they make much of their little knowledge; they have discarded many of their rites and good conduct of life; they have taken to agriculture as their profession; cruelty has become second nature to them; their ideas have become dirty and defiled.

Similarly the Ksatriyas also have discarded their duties; they associate with evil men; they indulge in sinful activities; vice and debauchery have become their main aim in life. They have ceased to be valorous; they never take interest in virtuous warfare; they flee from the battlefield; they follow the mean tactics of thieves and Sudras; they are mentally enslaved by base passions.

They have eschewed the practice of miraculous weapons; they never care to protect cows and brahmins; they no longer consider it their duty to protect those who seek refuge in them; they always indulge in brutish sexual dalliance with their damsels. The good virtue of protecting their subjects they have thrown over-board; they strictly adhere to sensual enjoyment; they are wicked annihilators of their own people; they rejoice in the harassment of all living beings.

VaiSyas too no longer perform holy rites; they have cast off their traditional virtue; they have taken to crooked ways to earn more and more; they are now notorious for their malpractices with the weighing balance. They are no longer devoted to preceptors, gods and brahmins; their intellect has become distorted; miserly and tight-fisted they no longer feed the brahmins.

They take delight in being the paramours of beautiful women; squalid and filthy in their ideas and deluded by cupidity they have lost clear thinking; they have abandoned their zeal for Pnrta and other holy rites such as digging wells, tanks, planting trees and parks. Similarly most of the Sudras have become depraved. Some of them show their interest in leading the life of brahmins with shining forms and features; they too in the confusion of their minds have abandoned their traditional practices. In their eagerness to appropriate a brahmanical splendour they frequently perform penances. They cause infantile and premature deaths by their chanting of mantras.

They worship the Salagrama stone and other things; they evince some interest in Homas too but in their thoughts and actions they are crooked and antagonistic; they calumniate the brahmins. Rich people indulge in misdeeds; learned people take perpetual delight in disputations; those who conduct discourses in holy narratives and expound virtuous rites of worship, themselves abandon virtuous practice of the same. Haughty persons assume the features of noble kings; those who liberally give, do so with a lot of fuss and haughtiness thinking themselves to be great lords and treating the brahmins and others as their servants.

Devoid of the strict observance of their traditional duties and virtues, the foolish people have brought about an admixture of various castes. Cruel in thought and obsessed by false prestiges, people have discarded the four-fold system of social classification.

Deluded people, wrongly considering themselves high-born, perform certain good rites which result only in the upset of the caste-order and down-fall of all people. Women, too, generally misbehave and err; they slight their husbands; they are inimical to their fathers-in-law; fearlessly they pursue their nefarious activities.

They indulge in foul coquettish gestures; they are carried away by amorous dispositions; their conduct is bad; they pursue illicit connections with paramours; they turn away from their own husbands.

As for sons, they are invariably wicked without any filial affection; they take lessons in ignorant activities and succumb to various ailments. O Suta, how can these deluded people who have abandoned their traditional virtues get salvation here and hereafter.

Hence our minds are always agitated. Indeed there is no virtue equal to helping others. Since thou art conversant with the essentials of all tenets, please tell us the easiest remedy for the immediate destruction of the sins of these people.

Vyasa said: —

On hearing these words of the sages of sanctified souls Suta thought of Siva and told them thus.

Answers Clarifying the Doubts of the Sages

Suta said: —

O saintly men, the question that you put me is very pertinent. Prompted by my love towards you all I shall, remembering my preceptor, the benefactor of the three worlds, tell you everything. All of you listen attentively.

The entire essence of Vedanta is contained in the excellent Sivapurana. It dispells all sins. It affords the attainment of the highest truth (Brahma) hereafter. O brahmins, the great glory of Siva, that destroys the sin of the Kali age, unfolds itself in the Purana and yields the fruits of the four varieties (Dharma, Artha, Kama and Moksa).

By the single-minded study of that most excellent Sivapurana excellent brahmins will attain salvation. It is only as long as the Sivapurana has not risen high in the world, that Brahma-hatya (the sin of slaying a brahmin) and other sins display themselves.

It is only as long as the Sivapurana has not risen high in the world, that the evil portents of Kali fearlessly roam about. It is only as long as the Sivapurana has not risen high in the world, that the different sacred texts clash together in disputation. It is difficult even to great men to comprehend Siva's features as long as the Sivapurana has not risen high in the world.

The cruel attendants of Yama roam about fearlessly as long as the Sivapurana has not risen high in the world. All the other Puranas roar loudly on the earth as long as the Sivapurana has not risen high in the world.

All the holy centres enter into mutual wrangles and disputes on the earth as long as the Sivapurana has not risen high in the world. All the mantras rejoice in mutual disputes as long as the Sivapurana has not risen high in the world. All the sectors of pilgrimage engage themselves in mutual disputes as long as the Sivapurana has not risen high in the world.

All the altars and pedestals engage themselves in mutual disputes as long as the Sivapurana has not risen high in the world. All the gifts engage themselves in disputes as long as the Sivapurana has not risen high in the world.

All those gods engage themselves in mutual disputes as long as the Sivapurana has not risen high in the world. All the philosophical tenets engage themselves in mutual disputes as long as the Sivapurana has not risen high in the world.

O foremost among brahmanical sages, I cannot adequately describe the fruit accruing from reciting and listening to this Sivapurana. Even then, O sinless ones, I shall succinctly describe its greatness as narrated to me by Vyasa. Please listen attentively.

He who reads a single stanza or even half of it piously becomes free from sin instantaneously. He who reads every day as much of Sivapurana as he can with devotion and alertness is called Jivanmukta (a living liberated soul). He who continues to worship this Sivapurana daily derives the fruit of horse-sacrifice undoubtedly. He who with a craving for an ordinary position in life listens to Sivapurana even from a person other than me is freed from sin. He who bows near this Sivapurana derives undoubtedly the fruit of adoration of all the gods.

Please listen to the meritorious benefit that accrues to the man who copies Sivapurana and gives the manuscript to the devotees of Siva.

He will have that benefit—very difficult to attain in the world—as that of the study of Sastras (sacred lore) and of commenting on the Vedas. He who observes fast on the CaturdaSi (fourteenth day in the lunar fortnight) and conducts discourses and comments on the Sivapurana in the assembly of the devotees of Siva is the most excellent of all. He shall derive the benefit of the repetition of Gayatri syllable by syllable. He will enjoy all worldly pleasures here and attain salvation hereafter.

I shall tell you the benefit derived by him who reads or listens to this after observing fast on the CaturdaSi day by keeping awake in the night. This is the truth, undoubtedly the truth that he will get the benefit derived by the man who makes gifts of wealth equal in weight to himself to brahmins with Vyasas at their head at the complete eclipse of the sun, many a time, in all holy centres, Kuruksetra, etc.

Indra and other devas wait eagerly for the directives of the man who chants day and night the verses of the Siva-purana.

The sacred rites performed by the man who regularly reads or listens to the Sivapurana are effective millions of times more than usual. He who reads the Rudrasamhita portion of Siva-purana with pure and concentrated mind becomes a purified soul within three days even though he might have killed a brahmin.

He who reads the Rudrasamhita three times a day near the image of Bhairava, refraining from useless talk, shall get all cherished desires fulfilled. If a slayer of brahmin circumambulates the trees of Vata and Bilva reciting the verses from Rudrasamhita he will become purified of the sin of Brahmin-slaughter.

The Kailasa samhita is even greater than that. It is of Vedic status and stature. The meaning of Pranava (the sacred syllable Om) is amplified in it.

O Brahmins, Lord Siva knows the greatness of KailaSasamhita in its entirety. Vyasa knows half of it and I am a moiety of the same. A part of it, I shall tell you, since it is impossible to say everything. On comprehending it people attain purity of their minds instantaneously.

O Brahmins, seeking for it ever and anon, I do not see a sin that cannot be quelled by Rudrasamhita.

Drinking that nectar prepared by Lord Siva after churning the ocean of the Upanisads (a class of Vedic literature) and handed over to Kumara (Lord Kartikeya) the devotee shall become immortal.

The person intending to perform expiatory rites for the sins of Brahma-hatya etc. should read that Samhita for a month. He shall be freed of that sin. By a single recital, that Samhita destroys the sin originating from the acceptance of monetary gifts from defiled persons, partaking of defiled food and indulging in foul talks.

The benefit derived by a person who reads that Samhita in the grove of Bilva trees in a temple of Siva is beyond description in words.

If a person reads that Samhita with devotion at the time of performing Sraddha and feeding the brahmins, all his Pitrs (manes) attain the great region of Siva.

The devotee who observes fast on the CaturdaSi day and reads that Samhita under the

Bilva tree is directly identified with Siva and is worshipped by the gods. The other Samhitas are no doubt the bestowers of the benefit of fulfilling all cherished desires. These two Samhitas are particularly excellent as they are full of divine sports and divine knowledge.

Such is the Sivapurana, extolled on a par with the Vedas, created by Lord Siva Himself at first and commensurate with the supreme Brahman.

Originally the Sivapurana was of very enormous size consisting of twelve sacred Samhitas: —(1) VidyeSvara (2) Rudra, (3) Vainayaka, (4) Aumika, (5) Matr (6) RudraikadaSa, (7) Kailasa, (8) Satarudraka, (9) Sahasrakotirudra, (10) Kotirudra, (11) Vayaviya and (12) Dharmasamjna.

O brahmins, I shall mention the number of verses in those Samhitas. Please listen with due attention.

The first Samhita of VidyeSvara, consisted of ten thousand verses. The Raudra, Vainayaka, Aumika and Matr Samhitas consisted of eight thousand verses each.

O brahmins, the Rudraikadasa samhita consisted of thirteen thousand verses; the Kailasa samhita of six thousand verses and the Satarudra of three thousand verses. The Kotirudra samhita consisted of nine thousand verses; the Sahasrakoti-Rudra samhita of eleven thousand verses.

The Vayaviya samhita consisted of 4000 verses and the Dharma samhita of twelve thousand verses. Thus the whole Sivapurana contained a hundred thousand verses.

That has been condensed by Vyasa to twenty-four thousand verses; that is to about a fourth of the original Purana and he retained seven samhitas.

The Puranic lore at the time of the first creation as conceived by Siva contained a thousand million (hundred crores) verses.

In the Krta age, Dvaipayana and others condensed it into four hundred thousand verses which in the beginning of Dvapara age was separated into eighteen different Puranas.

Of these the Sivapurana contains twenty-four thousand verses with seven Samhitas and the Purana is on a par with the Vedas (in excellence).

The first Samhita is called VidyeSvara, the second Rudra, the third Satarudra and the fourth Kotirudra.

The fifth is Aumi (of Uma), the sixth Kailasa and the seventh Vayaviya; these are the seven Samhitas.

Thus the divine Sivapurana with its seven Samhitas stands on a par with the Vedas, according salvation more than anything else.

He who reads this Sivapurana complete with the seven Samhitas devotedly is a living liberated soul.

Hundreds of other sacred texts as the Vedas, Smrtis, Puranas, Itihasas, and Agamas do not merit even a sixteenth of this Sivapurana.

Sivapurana is first expounded by Siva and then condensed by Vyasa, a devotee of Siva. It is pure and brief and as such it renders help to all living beings. As a queller of the threefold calamities (physical, extraneous and divine) it is unrivalled. It bestows welfare upon the good.

Undeceptive virtue is extolled herein; it is, in the main, of the nature of Vedantic wisdom. It contains mantras, and three aims of life and the thing knowable by wise men of unprejudiced mind. The Sivapurana is the best among the Puranas, extolling the great Being that glows in Vedanta and the Vedas. He who reads and listens to it with devotion becomes a favourite of Siva and attains the supreme position (here and hereafter).

The Deliberation on the Achievable and the Means of Achievement

Vyasa said: —

ON hearing the words of Suta, the great sages said: —
Please narrate the wonderful Purana that fully treats of the essence of Vedanta.

Very delighted at the request of the sages Suta meditated on Siva and spoke to them.

Suta said: —

Contemplating on Siva free from ailments may ye all hear this Sivapurana, the foremost among Puranas, that amplifies the essence of the Vedas.

Where the trio, Bhakti (Piety) Jnana (Wisdom) and Vairagya (non-attachment) has been proclaimed and the object which is knowable only through Vedanta, has been particularly described.

May ye all hear the Purana that embibes the essence of the Vedas. Formerly, when many Kalpas (Aeons) elapsed and this Kalpa started with the process of creation, a great dispute arose among the sages of six clans who held divergent views as to which is great and which is not. They approached Brahma the Creator, to ask him about the imperishable.

All of them with palms joined in reverence addressed him with words couched in humility—Thou art the creator of the entire universe, the cause of all causes. Who is that Being older than all Principles, the greatest of the great?

Brahma said: —

That from whom words recede, not approaching him even with the mind; that from whom this entire universe beginning with Brahma, Visnu, Rudra and Indra, along with all elements and all sense-organs, is evolved at first; he is the lord Mahadeva the omniscient, the lord of the universe. He can be realised by supreme devotion and not by other means.

Rudra, Hari, Hara and other lords of Devas are ever desirous of seeing Him, moved by great devotion. Of what avail is a verbose statement? One is liberated by devotion unto Siva. Devotion to the deity is due to His Grace; and His grace is due to devotion just as the seed gives rise to the sprout and the sprout produces the seed.

Hence, O Brahmins, all of you descend to the earth, to propitiate the Lord. You have to perform a sacrifice of long duration for a thousand years. It is by the grace of Siva alone who will be the presiding deity of this sacrifice that the means of achievement of the Achievable can be realised and that is the essence of the Vidya (mystic learning) mentioned in the Vedas.

The sages said: —

What is that great Achievable? What is that great means of achievement? Of what sort is the performer of the rite? Please mention these precisely.

The attainment of Siva's region is the Achievable. Means of achievement is the service rendered unto Him. Sadhaka (the performer of the rite) is the person who is free from desire even for permanence which attitude is the result of His grace. Rites mentioned in the Vedas should be performed with the fruits thereof dedicated to Him. Thence, through Salokya he attains the feet of the great Lord.

All attain the great fruit according to the standard in devotion achieved. The ways of achieving these standards are manifold as expounded by Isa Himself. I shall condense the same and tell you the essential means. Listening to the glory of Siva, glorifying him by means of words, and deliberation in the mind, these constitute the greatest of the means. MaheSvara is to be heard, glorified and meditated upon. Thus, Sruti is our authority. Resorting solely to this great means, all of you attain the Achievable.

Regarding visible things people see with their eyes and begin their activity. Concerning the invisible everywhere, they know through the ears and activise themselves. Hence Sravana (listening) is the first rite. The intelligent scholar must listen to the oral explanation of the preceptor and then practise the other rites.— Kirtana (glorifying) and Manana (deliberation).

When all the means upto Manana are well exercised, Sivayoga (unification with Siva) results gradually through Salokya etc. All the ailments of the body are nullified and supreme bliss is realised. Painful indeed is the process but later on everything becomes auspicious from beginning to end.

The Excellence of Listening and Deliberation

The sages asked: —

O holy one, What is Sravana? What is Manana? How is the Kirtana performed? Please expound these precisely.

Brahma said: —

The mind is fond of reasoning deliberation. The ability of the mind to ponder and evaluate the corresponding efficacy of the worship, Japa, the attributes of ISa, His form, His divine sports and multifarious names, is the result of the benignant glance of ISvara. Hence this steady continuance in the act of deliberation is the most important of all the means.

By Kirtana (glorification) is meant the clear expression of Siva's exploits, attributes, forms, sports, names etc. in good taste by reciting traditional lore, singing songs of praise even in mother tongue. It is the middle one of the three means.

O wise men, the means of Sravana famous in the world is the listening to words concerning Siva, in whatever manner, howsoever and wherever they are produced with the same steady attention as in the sporting dalliance of women.

Sravana (listening) is effected when one associates with good men. Then the Kirtana of PaSupati becomes steady. In the end is the Manana which is the most excellent. All these take place as a result of benevolent surveillance of Lord Siva.

Suta said: —

O saints, in the context of the elucidation of the greatness of the means, I shall narrate an anecdote of former days for your sake. Please listen to them attentively.

Long ago, my preceptor Vyasa, the son of Sage ParaSara, performed penance on the bank of the river Sarasvati with some mental agitation. The divine sage Sanatkumara who happened to go that way in an aerial chariot resplendent like the sun, espied my preceptor. Waking up from his meditation my preceptor saw the son of Brahma. The sage thereupon paid obeisance in a flutter and eagerness.

He offered Arghya and a seat befitting the divinity of the sage. Being delighted, the divine sage spoke to my humble preceptor in words of great profundity. O sage, you must meditate upon the True object. The great lord Siva can be realised and seen. But wherefore do you perform the penance here unattended?

When Sanatkumara addressed him thus, the sage Vyasa clarified his purpose. By the favour of divine elders like you I have almost established the four ways of virtue, wealth, love and salvation with due adherence to the Vedic path, in the world. I have become a preceptor unto all.

Still it is surprising that the knowledge of the means of liberation has not dawned on me. I am performing penance for the sake of salvation. But I do not know how it can be achieved.

O excellent brahmins, when thus requested by the sage Vyasa, the competent divine sage Sanatkumara told him of the sure way of realising salvation. It has already been mentioned that there are three means in conformity with Vedic ideal viz. Sravana, Kirtana and the highly efficacious Manana of Siva.

Formerly, I too, confounded by other means performed a great penance on the mountain Mandara. At the bidding of Siva, the divine attendant NandikeSvara arrived there. That sympathetic lord of Ganas, witness of all, lovingly told me about the excellent means of salvation. Viz.—Sravana, Kirtana and Manana all in conformity with Vedic ideals. Hence, O holy sage, as advised by Siva these are the three means of salvation. Please practise them.

He repeatedly advised Vyasa thus. After saying this to Vyasa, the son of Brahma mounted the aerial chariot accompanied by his followers and returned to his splendid and auspicious region.

Thus, in brief, I have told you the ancient anecdote.

The sages said: —

O Suta, you have narrated Sravana etc.—the three means of salvation. If a person is unable to practise these three, what shall he do to achieve liberation? What is that rite whereby salvation will be possible without stress or strain?

The Greatness of the Phallic Emblem (Liṅga) of Siva

Suta said: —

A person incompetent to perform the three rites of Sravana etc. shall fix the phallic emblem (liṅga) or the image of Siva and worship them every day. He can thus cross the ocean of worldly existence.

As far as he can afford, the devotee shall make gifts of wealth too without deceiving others. He shall offer them to the phallic emblem or the image of Siva. He must worship them constantly.

The worship must be performed elaborately. Construction of platforms, ornamental portals, monasteries, temples, holy centres, etc., offerings of cloth, scents, garlands, incense, lamps, with due piety; oblations of various cooked rice, pancakes, pies etc. with side dishes; umbrellas, fans, chowries with all paraphernalia—everything shall be maintained in the worship of Siva.

In fact, all royal homage shall be paid. Circumambulation and obeisance with Japas according to capacity shall be performed. All the different usual rites in worships like invocation shall be maintained with due devotion.

A person who worships the phallic emblem or the image in this manner will attain salvation even without Sravana etc. Many noble men of yore have been Uberated solely by this simple worship. Everywhere the deities are worshipped only in their image. How is it that Siva is worshipped both in the image and the phallus?

Suta said: —

O sages, this question is holy and wondrous. Here the speaker is Siva Himself and not any ordinary person.

I shall tell you what Siva Himself had said and what I heard from my own preceptor.

Siva alone is glorified as Niskala (nameless and formless) since He is identical with supreme Brahman. He is also Sakala as He has an embodied form. He is both Sakala and Niskala. It is in his Niskala aspect that the Liṅga is appropriate. In the Sakala aspect the worship of his embodied form is appropriate.

Since He has the Sakala and Niskala aspects He is worshipped both in the phallic and in the embodied form by the people and is called the highest Brahman. Other deities, not being Brahman, have no Niskala aspect anywhere. Hence the deities are not worshipped in the formless phallic symbol.

The other deities are both non-Brahman and individual souls. In view of their being embodied alone they are worshipped solely in the bodily form. Saṅkara has Brahmatva and the others Jivatva.

This has been explained in the meaning of the Pranava (Om), the essence of Vedanta, by NandikeSvara when asked by Sanatkumara, the intelligent son of Brahma, at the mountain Mandara.

Sanatkumara said: —

The embodied form alone is often observed in the worship of the deities other than Siva.

But both the phallic and the embodied forms are seen only in the worship of Siva. Hence O benevolent one, please tell me precisely making me understand the truth.

NandikeSvara said: —

It is impossible to answer this question without revealing the secret of Brahman. O sinless one, since you are pious I shall tell you what Siva Himself has said. Since Siva has the bodiless aspect in virtue of His being the supreme Brahman, the Niskala liṅga, in conformity with the Vedic implication, is used only in His worship.

Since He has an embodied form as well, His embodied form is also worshipped and accepted by all people. According to the decision in the Vedas, the embodied form alone is to be used in the worship of other deities who are only individual souls embodied. Devas have only the embodied aspect in their manifestation. In sacred literature both the phallic and the embodied forms are mentioned for Siva.

Sanatkumara said: —

O Fortunate one, you have explained the worship of phallus and image distinctly for Siva and the other deities. Hence, O lord of Yogins, I wish to hear the feature of the manifestation of the phallic aspect of Siva.

NandikeSvara said: —

O dear one, out of love for you I shall tell you the truth. Long long ago, in the famous first Kalpa, the noble souls Brahma and Visnu fought each other. In order to eradicate their arrogance lord ParameSvara showed his unembodied Niskala form in the form of a column in their midst. He showed his phallus emblem separate, evolved out of the column, with a desire to bless the worlds.

From that time onwards the divine phallus and the embodied image, both, were assigned to Siva alone. The embodied form alone was assigned to deities other than Siva. The different types of the embodied forms of the different Devas yield only enjoyments. In regard to Siva the phallic emblem and the embodied form together bestow auspicious enjoyment and salvation.

Battle Between Brahma and Visnu

(In the fight between Brahma and Visnu trying to establish themselves as the only lord, the Devas travel to Kailasa, terrified that they will use the Pasupata weapon in the fight. Nandikesvara narrates the story here.)

Once, a long time ago, the foremost among Yogins, Visnu was taking a nap on his serpent couch. He was surrounded by the goddess of fortune and his attendants. Brahma chanced to come there. He asked the lotus-eyed handsome Visnu who was lying there.

Brahma said: —

Who are you lying here like a haughty person even after seeing me? Get up, oh dear, and see me who is your Lord. I have come here.

Not getting any response from Visnu, Brahma continued with agitation. He said, 'You are to perform expiatory rites for being a spiteful wretch, behaving like a haughty fool when such an honourable elderly person is right in front of you.' On hearing these words, Visnu was angry. However, he assumed a calm exterior and said—'Oh dear, hail thee. Welcome. Please sit on this couch. How is it that thy face is agitated and thy eyes look curious?'

Brahma said: —

Dear Visnu, I have come with the speed of time. I am to be honoured greatly. Oh dear one, I am the protector of the world, Grandfather, and your protector as well.

Vishnu said: —

Oh dear one, the whole universe is situated within me and your way of thinking is like that of a thief. You are born from the lotus that sprung from my navel region. You are my son. Your words are futile, therefore.

Arguing with each other like this, saying that each is better than the other and claiming to be the Lord, they got ready to fight, desirous of killing each other. The two heroic deities, seated on their respective vehicles—the Swan and the Garuda, fought against each other. The attendants of Brahma and Visnu also clashed. In the meantime, the different groups of Devas moving about in aerial chariots came there to witness the great fight.

Witnessing from heaven, they scattered flowers everywhere. Visnu became infuriated and discharged numerous arrows and other weapons at Brahma's chest. The infuriated Brahma also hurled many arrows of fury and all sorts of weapons at Visnu.

Soon the Devas became agitated and started commenting on the hellish fight. Visnu, in his great fury, discharged the Mahesvara weapon at Brahma. Annoyed by this, Brahma aimed the terrible Pasupata weapon at Visnu's chest. The weapons rose high in the sky, blazing like ten thousand suns, with thousands of pointed spikes and roared awfully like a gust of wind. These two weapons of Brahma and Visnu thus faced each other in a terrible clash.

Such was the fight between Brahma and Visnu. Then, the Devas in their helplessness and vexation started talking amongst themselves like people do at the time of war between their monarchs.

The three-pointed-trident-bearing deity, the supreme Brahman, (i. e. Siva) is the cause of creation, maintenance, annihilation, concealment and blessing. Without his corroboration, even a blade of grass cannot be split by any individual anywhere.

Thinking thus in their fright they desired to go to Siva's abode and accordingly came to the summit of Kailasa where the moon-crested God resided.

On seeing that region of Paramesvara in the shape of Omkara, they bent their heads down in reverence and entered the palace. There they saw the supreme leader of the Devas seated on a gem-set chair in the company of Uma on an altar in the middle of the council-chamber.

His right leg was situated over the knee of the left; his lotus-like hands were placed over the legs; his attendants were all around him. He had all the good characteristic features. He was being fanned by the specialists in that art— ladies of pointed attention. The Vedas were extolling him. The Lord was blessing everyone.

On seeing the Lord thus, the Devas shed tears of joy. The hosts of Devas knelt down even from a great distance. The Lord, on seeing the Devas, beckoned them to him through his attendants. The Devas were delighted to be called by the crest-jewel of Devas. He addressed them with sweet auspicious words.

Siva Manifested Himself as a Column of Fire on the Battlefield

Isvara said: —

Dear children, hail to you. I hope the universe and the deities, under my reign, flourish in their respective duties. Oh, gods, the fight between Brahma and Visnu is already known to me. This agitation on your part is like a redundant speech.

Thus the consort of Amba consoled the concourse of devas with honey-like speech, smiling sweetly. In that very assembly, the Lord announced his desire to go to the battlefield of Hari and Brahma and accordingly issued a directive to hundreds of commanders of his attendants.

The Lord, consort of Ambika, mounted the holy chariot which was shaped like Omkara from front to back. It was embellished in five circular rings. He was accompanied by his sons and Ganas. All the devas, Indra and others, followed. Honoured suitably and accompanied by the great goddess Parvati, Pasupati (Siva) went to the battlefield with the whole army.

On espying the battle, the Lord vanished in the sky. The music stopped and the roars of the Ganas subsided. There in the battlefield, Brahma and Acyuta (Visnu) desirous of killing each other, were awaiting the result of the Mahesvara and the Pasupata weapons hurled by them. The flames emitted by the two weapons burned the three worlds. On seeing this imminent untimely dissolution, Siva took the form of a huge column of fire amongst them.

The two weapons that had the potential to destroy the entire world, fell into the huge column of fire that appeared instantly. Seeing that auspicious phenomenon assuaging the weapons, they asked each other: —

What is this wonderful form? What is this column of fire that has risen up? It is beyond the range of senses. We have to find out its top and bottom. Jointly deciding this, the two heroes immediately set about assiduously in their quest.

'Nothing will turn up if we are together. Saying this, Visnu assumed the form of a boar and went in search of the root. Brahma, in the form of a swan, went up in search of the top. Piercing through the netherworlds and going very far below, Visnu could not see the root of the fiery column. Utterly exhausted, Visnu, in the form of a boar, returned to the former battleground.

Brahma, who went high up in the sky, saw many Ketaki flowers falling from above. On seeing the mutual fight between Brahma and Visnu, Lord Siva laughed. When his head shook, the Ketaki flower dropped down. Although it had been in its downward course for many years, neither its fragrance nor its lustre had been diminished even a bit. The flower had been intended to bless them.

(Brahma said) O lord of flowers, by whom had you been worn? Why do you fall? I have come here to seek out the top, in the form of a swan. (The flower replied) I am falling down from the middle of this primordial column that is inscrutable. It has taken me a long time. Hence I do not see how you can see the top. Brahma said, Dear friend, hereafter you must do as I desire. In the presence of Visnu you must say this – 'Oh Acyuta, the top of the column has been seen by Brahma. I am the witness for the same.'

Saying this, he bowed to the Ketaki flower again and again. He assured himself that falsehood is justified in times of danger as suggested by the authoritative texts. Returning to the original place, and finding Visnu there, utterly exhausted and lacking pleasure, Brahma danced with joy. Visnu, in the manner of a eunuch admitting his inability (to a woman), told him the truth that he could not see the bottom.

But Brahma said, Oh Hari, the top of this column has been seen by me. This Ketaki flower is my witness.

The Ketaki flower repeated the falsehood, endorsing the words of Brahma in his presence. Hari, taking it to be true, made obeisance to Brahma. He worshipped Brahma with all the sixteen means of service and homage. The Lord then took up a visible form and came out of the column of fire to chastise Brahma for his deception.

On seeing the Lord, Visnu stood up and with his hands shaking with fear, caught hold of the Lord's feet.

Visnu said: —

It is out of ignorance and delusion about you, whose body is without a beginning or an end, that we indulged in this quest prompted by our own desire. Hence, Oh, the sympathetic being, forgive us for our fault. In fact, it is but another form of your divine sport.

Isvara said: —

Oh dear Hari, I am pleased with you because you strictly adhered to the truth in spite of your desire to be a Lord. Hence, among the general public, you will have a footing equal to mine. You will be honoured too in the same way. Hereafter, you will be separate from me, have a separate temple, have your idols installed, and festivities and people will worship.

Siva's Forgiveness of Brahma

NandikeSvara said: —

Mahadeva then created a wonderful person, Bhairava, from the middle of his brows, to quell the pride of Brahma. This Bhairava knelt before the Lord in the battlefield and said—

Oh Lord, what shall I do? Please give me your directives quickly.

To this, Shiva replied, 'Dear, here is Brahma, the first deity of the universe. Worship him with your sharp-pointed quick-moving sword.' With one of his hands, he caught hold of the tuft of Brahma's fifth head that was guilty of uttering a falsehood, and with the other hand, he furiously shook his sword in order to cut it off.

Brahma trembled like a plantain tree in a whirlwind, with his ornaments scattered here and there, his cloth ruffled and loosened, the garland displaced, the upper cloth hanging loose and the glossy tuft dishevelled. He fell at the feet of Bhairava.

Meanwhile, the sympathetic Acyuta, desirous of saving Brahma, shed tears over the lotus-like feet of our Lord and said with joined hands—

'Oh Lord, it was you who gave him five heads as a special symbol, long ago. Hence, please forgive him for his first guilt. Please favour him.'

The Lord, thus requested by Acyuta, relented and asked Bhairava to desist from punishing Brahma. Then the Lord turned to the deceitful Brahma, who bent down his neck and said, 'O Brahma, in order to extort honour from the people you assumed the role of the Lord in a roguish manner. Hence, you shall not be honoured, nor shall you have your own temple or festival.

Brahma said: —

Oh Lord, be pleased. Oh flourishing one, I consider the sparing of my head itself a great blessing and a boon. Obeisance to thee, the Lord, the kinsman, the originator of the universe, the forbearing, the forgiver of defects, the benevolent one, wielding the mountain as his bow.

Isvara said: —

Oh child, the whole universe will be ruined if it loses the fear of a king. Hence, you mete out punishment to the guilty and bear the burden of administering this universe. I shall grant you another boon which is very difficult to get. In all domestic and public sacrifices, you will be the presiding deity. Even though a sacrifice is complete with all the ancillary rites and offerings of monetary gifts, it will be fruitless without you.

Then the Lord turned to the deceitful Ketaki flower guilty of perjury and addressed him—

Oh you Ketaki flower, you are roguish and deceitful. Go away from here. Hereafter, I have no desire to include you in my worship.

Ketaka said: —

Obeisance to thee, Oh Lord, your bidding will mean that my very birth is fruitless. May the Lord be pleased to make it fruitful by forgiving my sin. You are known to quell all sins, committed consciously or unconsciously. How can my utterance of falsehood sully me?

Thus entreated in the middle of the council, the Lord said, 'It is not proper for me to wear you. I am the Lord and my words must stay true. My attendants and followers shall wear thee. Hence, thy birth shall be fruitful. Of course in the canopies over my idol you can be used for decoration'. The Lord thus blessed the three—the flower Ketaki, Brahma and Visnu. He shone in the assembly duly eulogised by the Devas.

The Proclamation of Siva as Mahesvara

NandikeSvara said: —

In the meantime, Brahma and Visnu had been standing silently on either side of the Lord with their palms joined in reverence. Then they installed the Lord with all the members of his family on a splendid seat and worshipped him with all holy personal things. Both of them adored the Lord with all these things worthy of the Lord and inaccessible to Pasu (the animal i.e. the individual soul).

In order to set up precedence, the delighted Lord handed over all those articles to the attendants assembled according to the order of priority. It was there that Brahma and Visnu adored Sankara at first. When they stood there humbly, the gratified Lord spoke smilingly, heightening their devotion.

Isvara said: —

Dear children, I am delighted at your worship on this holy day. Henceforth this day will be famous as 'Sivaratri', the holiest of holy days pleasing to me. He who performs the worship of my phallic emblem and the embodied image on this day will be competent to perform the task of creation and the maintenance of the universe.

The devotee shall keep fast on Sivaratri, both during the day and the night. He shall perfectly restrain his sense-organs. Festivities like the installation of my idols on that day are very auspicious. Since I manifested myself in the form of a phallic emblem in the field of battle, this place will be known as Lingasthana. Oh sons, this column without root or top will henceforth be very small in size for the sake of the vision and worship of the world. The phallic emblem is the only means of worldly enjoyment and salvation. May all of you achieve all your cherished desires.

NandikeSvara said: —

Thus blessing Brahma and Visnu who had been made humble, the Lord resuscitated all the soldiers of the two deities that had been killed in the battle and spoke to them in order to remove their foolishness and mutual enmity.

I have two forms: the manifest and the unmanifest. No one else has these two forms. Hence all others are non-Isavaras. Dear sons, I have shown you my formless Brahma-hood and embodied Isa-hood by being the column and then showing my physical form. These two forms are only present in me and no one else. Hence, nobody can claim Isatva (Isa-hood). It is out of your ignorance of this fact that you were swept away by your false prestige and pride of being Isa, surprising as it is. I rose up in the middle of the battlefield to quell the same.

Cast off your false pride. Fix your thoughts in me as your Lord. It is out of my favour that all the objects in the world are illuminated. Oh Brahma and Visnu, I am Brahman because of Brhatva (huge size) and Brmhanatva (causing it to grow). Oh children, similarly, I am Atman due to Samatva (equality) and Vyapakatva (pervasiveness). All others are Anatmans, individual souls undoubtedly.

There are five activities in respect of the universe beginning with Anugraha (liberation) and ending with Sarga (creation). Therefore, these activities devolve on me because

I am Isa and not on anyone else. The phallic symbol and the symbolised Siva are the same. Hence, this phallic emblem is identical to mine. It brings devotees quite near to me. It is worthy of worship, therefore.

Oh dear sons, if a phallic emblem of this sort is installed, I can be considered installed in the form of Siva. The result of installing the phallic emblem is the attainment of similarity with me. If a second phallic emblem is installed, the result is a union with me. A temple with the embodied idol of Siva is infructuous if it has no phallic image.

RUDRA-SAMHITA
CREATION

The Inquiry of the Sages
(Vyasa narrates the tale here)

I bow to Siva, the consort of Gauri, the sole cause of the origin, sustenance, and dissolution of the universe. I salute Siva who is prior to Prakrti, who is calm and tranquil. I salute Siva in his unmanifested form who stands in the middle of the entire creation while the worlds move around him.

Vyasa said: —

I describe this after bowing to Sambhu, the father of the universe Siva the mother of the universe and Ganadhisa their son. Once Saunaka and other sages living in Naimisa forest asked Suta with full devotion.

The sages said: —

Oh blessed Suta, live long. You will please tell us the great anecdotes of Siva. Oh sinless one, we are never satiated. Hence, we would like to know more. You know everything about the past, present and future. Now, oh wise one, please explain the excellent form of Siva. Please narrate the divine anecdote of Siva and Parvati without omitting anything. Mahesvara is Aguna (free from attributes).

How does he take up Saguna's form? Before the origin of creation, how does Lord Siva maintain his form? In the midst of creation, how does he maintain his sport? How does Lord Mahesvara stand at the moment of dissolution?

What benefit does the great Lord confer when he is pleased with his devotees? Please tell us. The three deities Brahma, Visnu and Mahesvara are born of Siva. Please explain his manifestation and tell us about his various activities. Please tell us about the birth of Uma and her marriage too.

Vyasa said: —

Being thus requested, Suta was delighted. Remembering the lotus-like feet of Siva, he replied to the sages.

Suta said: —

Oh Lordly sages, what you have asked for is very nice. Oh brahmins, I shall explain Siva's sports as far as my intelligence enables me. Please listen respectfully, replied Suta.

Induced by Lord Visnu, a manifestation of Siva, Narada had also posed the same question to his father Brahma as you are asking me now. On hearing the words of his son, Brahma, a devotee of Siva, was delighted. Out of love, he sang the glory of Siva, heightening the pleasure of sage Narada.

The sages said: —

Dear one, please tell us lovingly, when this highly pleasant conversation between Brahma and Narada took place, wherein Siva's glory was sung and the divine sport of Lord Siva, destructive of worldly existence, had been discussed. What were the questions and how were they answered, please explain.

On hearing these words of the sages, Suta was pleased and narrated everything about the conversation.

Indra Sends Kamadeva to Disturb the Penance of Narada

Suta said: —

Oh brahmins, once Narada, the excellent sage, son of Brahma, was inclined to perform penance to control himself. There is a magnificent cave in the Himalayan mountain, near which the celestial river flows rapidly. There was a great hermitage of divine splendour which was resplendent in many ways.

Narada, endowed with divine vision, went there to perform penance. On seeing the hermitage, the sage performed the penance for a long time, seated firmly and steadily, keeping silent, controlling the breath and retaining the purity of the intellect.

Suta continued: —

Oh brahmins, the sage performed meditation and contemplation, wherein the realisation 'I am Brahman' is generated leading to the direct perception of Brahman. When the great sage Narada was performing penance, Indra became excessively agitated and trembled.

Indra wanted to spoil the penance, thinking, 'This sage is yearning for my kingdom'. Indra, the leader of Devas, remembered Kamadeva (Cupid), who arrived there immediately, accompanied by his Queen (Rati) and spring (his friend). The king of Devas, endowed with crooked intelligence to achieve his interests, saw that Kama had arrived and addressed him thus.

Indra said: —

Oh friend, of great prowess, always doing good for me, please hear lovingly what I am going to say. Render me your help. Strongly supported by you, I have destroyed the pride of many ascetics. Oh friend, the stability of my kingdom is always due to your blessing. Narada, the sage, is performing a penance in the Himalayan mountain directing his mind towards the Lord of the universe with great mental control and firm resolve. I now fear he will beg for my kingdom from Brahma. You must go there now and hinder his penance.

Suta said: —

Being thus commanded by Indra, Kamadeva, accompanied by his wife (Rati) and Madhu, his friend, went haughtily to that place. He then prepared his own means of attack. He employed all his arts there immediately. Spring too, haughtily spread his prowess of diverse nature.

Oh great sages, the mind of Narada did not waver. Only the arrogance of these fellows suffered a setback and that too in the favour of Mahesa. Please listen to the reason. By the controlling power of the Lord, Kama could not exercise any influence. It was in this very place that Siva, the unfaltering enemy of Kama, had formerly performed a great penance. It was here that Kama was reduced to ashes—Kama who used to spoil the penances of sages. Rati wanted the resuscitation of Kama and requested the Devas. They appealed to Lord Siva, the benefactor of the whole world who said thus.

'Oh Gods, after some time Kama will come to life again. But none of his tricks will succeed here. Whatever space all around this spot is visible to people here, will be out of the influence of Kama forever,' said Siva.

It was due to this statement of Siva that Kama's tricks did not prevail upon Narada. From Siva's abode, he went to Indra. Kama then narrated everything about the sage and commended his power. At Indra's bidding, Kama returned to his own place.

Deluded by Siva's Maya (power of illusion), Indra was unaware of the true facts and was greatly surprised and he admired Narada. Backed by Siva's blessings, Narada stayed in the hermitage for a long time. Then, realising that his penance was complete, the sage concluded the same. Thinking that he had conquered Kama, he was puffed with pride. He was devoid of true knowledge and deluded by Siva's Maya. Oh great sages, blessed and very blessed is Siva's Maya. Even Visnu, Brahma and others do not know the turn it takes.

In that state of delusion and puffed-up arrogance, the great sage Narada went to Kailasa to expatiate on his own achievement. Bowing down to Rudra, the sage arrogantly spoke of his exploits with the conviction that he was equal to the noble-souled Lord, the conqueror of Kama, i.e., Siva. On hearing it, Rudra advised Narada, who was ignorant of the real cause, whose mind had strayed and who had been deluded by Siva's Maya, replied Suta.

Rudra said: —

Dear Narada, Oh wise sage, you are blessed. But please listen to me. Never speak like this anywhere else, especially in the presence of Visnu. Even when you are asked you should not mention your achievements as you have done just now. These should be guarded as close secrets and should never be expressed. I bid you specifically like this because you are a great favourite of mine. Since you are a devotee of Visnu, you are my follower, as all his devotees are, advised Rudra.

Suta said: —

Lord Rudra, the cause of creation, advised him in many ways like this. But Narada, who was still under the influence of Siva's Maya, did not take up this wholesome advice. Then, the great sage went to Brahma's world. After saluting Brahma, he told him about his conquest of Kama as a result of his penance. On hearing that, Brahma remembered the lotus-like feet of Siva and knew thereby the true cause. He then forbade his son.

Although foremost among the wise, Narada did not take up the advice of Brahma as he had been deluded by Siva's Maya. The sprout of arrogance had been fixed in his mind. Narada hastened to Visnuloka in the same state of senseless arrogance, to boast of his exploits in the presence of Visnu.

When Visnu saw Narada approaching, he could guess the purpose of his visit. He stood up and received him cordially. He walked forward and embraced him lovingly. He made Narada sit comfortably. After remembering the lotus-like feet of Siva, he frankly uttered these words intended to quell Narada's arrogance.

Vishu said: —

Oh dear Narada, foremost among sages, you are blessed. I am sanctified by your visit. May I know where you come from and why you have come?

Suta said: —

On hearing these words of Visnu, the sage Narada felt elated. He narrated his story in the same haughty manner. On hearing the arrogant words of the sage, Visnu understood the true cause. Then Visnu eulogised Paramesvara with his palms joined in reverence.

Visnu said: —

Oh Lord Mahadeva, Paramesvara, be pleased. Oh Siva, thou art blessed. Thy Maya enchants everyone.

Suta said: —

Having thus chanted the prayer to Siva, the supreme Atman, he closed his eyes and meditated on his lotus-like feet and stopped.

On coming to know what Siva was about to do, through Siva's bidding, he addressed the great sage pleasantly.

Visnu said: —

'Oh foremost among sages, you are blessed. You are the storehouse of austerities and large-hearted. Oh sage, lust and delusion rise only in the heart of that man who is devoid of the three types of devotion. But you are vowed to perpetual celibacy. You are ever endowed with knowledge and devoted to non-attachment. Unaffected by passion and highly intelligent by nature, how can you be swayed by lust?'

Narada said: —

'Oh Lord, what can Kama do to me if you remain favourable to me?'

Suta said: —

Saying so, the sage who had paid a casual visit, bowed to Visnu and left.

Narada Attends the Svayamvara
of a Virgin and Is Discomfited

The sages said: —

Suta, Oh blessed Suta, the disciple of Vyasa, our obeisance to thee. It is due to thy grace that this wonderful story has been narrated to us, Oh dear one. Now tell us in detail what Visnu did after Narada had left the place. And where did Narada go?

Vyasa said: —

On hearing these words of the sages, Suta the wise and excellent scholar of Puranas, remembered Siva, the cause of different kinds of creation and replied.

Suta said: —

When Narada went away casually, Visnu, skilful in wielding his Maya, spread his Maya, as Siva had willed. On the path taken by the sage, he created a big wonderful city.

It was a hundred Yojanas in extent and surprisingly beautiful. It was far more beautiful than heaven. Many articles were displayed there. Men and women of all four castes stayed there. The wealthy and prosperous king of that city named Silanidhi was preparing for the gorgeous celebration of Svayamvara of his daughter. Brilliant princes coming from all four quarters, eager to court the princess, had thronged there dressed in diverse ways.

On seeing such a splendid city, Narada was enchanted. With his love kindled, he eagerly went to the palace's threshold. When the sage reached the palace, king Silanidhi adored him, having offered him a seat on the splendid throne studded with precious gems. He called his daughter Srimati and asked her to kneel down at the feet of Narada. Narada was struck with wonder upon seeing the girl.

Narada said: —

Oh king, who is this lovely girl comparable to celestial damsels?

The king said: —

Oh sage, this is my daughter Srimati. She has attained a marriageable age. She is in search of a qualified bridegroom. She has all charms and accomplishments and her Svayamvara is imminent. Oh sage, kindly foretell her destiny, everything that is in her horoscope. Please tell me what sort of a husband she will get.

Suta said: —

By the time these words were spoken, Narada had become an agitated victim of love and desired her. Addressing the king, he said thus.

Narada said: —

Oh great king, this daughter of yours is endowed with all characteristics: She is highly fortunate and blessed like Laksmi. She is an abode of all qualities. Her future husband will certainly be a splendid God, Lord of all, heroic, on a par with Siva, and Vying with Kamadeva.

Having said this, the casual visitor Narada took leave of the king. Deluded by Siva's Maya, he was extremely oppressed by love. The sage began to muse— 'How shall I get her? How shall she woo me amongst the princes in the Svayamvara hall?'

Narada thought to himself, 'A comely appearance appeals to all women in every respect. Only by seeing a charming personality will she become enamoured.'

Thinking thus, Narada who was agitated by love, went to Visnuloka somehow to acquire Visnu's form to captivate her.

Narada said: —

I shall tell you secretly my affairs entirely. King Silanidhi is one of your devotees. He is a righteous king. His daughter Srimati is a maiden of very fair complexion and wide eyes. She has the lustre of Jaganmohini (enchantress of the universe—a manifestation of Visnu) and is the most beautiful woman in all three worlds. Oh Visnu, I wish to marry her without delay. The king, at the request of the princess, has arranged for a Svayamvara. Thousands of Princes have come from all four quarters.

If you can favour me with splendid form, I shall certainly be able to gain her. She will not put the wedding garland around my neck without your splendid form. Oh Lord! Give me your form. I am your servant and favourite. Give me your beautiful form so that princess Srimati may choose me.

Suta said: —

On hearing these words of the sage Visnu, the slayer of Madhu demon, laughed and sympathetically replied, bearing in mind the overwhelming power of Siva.

Visnu said: —

Oh sage, you can go to the place where you wish. I shall do what is beneficial to you in the manner of a physician doing what is good to the patient since you are a great favourite of mine.

Suta said: —

After saying this, Visnu blessed the sage with a form like his own and the face of Hari (i.e. the monkey, since the word Hari means a monkey also). The Lord then vanished.

The sage thus became highly delighted on receiving Hari's form. He was content but did not know the scheme behind the scene.

The great sage Narada hastened to the place where Svayamvarawas were to be held and where the princes had assembled. The Svayamvara hall splendidly decorated and graced by so many princes shone like another council chamber of Indra. Narada too went in and sat down in the hall of his king. With his mind surging with love, he began to think like this.

Narada thought, 'She will choose only me since I am in Visnu's form.'

Suta said: —

The poor sage did not know the ugly character of his face. The men assembled there saw the sage only in his old form. Oh brahmins, the princes and others did not know the difference created therein. Two of the attendants of Rudra knew this difference. They had come there in the guise of brahmins in order to protect him. Considering the sage a fool, the two attendants sat near the sage and began to mock him, seemingly conversing between themselves.

The two attendants said, 'See Narada's features as splendid as Visnu's, but the face as that of a monkey, deformed and awful. Being deluded by Kama, he wishes to marry the Princess.'

Suta said: —

With these and other veiled remarks, they mocked him. The sage, overwhelmed by love, did not heed their whisper. He went on gazing at princess Srimati and was eager to get her. In the meantime, the princess had come out of the harem, surrounded by ladies. The comely maiden came to the hall. With the beautiful golden garland in her hands, the princess shone in the middle of the Svayamvara hall like Goddess Laksmi. The princess, in search of a suitable bridegroom, went around the hall with the garland in her hands.

On seeing the sage with the face of a monkey and the body of Visnu, she was infuriated. Averting her eyes, she went elsewhere, being distressed in her mind. Failing to find a groom of her choice, she was afraid. She remained in the middle of the hall and did not put the garland around the neck of anyone.

Meanwhile, Visnu came there in the guise of a king. He was not seen by anyone. Only the princess saw him. Then, on seeing Visnu, her lotus-like face beamed. The comely lady put the garland around his neck. Lord Visnu, in the guise of a king, took her with him and vanished from there immediately back to his own abode. The assembled princes lost their hope of getting Srimati. The sage, oppressed by love, became excessively agitated. Immediately, the two attendants of Rudra, of perfect wisdom, disguised as brahmins, spoke to Narada.

The attendants said: —

Oh sage Narada, being deluded by love, you are desirous of getting her. Your effort is in vain. See, your face is as despicable as that of a monkey.

Suta said: —

On hearing their words Narada was surprised. Deluded by Siva's maya, he looked into a mirror. On seeing his face like that of a monkey he became infuriated. The deluded sage cursed the two attendants.

Narada said: —

Since you had mocked me, you will become demons born of brahminical semen and of that form.

Suta said: —

On hearing the curse, the two attendants of perfect wisdom remained silent because they knew that the sage was deluded. The brahmins returned to their abode and sitting there quietly, went on eulogising Siva. They considered everything as Siva's will.

Narada Went to Vaikuntha and Curses Visnu There

The sages said: —

Suta, Oh Suta of great intellect, a wonderful tale has been narrated by you. When the two attendants of Lord Rudra had left at their own will, what did the infuriated Narada do?

Suta said: —

After cursing the two attendants of Siva suitably, the sage, still under the earlier delusion, looked into the water and saw that his face was quite normal. It was also due to Siva's will. He did not wake from the delusion still due to Siva's will. Thereupon, recollecting that it might have been a deception of Hari, he became unbearably infuriated and went to Visnuloka. There, he angrily poured abusive words blazing like kindled fire.

Narada said: —

Oh Visnu, you are an extremely wicked, deceptive enchanter of the world. You are unable to stand others' success. You dabble in illusory tactics and your intentions are always dirty. Formerly you assumed the form of an enchantress and showed your deceptive power. You made the demons drink liquor and not the nectar.

If out of pity, Siva had not drunk poison, all your illusory tactics would have been quelled since you take pleasure only in deception. Oh Visnu, a deceptive path is extremely attractive to you. You had never been of saintly nature, but the Lord made you free from control. Siva must be repenting of the powers he gave you. Oh Visnu, I shall now teach you a lesson so that you will never do such a thing again. You are fearless because till now you have not come into conflict with an equally powerful person. Now you will derive the fruit of your own deeds.

Suta said: —

After saying this, the sage, still under the influence of Maya, furiously cursed Visnu, thereby exhibiting the superiority of his brahminical power.

Narada said: —

Oh Visnu, the enchanter that you are, you made me distressed for the sake of a woman. You shall experience misery in that human form which you imitated while proceeding with your deceptive tactics. Your allies will be those whose faces you assigned to me. Oh inflictor of miseries upon others, you shall get the misery of separation from a woman. You shall have the travails of a human being deluded by ignorance.

Suta said: —

Thus Narada cursed Hari. Visnu quietly accepted the cause, praising the Maya of Sambhu. Thereafter Siva, of great divine sport, withdrew his enchanting Maya, whereby Narada became wise (as before) and free from delusion.

When the Maya vanished, he became as intelligent as before, regaining perfect knowledge and becoming free from distress. He was surprised at his own actions. He cursed himself after repenting again and again. He praised the Maya of Siva which could enchant even wise people. On realising his mistakes due to illusion, Narada fell at Visnu's feet. Consoled by Hari and freed from wicked ideas, he spoke to Visnu.

Narada said: —

Being deluded and evil-minded, I have spoken many wicked words to you. Oh Lord, I heaped curses on you. Oh master, please make them ineffective. I have committed a great sin. Certainly, I will be falling into hell. Oh Hari, I am your slave. Please direct me on what to do whereby I may destroy my sins and prevent my downfall into hell.

Visnu said: —

Do not be sorry too much. Undoubtedly you are my true devotee. Dear sage, now listen. You will not fall into hell. Siva will make you happy. Deluded by your haughtiness, you disobeyed the instructions of Siva hence he taught you a lesson. Be sure in your mind that everything has happened in accordance with Siva's wish. That Lord Siva removed your haughtiness.

Oh sage Narada, cast off all your doubts. Sing the songs of the noble glory of Siva. Repeat a hundred names of Siva and his hymns. By his Japa, all of your sins will perish. Oh sage, do not be grief-stricken. Nothing has been perpetrated by you. It was Siva who did everything. It was Lord Mahesvara who deluded your splendid intellect and made you suffer on account of love. It was he who made you his mouthpiece and cursed me. From now onwards you shall always worship Lord Siva with care and utter devotion.

Suta said: —

After advising the sage thus, Visnu was pleased. Remembering, saluting and eulogising Siva, he vanished from that place.

Narada Goes to Kasi

Suta said: —

Oh brahmins, when Visnu vanished, sage Narada roamed over the Earth seeing Siva Lingas with piety. While he wandered all over the Earth, with his mind full of devotional pleasure, he saw many forms of Siva that confer worldly pleasures and salvation on the devotees. On knowing that Narada was wandering over the Earth, the two attendants of Siva approached him, who by that time had become pure in mind. They bowed to him and touched his feet. With a desire to secure release from the curse, they spoke to him respectfully.

The attendants of Siva said: —

Oh celestial sage, son of Brahma, please hear us. We who formerly offended you are really not brahmins. We, your former offenders, are the attendants of Siva. Induced by Siva you had cursed us when your mind was deluded by the illusory infatuation for the princess at the Svayamvara. Realising that the occasion was inopportune, we kept quiet then. We reaped the fruit of our own actions. No one is to be blamed for it. Oh Lord, be pleased. Bless us now.

Suta said: —

On hearing the words of the attendants uttered with devotion and respect, the sage replied lovingly, repenting (for his previous fury).

Narada said: —

Oh attendants of Lord Siva, most worthy of the respect of good people, please listen to me, it will make you happy. Formerly, my mind had been deprived. Certainly, it was Siva's will. In that state of delusion and crookedness, I had unfortunately cursed both of you. What I have said is bound to happen.

Still, oh Ganas (attendants) listen. I shall tell you the way of redemption from the curse. Please forgive my sin now. You will be born as demons from the semen virile of a great sage and due to his power, you will secure the commanding position of the king of demons. You will be endowed with prosperity, strength and valorous exploits. You will rule over the whole of the universe as devotees of Siva. You will gain your former position after courting death at the hands of a manifestation of Siva.

Suta said: —

On hearing this the two attendants of Siva became delighted and went back to their abode joyfully. Narada too was delighted. Meditating exclusively on Siva, he continued his wanderings over the Earth, seeing the various holy centres of Siva personally.

Reaching Kasi, which is a favourite resort of Siva, the sage became content. He saw Siva, the Lord of Kasi and worshipped him with great pleasure and love. He stayed in Kasi for a long time. Narada then went to the region of Brahma, his mind being highly purified by remembering Siva. He then asked Brahma to tell him the good principles of Siva.

Narada said: —

Oh Brahma, the Lord of the universe, by your grace I have heard the greatness of Visnu entirely and also the path of devotion. But I have not understood the principle of Siva.

Hence, Oh Lord, please explain the rules of his worship and also the various activities of the Lord. How did Siva remain in his pure form before creation? In the middle of creation, how did he sport? At the time of dissolution, how does he remain? How is he, the benefactor of the world, propitiated? Please tell me all about his manifestation and especially his exploits. Tell me about the manifestation of Uma and her marriage. Narrate to me Parvati's birth and her marriage as well as Guha's birth.

Suta said: —

On hearing these words of Narada, his own son, Brahma, the grandfather of the world, spoke to him.

Description of the Nature of Mahapralaya and the Origin of Visnu

Brahma said: —

Oh Brahmin, foremost among the celestial beings, a good matter has been enquired by you. I shall explain to you the wholesome and salutary principles of Siva.

At the time of great dissolution, when all the mobile and immobile objects of the world are dissolved, everything gets enveloped in darkness, without the sun, moon, planets and stars. The day and the night are not demarcated. There is no fire, no wind, no earth and no water. The whole firmament is one but void. There is no Dharma or Adharma, no sound, no touch. Smell and colour are not manifest. There is no taste.

Thus when there is pitch darkness and what is mentioned in the Vedas as 'The Existent and the Brahman' is alone present. It is incomprehensible to the mind. It cannot be expressed by words. The Veda says that it envelops whatever is in a surprising way. It has no beginning or end. It is in the form of pure knowledge.

People have doubts about giving it a name. That 'Being', then after some time, it is said, wished for a second. The Being, having no form of its own, wished to create an auspicious form of its own endowed with all power, qualities and knowledge. The Being was created in the form of Isvara of pure nature. The original Being without a second, who was termed Supreme Bahman, vanished. The manifest form of the formless Being is Sadasiva.

Isvara thought alone, then created the physical form Sakti from his body. That Sakti is Ambika, Prakrti and the goddess of all. She is the prime cause and the mother of the three deities. The supreme Purusa is Siva. He is called Sambhu. He holds the Mandakini (Ganga) on his head, and the crescent moon on his forehead. He has three eyes. The Brahman in the form of Kala (Time) together with Sakti, created the holy centre called Sivaloka. The same is called Kalika, the excellent holy centre. Oh sage, that holy centre is never free from Siva. Oh celestial sage, the blissful two deities then wished for another Being to be created.

Siva thought within himself — 'Another being shall be created by me. Let him create everything, protect it and in the end, let him dissolve it with my blessing. Having entrusted everything to him, we two, remaining in Kasi, shall roam as we please. We can stay happily in this blissful forest being free from worries (of creation).' Thereupon a person came into being who was the most charming one in the three worlds, who was calm with Sattva Guna being prominent, and who appeared to be the ocean of immeasurable majesty.

Oh sage, he was endowed with patience. There was no one comparable to him. He had the lustre of sapphire. He was glorious with his excellent eyes shining like a lotus. He bowed to Siva Paramesvara and said— 'Oh Lord, give me names and assign me my task.' On hearing this, Lord Siva laughed. With words thunder like in resonance, Lord Siva addressed the person thus.

Siva said: —

You will be famous as Visnu by name as you are all-pervasive. You will have many other names conferring happiness on devotees. Perform penance. Be firm in it.

Brahma said: —

After bestowing all the Vedas into him, Siva vanished, accompanied by Sakti and his attendants. After due obeisance to Siva, Visnu began his great penance. Even after performing penance for twelve thousand divine years, Visnu could not achieve his desire, the vision of Siva that confers everything. He became suspicious and respectfully meditating on Siva pondered, 'What shall I do now?'

In the meantime, the auspicious voice of Siva was heard.

Siva said: —

Perform penance again to remove your doubts.

Brahma said: —

On hearing this, Visnu performed a terrible penance, for a long time, following the path of meditation. Then Visnu became enlightened, following the path of meditation. He was delightfully surprised. From the body of Visnu who exerted himself, water currents of various sorts began to flow as a result of Siva's Maya. He came to be known as Narayana. Oh great sage, the Supreme Brahman in the form of divine waters pervaded the entire void. This water could destroy all sins.

Visnu, the weary person, went to sleep amidst the waters. He was in that blissful state of delusion for a long time. In the meantime, the principles too evolved out of the great soul. The essences, the five elements, the senses of knowledge and action too came into being then.

The Dispute between Brahma and Visnu

Brahma said: —

When Lord Narayana continued to sleep, an excellent lotus of huge size came out of his navel as desired by Siva. It was wonderful, excellent and worthy of vision containing Tattvas. Exerting himself as before, Siva created me from his right limb. Oh sage, having deluded me with his illusion immediately, Siva produced me through the umbilical lotus of Visnu. Thus, I came to be known as lotus-born and conceived in a golden womb.

Deluded by his illusion and weakened in knowledge, I did not know who the progenitor of my body was, other than the lotus. I questioned myself thus. 'Who am I? Where did I come from? What is my duty? To whom was I born a son? By whom have I been created?'

My intellect became confused with these doubts. Then I thought, 'Why shall I be under a delusion? It is easy to gain that knowledge. The place of growth of this lotus is below. My progenitor will undoubtedly be there.' Thinking thus, I descended from the lotus. Oh sage, for a hundred years, the downward trend continued. The source of the lotus was not attained by me. In the doubt-tormented state, I became eager to go up to the top of the lotus.

I climbed up to the lotus by the stalk. But the upper part of the lotus I could not reach. I was disappointed. Another hundred years elapsed in my wandering up the lotus. I stopped for a while in that confused state. Then, by the will of Siva, an auspicious voice from the sky said, 'Perform Penance'. On hearing the voice, I exerted myself for twelve years in performing a terrible penance in order to see my progenitor. At the same time, the four-armed Lord Visnu suddenly appeared before me in order to bless me.

The great Lord was holding the conch, the discus, the mace and the lotus in his hands. He had a crown. Deluded by the illusion of Siva, I could not recognise my progenitor in him. I asked him who he was. Saying that I tried to wake the eternal being. When he did not wake up, I tried to wake him up with fiercer and firmer beatings of the hand. Then the Lord, who had self-control, woke up from his bed and sat. He looked up with his pure eyes resembling a wet lotus, due to sleep. As I stood there quietly, Lord Visnu spread his brilliance over me. Standing up, he smiled once and spoke sweet words.

Visnu said: —

Welcome, welcome to you, dear child, Oh Pitamaha of great brilliance. Do not be afraid. Undoubtedly, I shall confer on you all that you desire.

Brahma said: —

Oh faultless one, how is it that you speak of me trivially as 'Dear child?' I am the creator of worlds, unborn, the eternal, all-pervasive Brahma. I was born of Visnu. I am the soul of the universe, the originator, creator, and the lotus-eyed. You must explain to me quickly why you speak like this. The Vedas speak of me invariably as self-born, all-pervasive, grandfather, self-governed and the excellent supreme being.

Visnu said: —

I know you as the creator of the world. For the sake of creation and support, you are descended from my undecaying limbs. You have forgotten me, who is the Lord of the universe. There is no doubt in this that you are born of the lotus from my umbilicus. Of course, it is not your fault. I have exercised my power of illusion over you. I am the Lord of all Gods. I am the creator, sustainer and destroyer. There is no powerful person equal to me. Realising this, Oh Brahma, the Lord of subjects, seek refuge in me. I shall certainly protect you from all miseries.

Brahma said: —

On hearing these words, I became angry. Being deluded by illusion, in a threatening attitude, I asked him, 'Who are you? Why do you talk so much? Your words will bring up a disaster. You are neither the Lord nor the supreme Brahman. There must be a creator of yours.'

Deluded by the illusion created by Siva the great Lord, I fought a terrific battle with Visnu. We fought a fierce battle in the middle of that vast expanse of the sea of Dissolution. Meanwhile, a phallic image appeared before us in order to enlighten us and settle our dispute. It was as furious as hundreds of the fire of death with thousands of leaping rows of flames.

The Lord Visnu became unconscious by its thousand flames. When I too became senseless, Visnu said to me, 'Oh, why do you contend with me now? A third person has now come. Let our quarrel cease. Let us examine this fire being. I shall go down to find the root of this matchless column of fire. Please go up to the top to examine.

Having said so, Visnu assumed the form of a Boar. Oh sage, I became a swan immediately. From that time onwards, people call me HamsaHamsa, a supreme being.

I flew up and up with the speed of the mind and wind. Narayana, the soul of the universe too, became white then. His body was ten yojanas wide and a hundred yojanas long, as huge as the mountain Meru. He had white sharp teeth. His snort was long and his roar tremendous. His form as the boar was of matchless firmness and he went down quickly. For a thousand years, his downward course continued. From that time onwards Visnu came to be called Svetavaraha (white Boar) in all the worlds.

A Kalpa had elapsed according to the human calculation when Visnu went down and wandered in his eagerness to come out victorious. The Boar did not find even the smallest trace of the root of the Linga. Oh destroyer of enemies, I too spent the same time going up. Unable to see the top, I came down after some time.

Similarly, Lord Visnu, the lotus-eyed, too became weary. Appearing like the Lord of everything in his huge body he too rose up. As soon as he came up, we bowed to Siva again and again. He stood aside with a gloomy mind as he too was deluded by the illusion of Siva. We bowed down to Linga at his back, sides and in front. Both of us, Hari and I, with the peace of our minds, became eager to perform obeisance and spent a hundred autumns therein.

The Friendship of Siva and Kubera

Brahma said: —

In the Kalpa called Padma, I created my mental son Pulastya whose son Visravas had a son named Vaisravana. He propitiated the three-eyed God Siva, with very severe penance and enjoyed the city of Alaka built by Visvakrt.

When that Kalpa was over and the Meghavahana Kalpa had started, the son of Yajnadatta, Srida, performed a severe penance. He reached Kasi after performing his penance. Under the lustre of the gems of the mind, he repeated the mantras of eleven Rudras with loyal devotion and concentration. Then he performed a very severe penance for two hundred thousand years—a penance which was pure in every aspect.

He set up the linga of Siva and worshipped it with the same devotion. The penance was so severe that his body was reduced to skin and bones. Then, in the company of the Goddess Parvati, the Lord Visvesvara addressed the devotee, the Lord of Alaka— 'I am ready to grant you a boon. Choose it, Oh Lord of Alaka'.

The devotee opened his eyes and gazed at Lord Siva. Dazzled by the brilliance, he closed his eyes and addressed him, 'Oh Lord, please give my eyes the power to see your feet. This itself is a great boon, Oh Lord, that I see you present. Oh Lord, obeisance be to you. Of what avail are other boons?'

On hearing his words, the Lord of devas touched him with his palm and gave him the requisite vision. After securing the power, Yajnadatta's son opened his eyes and saw Uma alone at first. He asked, 'Who is this beautiful lady near Siva the Lord? What penance did she perform more difficult than mine? What a form! What love! What good luck! What a fine glory!' He repeated these words several times.

While he was doing this and glancing cruelly at Uma, his left eye, as a result of seeing the lady, burst. Then the Goddess told Siva — 'Why does this wicked man look at me often and say, 'You make my penance shine!' and see me with jealousy? Why does he marvel at my beauty, love and good luck?'

On hearing the words of the Goddess, Lord Siva laughed and said 'Oh Uma, he is your son. He does not look at you angrily or with jealousy. He is describing your glory of penance.' After saying this to the Goddess, Isa told him again.

Siva said: —

Dear son, I am delighted at your penance. I shall give you the boon you desire. You will be the Lord of treasures and the Lord of Guhyakas. You will be the king of Yaksas, Kinnaras and rulers. You will be the leader of Punyajanas and the bestower of wealth to all. My friendship with you shall remain forever. I shall stay near you, very near Alaka, dear friend, in order to increase your love. Oh son of Yajnadatta, great devotee, come on. This is your mother. Fall at her feet with a delighted heart.

Brahma said: —

After granting him boons, Lord Siva told Uma, 'Oh Goddess, be pleased with him. This ascetic is your own son.' On hearing these words of Siva, Parvati, the mother of the universe said to the son of Yajnadatta with a delighted mind.

The Goddess said: —

Dear son, may your pure devotion to Siva remain forever. With your left eye burst you will be Ekapinga, (having a yellow mark in place of an eye). May all the boons granted to you by the Lord fructify. You shall be called Kubera (possessed of an ill-shaped body) since you jealously looked at me.

Brahma continued: —

After granting these boons to Kubera, Lord Mahesvara, in the company of the Goddess Parvati, entered his Visvesvara abode. Thus Kubera attained the friendship of Siva. Very near his city Alaka was Kailasa, the abode of Siva.

Siva Goes to Kailasa

Brahma said: —

Oh Narada, hear the story of Siva's arrival at Kailasa. The Lord of the universe, after bestowing the boon of the Lordship of treasures upon Kubera, returned to his excellent abode and thought within himself thus — 'My complete manifestation, born of Brahma, can look after the activity of dissolution. Now, assuming that form I shall go to Kailasa, the residence of Guhyakas. Rudra, my perfect manifestation, is the single supreme Brahman. He is worthy of being served by Visnu, Brahma and others. In that form I shall become that friend of Kubera, shall remain near him and perform great penance.' Thinking thus, Rudra, desirous of carrying out the wish of Siva, sounded his drum that gave out the divine Nada.

On hearing that, Visnu, Brahma and other deities, sages, and others came there with great delight. The Pramathas too reached that place from different quarters. The leaders of Ganas, revered by the whole world, arrived there. All of them arrived in thousands and crores. The place was able to accommodate everyone.

Then they all lovingly went to Kubera's residence. Kubera and his attendants received the distinguished guest with great respect and worshipped him with devotion. He also worshipped Visnu and other Devas, the Ganas and the followers of Siva.

Siva was highly delighted and he embraced Kubera and kissed him on the head. With all his followers, he stayed near Alaka. The Lord commanded Visvakarma to erect buildings on the mountain for his own residence and that of everyone else. Visvakarma swiftly made all the arrangements. Then at the request of Visnu, Lord Siva went to Kailasa after blessing Kubera and entered his residence at an auspicious hour.

Seated in his throne, Siva then shone all the more. He was duly served by everyone. Everyone eulogised him and Siva blessed them all. Then everyone returned to their abode. When everyone was leaving, Lord Siva asked Visnu and me to sit down. Then He lovingly blessed us.

Siva said: —

Dear sons, you are great favourites of mine, entrusted with the work of creation and sustenance of the three worlds. You are the best of the Devas. Go back to your abodes without any fear. I shall always provide you with happiness. I shall particularly look after you both.

Brahma said: —

On hearing the words of Siva, Visnu and I duly bowed to him and though not delighted (in leaving him), returned to our abodes. At the same time, Siva delightfully made the Lord of treasures sit down and held his hands with his own and said some auspicious words.

Siva said: —

Dear friend, I am charmed by your love. I have become your friend. Go to your place fearlessly. I shall always assist you.

Brahma said: —

On hearing these words of Siva, Kubera was highly delighted. At his bidding, he returned to his abode. Siva stayed on Kailasa, the best of all mountains, along with his Ganas. In some places, he meditated upon his own soul. In some places, he practised Yoga. At times, of his own accord, he gave discourses on ancient historical tales. Thus Lord Siva who had assumed the form of Rudra performed divine sports on mount Kailasa. After some time, he married Sati, the daughter of Daksa Prajapati. Lord Siva sported with her. Following the conventions of the world, he became happy.

RUDRA-SAMHITA
Satikhanda

Summary of Sati's Life

Narada said: —

Oh Brahma, thanks to Siva's favour, you know everything. Now please also tell me how Lord Siva became a householder. Tell me about the story of Siva and Parvati now. I wish to know everything. How did Sati become Parvati and attain Siva again? Oh Brahma, please explain all these and other points relating to this episode.

Brahma said: —

Oh best of sages, listen then. I shall narrate the auspicious story.

Formerly, on seeing my daughter Sandhya in the company of my sons, I was afflicted by the arrows of the cupid and was upset. When remembered by Dharma, Rudra, the highest Lord, came there. He reproached me as well as my sons and went back to his abode. A serious offence was committed by me against Siva, by whose Maya I was subjected to great delusion. Under great delusion and goaded by envious feelings towards the Lord, I conspired with my sons to find out ways and means to delude the Lord himself.

Here again, I was deluded by Siva's Maya. All our ways and means to delude the Lord became ineffective. When my strategy failed, I remembered the Lord Laksmi (Visnu) in the company of my sons. The intelligent Lord Visnu came there and advised me. Instructed by Visnu, who demonstrated Siva's principles, I cast off my envy, but since I still was under delusion I did not abstain from my stubbornness.

I humbly served Sakti and when she was pleased, I created her as the daughter of Daksa and Asikni (Daksa's wife). Daksa, you remember, was my son. The goddess Uma became Daksa's daughter, performed severe penance and thanks to her great devotion, became Rudra's wife.

In the company of Uma, Rudra became a householder and the great Lord performed divine sports. He deluded me even at the time of his marriage. The independent Lord, assuming his own body, married her and returned to his mountain. In her company he sported much, deluding many. Oh sage, much time was happily spent by Siva, free from all depraved feelings and indulging in noble dalliance with her.

Then a feeling of rivalry arose between Daksa and Rudra; Daksa was excessively deluded by Siva's illusion and so, becoming extremely haughty, he censured the quiet Siva. Then Daksa, the haughty, performed a sacrifice without Siva, although he had invited Visnu, me and all other devas.

Since he was in delusion he did not invite Rudra and his own daughter Sati. When she was not invited by her father Siva (Sati) of perfect knowledge and purest chastity played a divine sport. Though not invited by her haughty father, she did go to her father's house, securing the reluctant permission of Siva. Seeing no share of Rudra set apart and being slighted by her father, she reproached all those who were present there and cast off her body. On hearing that, Lord Siva became unbearably furious and pulling at his matted hair he created Virabhadra from his locks.

When he was created, along with attendants, he began asking, 'What shall I do?'. The entire annihilation of Daksa's sacrifice and the disgrace of everyone present there was the order issued by Siva. The Lord of the Ganas (Virabhadra), accompanied by his soldiers, reached the place immediately after receiving the orders. They wreaked havoc there. Virabhadra chastised everyone and spared none. After defeating Visnu and the Devas with strenuous effort, the chief of Ganas cut off the head of Daksa and threw it into the sacrificial fire. By doing so, he destroyed the sacrifice. Then he came back to the mountain and bowed to Lord Siva.

It is said in the Vedas that the world cannot be happy if Lord Rudra is angry. On hearing his song of praise, Rudra relented. He granted their request. Siva became sympathetic and merciful as before. Daksa was resuscitated. The whole sacrifice was renewed under the instruction of the merciful Lord Siva. The Goddess Sati then became the daughter of Himalaya in her next birth. As such, she became famous as Parvati. She propitiated Lord Siva with a rigorous penance and attained him as her husband.

Kama Is Cursed but Blessed Later

(After Brahma creates Sandhya and Cupid out of his mind (Kama), he moves on to tell the rest of the tale. Sandhya is considered as the most beautiful woman to ever exist.)

Brahma said: —

The brahmins Marici and others, my sons, decided on suitable names for the Being that was created out of my mind.

The sages said: —

You will be famous in the world as Manmatha. You will be able to assume any form you wish. Hence, Oh mind-born God, you will be known as Kama too. There is no one equal to you. Causing elation in others you will be known as Madana. The collective power of all the Devas will not be equal to yours. Therefore you will be omnipresent.

Daksa here, the first Prajapati, will give you a suitable wife. This girl of handsome features, born of Brahma's mind, shall become famous in the world as Sandhya. She will be as lustrous as the jasmine flower.

Brahma said: —

Taking his five flower arrows, Kama decided on his future course remaining invisible in form. He thought like this — 'I shall begin my career as assigned by Brahma himself as my eternal task, here itself in the presence of the sages and Brahma. They shall witness my resolution and performance. Sandhya who was referred to by Brahma is also present here. She shall be my mouthpiece. I shall test my power here and then only carry on my work elsewhere.'

After thinking like this and deciding on his further activity, Kama fitted his flower arrows. He got ready to shoot his love arrows at Brahma and others. The enchanter then charmed Brahma and others, the mental sons with several sharp flower arrows.

Oh sages, we felt instantly enamoured. We began to stare at Sandhya frequently, passion depriving our minds. Our lust was heightened. When on seeing her, my vital elements became displaced, and the forty-nine animal Bhavas came out of my body. She too began to manifest the instinctive gestures of side glances, pretences of concealing feelings, as a result of being hit by Kama's arrows.

All the sages, Marici, Atri, Daksa and others, attained a state of sensuous excitement. Then Kama thought to himself — 'The work entrusted to me by Brahma can easily be performed by me.'

On seeing the sinful proclivities of his brothers and father, Dharma remembered Lord Siva. Mentally meditating on Siva, eulogised Siva with different prayers in his state of sorrow.

Dharma said: —

Oh Mahadeva, obeisance be to thee. You are devoid of all attributes. You are Siva, free from the influence of the three Gunas, the fourth Being. Great Lord! Save me from this impassable ocean of sin. My father and my brothers are now sinfully inclined towards me.

Brahma said: —

Thus eulogised by Dharma, the great Lord came there immediately to protect Dharma. Stationed in the ether, Siva saw me, Brahman, Daksa and others in such a mental state and laughed mockingly. The full-emblemed deity spoke these consoling words.

Siva said: —

Alas! Oh Brahma, how is it that you were overwhelmed with lustful feelings on seeing your own daughter? This is highly improper for those who walk on the line of the Vedas. Sister, brother's wife and daughter are like one's mother. A sensible man shall never look at them with a reprehensible vision. The Vedas clearly mention these principles.

Oh Brahma, how can you forget them? How is it that your sons who practise Yoga and meditate, fall for their sister like such? This Kama is a fool, deficient in sense and ignorant of proper occasion. How is it that he has begun to torment them with excessive power?

Brahma said: —

On hearing these words of Siva, I perspired profusely in an instant, on account of shame. Although the desire to seize Sandhya still lingered, I curbed the upset senses, fearing him (Siva). From my sweat were created manes of extraordinary powers. Daksa also perspired. From the drops of sweat that fell from Daksa's body, a splendid woman endowed with good qualities was born. Her face shone like the full moon and full-blown lotus. Her name was Rati. She was capable of captivating even the sages.

Then, all others curbed their senses and their activities. The semen virile of the four — Kratu and others — fell on the ground from which other types of manes were born. Sandhya, whose senses were also twisted, regained her original senses. Since she was glanced at kindly by Siva, she became free from defects and devoted herself to virtuous rites.

In the meantime after blessing all the brahmins and protecting virtue duly, Siva vanished suddenly. I, the grandfather of the world, snubbed and put to shame by Siva's words, turned my anger against Kama. Seeing my face and realising my hint, Kama withdrew his arrows. He was so terribly afraid of Siva. I then said — 'After playing this same trick on Siva, Kama will be consumed in the fire of Siva's eye and freed of his arrogance.'

It was in front of everyone, including the manes, that I spoke to Kama this way. On hearing this curse of terrible nature, Rati's husband was frightened. He abandoned his arrows and became visible.

Kama said: —

Oh Brahma, why have I been so terribly cursed by you? Oh Brahma, you have assigned me my task. I have only carried it out. Hence this curse is not proper. I have not done anything else. You had said — 'All of us, I, Visnu and Siva are targets of your arrows.' I only tested your statement.

Brahma said: —

I cursed you because you have aimed at us—this Sandhya who is my daughter and me her father. But now I am free from anger. In this state, I tell you Oh Kama, do not be under any suspicion. Cast off your fear. Be happy. Oh Kama, he will reduce you to ashes in the fire of his eye. But he will give you another similar body afterwards. Saying this, I vanished. Kama also got mental peace and everyone returned to their abodes.

The Hymn Sung by Sandhya.
Sandhya Acquires the Boon from Siva

Bhrama said: —

Oh best of my sons, listen to the description of the great penance of Sandhya. Vasistha had formerly instructed Sandhya in the rites of penance that she wanted to perform after being deluded by Kama's arrows. Sandhya was greatly pleased on learning the procedure. On the bank of the lake Brhallohita, she began to perform penance. She worshipped Siva with the mantra taught by Vasistha. A period of four Yugas elapsed while she performed penance. Propitiated by her penance, Siva was greatly delighted. He revealed himself to her. She rejoiced much on seeing in front of her, the Lord Siva with a face beaming with delight, in the same form as she was meditating on.

Sandhya thought to herself, 'What shall I say? How shall I eulogise?' In this agitation, she closed her eyes with fear. As she remained with eyes shut, Siva entered her heart and blessed her with divine wisdom, divine speech and divine eyes. Directly perceiving the Lord Durga, she eulogised the Lord of the worlds.

Sandhya said: —

Obeisance be to you who is the creator of the worlds. Obeisance to you whose form can be imagined in the nature of Vidya, which is different from insentient things. Obeisance to you who created this universe in the form of Brahma, who sustains it in the form of Visnu and who destroyed it in the form of Rudra.

Bhrama said: —

Being thus eulogised and having heard her words, Siva became highly pleased. Her body, originally clad in barks of trees and deer-hide, had, by this time, been completely covered by clusters of matted hair hanging down from the head and her face appeared like a lotus threatened by frost. On seeing her Siva melted with pity and addressed her.

Siva said: —

Oh gentle lady, I am delighted by your great penance and this eulogy. Oh auspiciously intelligent woman, you can choose your boon. Whatever boon seems to be useful to you and is desired by you, I shall grant it to you. I am delighted by your rites, said Siva.

Sandhya said: —

Oh Lord Siva, let the first boon chosen by me be granted. Let no living being, born in this atmosphere, be full of lust at the time of its nativity. This is another boon chosen by me that no other woman shall become so famous in the three worlds as I have become or shall become. No creation of mine shall become lustful or fall anywhere degraded. He who becomes my husband shall be my intimate friend with pure mind. Any person who looks at me with lustful eyes shall lose his manliness and become a eunuch.

Shiva said: —

Oh lady Sandhya, listen. Your sin has been reduced to ashes. I have abandoned my anger towards you. By this penance you have become pure. Whatever you have asked I grant you entirely. In all living beings the first stage shall be infancy, the second childhood, the third youth and the fourth stage shall be old age. When the third stage in life is reached, the living beings shall become lustful. In some cases it shall be at the end of the second stage.

This new limitation is imposed by me as a result of your penance. No living being shall be lustful at the time of its nativity. You will attain such a pure chastity as will not be attained by any other woman in the three worlds. Except Your husband, whoever looks at you with lustful eyes, shall immediately become impotent and weak. Your husband shall be the one endowed with great fortune, penance and comely features. He shall live for a period of seven Kalpas along with you.

Thus I have granted you all the boons requested by you. I shall tell you another incident that transpired in the previous birth. That you would cast off your body in the fire has been foretold. I shall tell you the means thereof. You will certainly carry it out. Let that be performed by you at the twelve-year sacrifice of the sage Medhatithi in the blazing sacrificial fire.

In the ridge of this mountain, on the banks of this river Candrabhaga, Medhatithi is performing a great penance in his hermitage. You go there, unobserved by the sages. Thanks to my favour, you will become his fire-born daughter. If you have chosen in your mind a desirable bridegroom as your husband, you shall think of him while you consign your body into the fire.

Oh Sandhya, while you were performing severe penance, Daksa had begotten many chaste daughters who were also duly married. He gave twenty-seven of his daughters to the moon in marriage. But the moon had a special liking for only Rohini and he neglected others. Hence, the moon was cursed by Daksa. The redemption being, when he sees the Ether, he would find her there. At that time the Gods had come near you but since your mind was fixed in me, they couldn't see you.

The river Candrabhaga arose, being created by Brahma for the redemption of the moon from the curse. It was then that Medhatithi arrived here. There is none equal to him in penance. There has never been such a person, nor will there ever be one. He has now started the sacrifice of Jyotistoma of many great rites. In that blazing sacrificial fire, you shall cast off your body. You are pure now. May your other desires be also fulfilled.

The Sacred Rites of Nanda
and Hymn to Siva

Brahma said: —

Oh sage, once I saw Sati standing near her father along with you. When she saw both of us being honoured and bowed to by her father, Sati also did the same. At the end of obeisance, Oh Narada, you and I sat in the fine seat provided by Daksa. When she humbly bowed again, I spoke to her. I said, 'Oh Sati, secure, as your husband, the Lord of the universe (Siva), who desires only you and whom you too desire. Oh auspicious lady, you shall secure, as your husband, the person who has not taken, does not take, and will not be taking another wife. He will be unlike others.'

After saying this to Sati, we stayed in Daksa's abode for a long time. He bid farewell to us and we went to our respective places. On hearing what I had to say to Sati, Daksa became delighted and free from all worries.

After passing her girlhood and reaching the state of early youth, she attained beauty in every limb which blazed forth brilliantly. Daksa, the Lord of worlds, on seeing her blooming in the proper age thought within—'How shall I give my daughter to Siva?' She too desired to attain Siva. Her desire grew every day. After knowing her father's idea, she approached her mother.

Sati sought the permission of her mother to perform the penance with Siva as the goal. Firmly resolved in her desire to secure Siva as her husband, she propitiated him in her own house with the permission of her mother. She offered him cooked rice, sweet pies, puddings, cooked barley and much more. This she did each month.

With every passing month and season, she had offered various food items to Siva along with sweet smelling flowers. Sati ensured to keep fast as directed by the rituals and lay awake for as long as it was said. All the while, she kept worshipping Siva in her heart.

She was steady and she never thought of anyone else. In the meantime, devas and sages with Visnu and I, at their home, came to see the penance of Sati. On arrival, Sati was seen by the devas as an achievement in embodied form. She was completely engrossed in meditating on Siva. She had reached the stage of the enlightened seers.

With palms joined in reverence, the devas paid respects to Sati joyfully. Visnu and others joyously praised Sati's penance. They then went to Kailasa, the great mountain dear to Siva. The Lord Visnu approached Siva with great joy, accompanied by Laksmi, and I too along with Savitri. On arriving there and after paying respects to the Lord with great excitement we lauded him with various hymns.

The Devas said: —

Obeisance to thee, Oh Lord, from whom the mobile and the immobile beings have originated. Obeisance to the great Purusa, Mahesa, the supreme Isa and the great Atman. Obeisance to the primordial seed of every one. We have sought refuge at his feet who is the supreme Brahman, who is the soul of everyone, who is the greatest witness with unbarred vision and who assumes various forms.

Brahma said: —

After eulogising the great Lord, all the Devas, Visnu and others, stood silently in front of the Lord with their shoulders stooping down with great devotion.

Prayer to Siva Offered by Brahma and Visnu

Brahma said: —

On hearing the song of praise offered by Visnu and others, Siva became delighted and smiled broadly. On seeing Brahma and Visnu in the company of their consorts, Siva addressed them suitably and asked them the purpose of their visit.

Oh Visnu, Oh Brahma, Oh devas and sages, please tell me precisely and without fear the purpose of your visit. I am delighted at the hymn sung by you all. I wish to hear why you have all come here and what is the work to be done here, said Siva.

Brahma said: —

Oh great Lord, please listen to why we both have come here in the company of devas and sages. Visnu and I have become united with our wives. With great pleasure, we carry on our activities in the world at your bidding. Hence, for the benefit of the universe, for the happiness of the devas, you must accept an auspicious lady as your wife.

Oh great Lord, please listen to another incident of bygone days, just recollected by me. You yourself as Siva mentioned this to us formerly. You had said, 'Oh Brahma, this my great form, exactly as this, will be manifested through your limb. He will be known as Rudra in the world. Brahma is the cause of creation, Visnu is the sustainer. I shall be the cause of dissolution in the form of Rudra, a Saguna form. I shall marry a woman and perform an excellent function.'

These are your words. Remembering these words please fulfil your promise. Oh Lord, this is your own directive that I be the creator and Visnu the protector. We two are unable to perform our duties without you. Hence, take up a beloved consort who too will be engaged in the activities of creation.

Siva said: —

Oh Brahma, Oh Visnu, both of you are always dear to me. What you say is indeed weighty since you two are engaged in Siva's work. Oh best of Devas, it is not proper for me to marry as I am detached from the world and engaged in penance. Besides, I am always unclean and inauspicious. Hence say, now what can I do with a loving wife? None of my activities are pursued with self-interest. Yet I shall carry out what you have suggested for the benefit of the universe. Considering your weighty words for the fulfilment of my promise and the goal of my task, I shall marry.

You must hear what sort of a wife I will be taking in accordance with that promise. What I say is indeed proper. Suggest a woman of comely features and Yogic practice who will be able to receive my semen virile in parts. She must be a Yogini when I practise Yoga and a loving woman when I indulge in love. I shall also be deep in meditation from time and again. Damned be she if she comes in the way. It is these worries that kept me unmarried. Hence, get me a wife who will follow my activities ever. There is another condition to which please also listen, O Brahma. If she evinces a disbelief in me or in what I say, I shall abandon her.

Brahma said: —

Oh Lord Siva, I shall suggest such a woman as you desire for yourself. She is Uma.

Formerly she manifested herself in the forms of Sarasvati and Laksmi in order to fulfil her task. Laksmi became the wife of Visnu and Sarasvati became mine. From her desire for the welfare of the world she has taken a third form. She is born now as Daksa's daughter in the name of Sati. Oh Lord, she will be an ideal wife rendering wholesome service.

Oh great Lord, there is no doubt in this that what Brahma has said constitutes what I have to say. Hence, Oh great Lord, be merciful to me and carry out this request. said Visnu.

Brahma said: —

After hearing both of us, great Lord Siva agreed and said, 'So be it'.

Sati is Granted the Boon

Brahma said: —

Oh sage, now listen to how Sati obtained a boon from Siva.

In the month of Asvina (September-October), Sati kept a fast on the eighth day of the bright half and worshipped Siva with great devotion. When her Kanda rites were concluded on the ninth day (Navami), while she was engrossed in meditation, Siva became visible to her.

He was fair-complexioned, handsome in appearance, had five faces and three eyes. The crescent moon adorned his forehead. He was in a joyous mood. He had four arms and His neck was blue in colour. He was holding a trident and an amulet for protection. On seeing Siva directly in such a form, she bent her head from shyness and she knelt at his feet. Although he desired her to be his wife, he wished to bestow on her the fruit of her penance. Thus he spoke to her in the state of her penance.

Siva said: —

Oh daughter of Daksa, of good rites, I am delighted by these rites you have observed. Choose a boon. I shall grant it whatever it may be, said Siva.

Brahma said: —

Although Siva, the Lord of the universe, knew her desire, he said—Choose a boon. It was because he desired to hear her speak. She too, who was highly bashful, could not speak out her mind as it was covered up by bashfulness. He repeatedly urged her to tell him the boon she desires. Somehow suppressing her bashfulness, Sati spoke.

'As you please, give unto me, the desired boon or the bridegroom of my desire, without any hindrance,' replied Sati.

'You be my wife,' said Siva.

'Oh great Lord of Devas, Lord of the universe, please take me with due marital rites in the presence of my father,' replied Sati.

Brahma said: —

On hearing these words of Sati, Siva glanced lovingly at her and said— 'So be it.' The daughter of Daksa bowed to Siva with devotion, sought and received his consent and returned to her mother with a fascinating gaiety. Siva returned to his hermitage on the ridges of the Himalayas and began meditations though with difficulty, as he still felt the pangs of love in separation from Sati. Calming his mind somehow, he thought of me in the usual conventions of the world. I approached him immediately.

Accompanied by Sarasvati, I reached that place on the Himalayan ridge where Siva stayed pining in the anguish of love for Sati. On seeing me, he spoke.

Siva said: —

Oh Brahma, since, in the matter of accepting a wife, I showed a little selfishness. I have been propitiated by Sati, the daughter of Daksa, with devotion. Thanks to the sacred Nanda rites, I have given her a boon. The boon 'Oh be my husband' was asked by her.

I granted her the boon.

Then Sati said, 'Oh Lord of the universe, please accept me in the presence of my father.' Oh Brahma, that too I granted her as I was satisfied with her devotion, he returned to her mother's house, and I returned here. At my bidding you must approach Daksa. Speak to him so that he shall give his daughter in marriage to me at once. Exploit all means to cut short her days of separation. Oh adept in every lore, console Daksa.

Brahma said: —

Saying thus in my presence I was happy to be of assistance. I told Lord Siva that Daksa himself will offer him his daughter. Then I went to Daksa's residence by a speedy flight.

Narada said: —

Oh Brahma, please tell me. When Sati returned to the house what did Daksa do thereafter? asked Narada.

Brahma said: —

Having concluded the austerities, and secured what she desired as a boon, Sati went home and made obeisance to her father and mother. Her girlfriends informed her mother and father about the acquisition of boon by their friend Sati from Lord Siva who was glad at her devotion.

The parents who obtained the news through her friends were very glad and celebrated a great festival. Virini embraced her daughter on the head and delightfully praised her frequently. After some time had elapsed, Daksa thought of the procedure of handing over his daughter to Siva. The great Lord Siva had come here himself. But he has gone back. How will he come again to woo his daughter?

Daksa thought, 'Can a person be sent to Siva immediately? No, this is not proper. If he spurns the offer it will be a fruitless torment.'

Even as Daksa was constantly thinking like this, I suddenly appeared before him along with Sarasvati. On seeing me Daksa, my son, paid due respects and stood waiting. He gave me a fitting seat to sit on. Daksa was worried with thoughts. But he became greatly delighted at my sight. He asked me the purpose of my visit.

Siva said: —

Oh creator, preceptor of the universe, be kind and tell me the purpose of your visit.

Brahma said: —

Oh Daksa, listen. I shall tell you why I have come here. The wholesome benefit of your progeny is what I desire and what you must also desire. Your daughter has propitiated Siva, the Lord of the universe and has secured a boon.

The opportune moment for the same has arrived now. After granting the boon, Siva returned. But, ever since, he has not had any mental peace due to separation from your daughter. He is unable to find any peace in Yoga and meditation. It is only Sati that he desires now.

Hence, Oh Daksa, offer your daughter immediately to Siva for whom she has been intended. Thereby you will get contentment and relief. Through Narada I shall bring him here.

'It is so. It is so,' said Daksa.

Marriage of Siva and Sati

Narada said: —

When you approached Siva, what was it that transpired? What were the events? What did Siva himself do?

Brahma said: —

I approached Lord Siva who was staying in the Himalayan mountains in order to bring him (to the house of Daksa). I was in a joyous mood. On seeing me approach, the bull-emblemed Siva had doubts about the acquisition of Sati. He immediately spoke to me.

Siva said: —

Oh eldest of devas, what did your son (Daksa) say? Tell me lest my heart should be severed by the cupid. This anxiety of separation is truly unbearable now. Oh Brahma, respect the name Sati. Let me do what shall be done. She is not different from me. She has to be attained by me.

Brahma said: —

O sage Narada, on hearing the words of Siva best speaking of His strict adherence to the conventions of the world I told Siva, consoling Him.

Oh bull-emblemed God, hear what my son told me regarding Sati. Rest assured that what you wanted to achieve has been achieved.

Daksa has said, 'My daughter shall go to him. She has been intended for him. This has been my desire. For this purpose, Siva had been propitiated by my daughter. Now he too seeks her. Hence she has to be offered to him by me. Let him come to me in an auspicious conjunction of stars. Then I shall offer my daughter to him in the form of Alms.'

Oh bull-emblemed God, Daksa has told me so. Go to his house at an auspicious hour and bring her here.

Siva said: —

I shall go to his house accompanied by you and Narada. Hence, Oh creator of the universe, you remember Narada. Remember your mental as well as physical sons — Marici and others. Oh Brahma, with all my attendants and with them, I shall go to Daksa's house.

Brahma said: —

Thus commanded by Siva following the conventions of the world, I remembered you, Narada and my other sons. Everyone arrived delightedly as soon as I remembered them. Vishnu also arrived accompanied by Laksmi and his entire army.

Siva started his journey to Daksa's place on the thirteenth day in the bright half of the month of Caitra (March-April). He went ahead with all his companions and animals. Siva reached Daksa's abode seated on his speedy bull and along with Visnu and others. With great humility and boundless joy, Daksa along with his people welcomed him. Daksa honoured everyone.

The sages were seated in their due order. Then Daksa took Siva inside the house along with the devas and the sages. The delighted Daksa worshipped Lord Siva, after offering him an excellent seat. He worshipped Visnu, me, the brahmins, devas and the Ganas of Siva, with great devotion. After performing the suitable worship, Daksa in the presence of respectable sages, announced the marriage agreement.

Then Daksa knelt before me, his father, with pleasure and said — 'Oh Lord, the marriage rites shall be performed by you.' Saying 'Amen', I got up with a delightful heart and performed the preliminary rites.

Then in an auspicious conjunction of stars with the planets in a propitious position, Daksa joyfully gave his daughter Sati to Siva. As a part of the rites of marriage, Siva held the hand of Sati. We all, Visnu, I, you and other sages, bowed to Siva and delighted him with laudatory hymns. After offering his daughter, Daksa, my son was extremely satisfied, Sati and Siva were in a happy mood. Everything concluded auspiciously.

Description of Siva's Sports

Brahma said: —

After giving his daughter in marriage, Daksa gave her different articles in the form of dowry. Many gifts were given to Siva. Daksa gave monetary gifts to the brahmins with great delight. Then Visnu stood up and spoke thus.

Visnu said: —

Oh great Lord, you are the father and Sati is the mother of the world. You have taken incarnation out of sheer sport for the welfare of the good and suppression of the wicked—so says the eternal scripture. You two shine in juxtaposition with us. Always bestow auspicious goodness upon the people of this world. Oh Lord of living beings, this is my humble submission. You shall kill the man, whoever it may be, who sees or hears her with lust in his mind.

Brahma said: —

On hearing these words of Visnu, Lord Siva laughed. The omniscient Lord told the slayer of Madhu, 'Be it so.' Oh great sage, after this, Visnu returned to his abode. He kept the incident quite secret but asked the people to continue the festivities. Then at my bidding in the capacity of the main priest, Siva duly and with great delight, performed the circumambulation of the sacred fire. Then a surprisingly strange event occurred there.

Siva's power of illusion is inscrutable. Oh sage, while going round the fire, the feet of Sati protruded out of the cloth that covered them. I looked at them. My mind being afflicted by love, I stared at the limbs of Sati. Oh excellent brahmin, I was deluded by Siva's Maya. The more I stared at the beautiful limbs of Sati eagerly the more I became thrilled like a love-afflicted man. Staring thus at the chaste daughter of Daksa and being afflicted by the cupid, I craved to see her face.

Since she was bashful in the presence of Siva I could not see her face. Then I began to consider proper means whereby I could see the face.

Afflicted much by the cupid, I pitched upon the production of smoke as the means thereof. I put many wet twigs into the fire. Only very little ghee did I pour into the fire. Much smoke arose out of the fire from the wet twigs, so much so that darkness enveloped the whole altar ground (and the neighbourhood). Then Lord Siva, covered his eyes affected by smoke.

Then, afflicted by cupid, I lifted her veil and stared into the face of Sati. I looked at Sati's face many times. I was helpless in curbing the onset of a sensuous orgasm. Four drops of my semen virile got displaced and fell on the ground like drops of dew as a result of staring into her face.

I was stunned into silence. I was surprised. I became suspicious. I covered up the semen drops lest anyone should see them.

But Lord Siva saw it through his divine vision. The trickling down of the semen excited his fury and he said thus to me.

Siva said: —

Oh sinful wretch, what a despicable mess you have perpetrated! At the time of her marriage you have passionately gazed at the face of my beloved. You think that this blunder has not been known by me at all. There is nothing that is unknown to me in the three worlds. Tell me how can it then remain hidden?

Brahma said: —

Saying thus, and remembering the words of Visnu, Siva who dearly loved Visnu, lifted his trident and wished to kill me. When the trident was lifted to kill me, Marici and others raised a hue and cried. Then all the devas and the sages, extremely terrified, began to eulogise him who was blazing there.

Devas said: —

Oh great Lord, save me. Be pleased. Oh Lord of Devas, Visnu, Brahma and others are all your slaves.

Brahma said: —

Thus in many ways, the timid and frightened devas and the sages eulogised the Lord of devas who was furious. Suspecting some terrible disaster, Daksa raised his hand and rushed at Siva, preventing him with shouts of, 'Oh don't do this, Oh don't do this'. Seeing Daksa in front of him in a state of excited suspicion, and remembering the request of Visnu, Lord Siva spoke displeasing words.

Lord Siva said: —

Oh patriarch Daksa, what has just been requested by Visnu, my great devotee and agreed to by me shall be done here. Whoever stares at Sati lustfully shall be killed by me. I shall make the words of Visnu true by killing Brahma. Why did Brahma stare at Sati lustfully? Moreover, he has committed a sin by discharging his semen. Hence I shall kill him.

Brahma said: —

Then the intelligent Visnu, the great favourite of Siva and very clever in managing all affairs, bowed down and lauded Rudra who spoke as before. Standing in front of him and singing various songs of praise to Siva, he prevented him.

Visnu said: —

Oh Lord Siva, do not kill Brahma, the creator and Lord of the worlds. He has sought refuge in you and you are reputed to be favourably disposed to those who seek refuge in you. Oh Lord, I am a great favourite of yours and am called the chief of Devotees. Keeping my submission in mind, be merciful towards me.

This four-faced deity has manifested himself to create the subjects. If he were killed, there would be none to create the subjects. Oh Lord, we three are carrying out the functions of creation, sustenance and dissolution repeatedly as you bid us. If he is killed, who will carry out your directives? Hence Oh Lord, you shall not kill this creator. It was by him that Sati, the daughter of Daksa, was fixed up as your wife by good means.

Brahma said: —

On hearing this entreaty of Visnu, Siva finally spoke.

Lord Siva said: —

Oh Visnu, Lord of devas and as dear to me as my vital airs, do not prevent me from killing him. He is a rogue. I shall fulfil your first entreaty already accepted by me. I shall kill this wicked four-faced one who has committed a great sin. I shall myself create all living beings — mobile and immobile. Or by my splendid power I shall create another creator. Killing this Brahma and keeping up my plighted word, I shall create another creator. Do not prevent me.

Brahma said: —

On hearing these words of Siva, Visnu spoke again, smiling to himself and saying, 'Oh Lord, don't do this.'

Visnu said: —

Fulfilling the promise is but proper in you, the great Being. We three, Oh Siva, are your own selves. We are not different. We are of the same form. Think over the exact state.

Siva said: —

Oh Visnu, Lord of all devotees, how can this Brahma be my own self? He is observed as different, standing before me.

Visnu said: —

Oh Sadasiva, Brahma is not different from you, nor are you different from him. I am not different from you, nor are you different from me.

Who are you? Who am I? Who is Brahma? Your own three parts—you being the supreme soul. They are different only as the cause of creation, sustenance and dissolution. Just as the body has the parts of head, neck, so also we are the three parts of Siva.

Brahma said: —

Oh excellent sage, on hearing these words the great Lord Siva was delighted. He did not slay me.

Siva's Marriage Festival

Narada said: —

Oh Lord Brahma, what happened after that? Please continue to narrate the story of the moon-crested Siva and Sati, the wonderful story that quells all sins.

Brahma said: —

When Siva, who is sympathetic towards his devotees, desisted from killing me, all became fearless, happy and pleased. They lauded Siva with devotion. They shouted cries of victory with pleasure. At the same time, delighted and fearless, I eulogised Siva with devotion by means of auspicious prayers. Then Lord Siva spoke to me.

Rudra said: —

Dear Brahma, I am glad. You can be free from fear. You touch your head with your hand. Unhesitatingly carry out my request.

Brahma said: —

On hearing these words of Lord Siva, I touched my head and in the same manner bowed to Siva. When I thus touched my head I assumed the shape of his vehicle, the bull. Then I was very ashamed. I stood with my head bent down. Indra and other devas standing around saw me in that plight. Ashamed that I was, I repeatedly bowed to him and asked for his forgiveness. I asked for the mode of atonement for my sin. I was ready to die too.

Siva said: —

In this very form (of a bull) whereon I sit, you shall perform penance with pleasure in your heart and desire for propitiating me. You will acquire the glory of being called 'The head of Rudra' in the world. You will be the accomplisher of rites for brahmins of great repute.

Discharge of semen is the act of human beings and as you have done the same, you will be born as a man and be roaming over the earth. When you wander over the earth in this form, people will be asking, 'What is there on the head of Brahma?' and you shall reply 'Siva'.

Anybody who has committed the sin of outraging the modesty of another man's wife will be free from that sin if he eagerly hears your story. Whenever people thus repeat your wicked action, your sin will gradually subside and you will become pure.

Oh Brahma, this is the atonement I lay down for you, being laughed at by the people and ridiculed by them. The semen drops that fell in the middle of the altar-ground when you were excited by lust and seen by me will not be retained by anyone. Four drops of your semen fell on the ground. Hence so many terrible clouds causing dissolution shall rise up in the sky.

[In the meantime, (when Siva said so) in front of the devas and the sages, so many clouds emanated from the semen drops.]

Brahma said: —

Oh excellent sage, those clouds rumbling and roaring with hideous sounds, dropping showers at the slightest wish of Siva, burst asunder in the sky. When the sky was covered by those roaring clouds, Siva was quite calm.

After becoming fearless, I concluded the remaining rites of the marriage at the bidding of Siva. Everyone was overjoyed. Music and festivities continued. Flowers were showered on the happy couple. Then the delightful Lord spoke to me as I was standing with palms joined in reverence.

Siva said: —

Oh Brahma, all the rites of marriage have been performed extremely well. I am pleased. You officiated as the priest. What shall I give you as the nuptial fee? You can demand it even if it is hard to get. Tell me quickly, for there is nothing which cannot be granted by me.

Brahma said: —

Oh Lord of Devas, if you are pleased, if I deserve your blessings, please grant me this wish. Oh Lord Siva, for the purification of men from sins, please stay forever in this altar in this self-same form. I shall make my hermitage in its vicinity and perform penance to destroy my sin. If anyone visits this holy site on the thirteenth day in the bright half of Caitra the day is Sunday, may all his sins be quelled. If a woman who is barren, one-eyed, ugly or unfortunate, visits this place she shall be freed from all these *defects.*

Siva said: —

For the benefit of the people, I shall stay in this altar, with my wife Sati in accordance with your words of request.

Brahma said: —

After saying this, Lord Siva, in the company of his wife, stayed in the middle of the altar creating a partial image of himself. Then taking leave of Daksa, Siva desired to depart along with his wife Sati. Daksa bowed humbly to both Siva and Sati and eulogised Siva with devotion.

With the joyous consent of Daksa, Siva seated Sati on the bull and then sitting himself on it went to the Himalayan ridges. Half the way Siva took leave of Daksa with pleasure. Siva soon reached his abode in the beautiful surroundings of the Himalayas with great delight. After reaching his abode Siva honoured the devas and the great sages and then bade farewell to them with respect. Then everyone returned to their humble abodes and Siva entered his residence with Sati.

The Dalliance of Sati and Siva

Narada said: —

Oh dear, I wish to know more of the auspicious story of Siva and Sati, hence having unequalled consideration for me, please narrate the same.

Brahma said: —

our enquiries for the history of the merciful lord are pursued well, since you have prompted me to narrate the divine sports of Siva. Know from me what Siva did with pleasure on reaching His abode after His marriage with goddess Sati, Daksa's daughter and the mother of the three worlds.

Oh celestial sage, after entering his apartment in a befitting manner, along with Sati, Siva, assuming worldly conventions, rejoiced very much. Then after approaching Sati, Siva sent out his attendants—Nandin and others, from the cave in the mountain. He said some words to Nandin and others.

Siva said: —

Oh my attendants, with minds respectfully concentrated in thinking upon me, you shall come to me only when I remember you.

Brahma said: —

Everyone was pleased to hear these words. Then they all went away and he was left alone with Sati. He sported with her with great pleasure. He would make garlands that he would put around her neck. He would sometimes play with her ear rings, bracelets and bangles. He would say things in her ears that made her blush.

Sometimes Lord Siva would become invisible and appear suddenly, embracing her from behind. Sometimes with musk, he would make marks like bees on her breasts that resembled the buds of a golden lotus. Sometimes he would take the necklace off her breasts and press them with his hands.

Sometimes he would come to her lofty breasts saying with laughter, 'this dark spot Kalika on your breasts is your companion of the same colour as it contains the same letters that are found in your name Kalika.' Sometimes when he was overwhelmingly excited with love, he would exchange pleasantries with his beloved.

After dallying among the hedges and grottos in the Kailasa mountain for a long time he went to the Himalayan ridges where he remembered Kama out of his own accord. When Kama reached the vicinity of Siva, Spring spread all his splendour in accord with the inclination of the Lord.

Oh sage, then Sati so exercised her splendid influence on Siva that he did not have mental peace without her even for a moment. The goddess satisfied him completely in the matter of intercourse. She seemed to enter his body. He made her drink that juice. With garlands of flowers wreathed by himself he decorated her and felt new pleasures.

Thus in the ridges and caverns of the Himalayan mountains, the Lord sported about in the company of Sati every day. According to the calculation of the Devas, twenty-five years elapsed, during which he dallied thus.

The Dalliance of Siva and Siva on the Himalayas

Brahma said: —

Once at the advent of clouds, Daksa's daughter said to Siva, who was halting on the ridge of Kailasa mountain.

Sati said: —

Oh Siva my dear husband, please hear my words and do accordingly. The most unbearable season of the advent of clouds has arrived. The speedy gusts of wind scattering sprays of water mingled with nectarine drops from the Kadamba flowers captivate the heart as they blow.

Whose mind will not be agitated by the loud and forceful rumblings of the clouds? In this troublesome time, even crows and Cakora birds build their nests. But you don't. Without a home how will you be happy? Hence endeavour for a residence. Do not delay. Heed my words.

Brahma said: —

Thus advised by Sati frequently Siva laughed provoking a smile from the moon. Then Siva spoke to her on his head by way of its beams.

Siva said: —

Oh my beloved, beautiful woman, clouds will not reach the place where I have to make an abode for you. The clouds usually come only up to the foot of Kailasa. They never go above it. Of the mountains I have mentioned, you can choose one for residence as you desire. Please tell me quickly where you wish to reside.

Oh beloved, do you wish to go to the Himalayas, the king of mountains wherein there is spring for ever, which contains many lakes filled with cool water and hundreds of lotuses? It is full of grassy plains and trees. You can see plenty of flowers, horses, elephants and cows there.

Do you wish to sport about on this great mountain which is very beautiful and which appears to contain the essence of all mountains? Or do you wish to have an abode in my own Kailasa, the great mountain affording shelter to the good and enhanced in beauty by the luminous city of Kubera? Oh beautiful lady, tell me quickly where you wish to stay among these places? I shall make arrangements for your residence.

Brahma said: —

When Siva said this, Sati slowly told Lord Siva revealing her desire.

Sati said: —

I wish to stay only in the Himalayas along with you. You please make arrangements for a residence on that mountain at once.

Brahma said: —

On hearing her words, Siva was fascinated and he went to the summit of the Himalayas along with her. On the top of the mountain near the city of Himalaya, Siva sported about for a long time in the company of Sati. It was a very beautiful place which abounded in crystalline clouds. It shone with grassy plains and plenty of trees. There were various flowers in abundance. It had many lakes. In that heaven-like spot Siva sported with Sati for ten thousand years according to divine calculation.

Siva found peace and pleasure only with Sati. He found no pleasure in sacrifices or the Vedas or penances. Day and night, Sati stared into the face of Siva and he stared at hers. Thus by their mutual association, Kali and Siva nurtured the tree of love, sprinkling it with waters of emotion.

Sati's Test of Rama's Divinity

Narada said: —

Oh Brahma, you have narrated the benevolent glory of Sati and Siva. Now, please tell me more of their glory. What did the couple Siva and Siva do further, stationed on that mountain?

Brahma said: —

Oh sage, listen to the story of Sati and Siva. Having resorted to worldly conventions they continued their sports every day. Thereafter, according to a tradition, it is said that the great Goddess Sati was separated from her husband Siva. She was forsaken by her husband at the time of her father's sacrifice. In view of the disrespect shown to Siva, she cast-off her body there. She was born again as Parvati, daughter of the Himalayas. She performed penance for several years and attained Siva as her husband.

Suta said: —

After hearing these words of Brahma, Narada asked the creator about the glory of Siva and Siva.

Narada said: —

Oh Brahma, disciple of Visnu, please explain in detail the story of Siva and Siva who followed the conventions of the world. Why did Siva abandon his wife who was dearer to him than his life? It looks rather strange. Why did your son Daksa disrespect Siva at the time of sacrifice? How did she abandon her body at the sacrifice of her father? What happened after that? What did Siva do? Please explain everything to me.

Brahma said: —

Oh dear Narada, listen with pleasure to the story of the moon-crested Lord.

Once Siva, accompanied by Sati an of Bharata. He had become cheerless and devoid of lustre. The great liberal-minded Lord Siva bowed to Rama. He said, 'Be victorious'. While he was going elsewhere in the forest he revealed himself to Rama. Sati was surprised at this charmingly strange sport of Siva. She was deluded by Siva's Maya and spoke to him.

Sati said: —

Oh Lord, the Lord of all, the Supreme Brahman, thou art worthy of being served and bowed to. Who are these two people apparently grief-stricken from pangs of separation? Though heroic archers, they are greatly distressed. They seem to be roaming about in the forest. How is it that thou becomest highly delighted and behaved like a devotee? Oh Lord Siva, may this doubt of mine be kindly heard. Oh Lord, the kneeling down of the master at the feet of a servant is not quite befitting.

Brahma said: —

The great Goddess Sati put this question to Siva on being deluded by Siva's illusion. On hearing these words of Sati, Lord Siva laughed and told Sati something she needed to know.

Lord Siva said: —

I shall truly explain it. There is no deception. I bowed thus with respect due to the power of the boon (granted by me). They are two brothers, Rama and Laksmana. They are heroic, intelligent sons of Dasaratha, born of the solar dynasty. The fair-complexioned one is the younger brother Laksmana. The elder one is the complete incarnation of Visnu. He is called Rama. He is incapable of being harassed.

Siva said again: —

Oh goddess, if your mind is not convinced, listen to my words. You can test the divinity of Rama yourself, using your own intelligence.

Brahma said: —

Going there at Siva's bidding, Sati thought — 'I shall assume the form of Sita and shall go to him. If Rama is Visnu, he will know it and otherwise not.' Deciding this she became Sita and went there to test him. On seeing Sati, in the guise of Sita, Rama the scion of Raghu's race, repeated the name Siva, realised the truth and laughed. He bowed to her and spoke humbly.

Rama said: —

Oh Sati, Obeisance to you. Where has Siva gone? Please tell me affably. How is it that you have come here alone without your husband? Oh goddess Sati, why have you cast off your own form and assumed this guise? Take pity on me and tell me the reason thereof.

Brahma said: —

On hearing these words of Rama, Sati was stunned. Remembering Siva's words and realising the truth of the same she felt ashamed. Realising Rama to be Visnu she re-assumed her own original form. Sati spoke delightedly.

Sati said: —

Wandering over the earth along with me in the company of his attendants, the great Lord Siva came here in the forest. Here he saw you searching for Sita in the company of Laksmana. You were highly distressed on account of separation from Sita. At the root of the Vata, he came and bowed to you, glorifying your greatness with pleasure. He was not so happy on seeing the four-armed Visnu as on seeing this simple pure form of yours.

On hearing those words of Siva, my mind became suspicious and at his bidding I desired to test your divinity. Oh Rama, I have realised your Visnuism. I have seen your over-all Lordship. I am now free from doubts. But, still please listen to this. How is it that you became worthy of being saluted by him? Please tell me the truth. Make me free from doubt. Thus, you shall be happy.

Brahma said: —

On hearing her words Rama became happy, his eyes shining with brilliance. He thought upon his Lord Siva. Emotions of love swelled in his heart. Describing Siva's greatness Rama spoke to Sati again.

Separation of Sati and Siva

Rama said: —

Oh Goddess, once Siva called Visvakarman his highest region. He made him erect a large hall of great beauty in his cowshed, and an exquisite throne there. Siva caused Visvakarman to make an excellent, divine, wonderful umbrella for warding off obstacles. He invited Indra, other gods, sages, Brahma and his sons and many more. Sixteen virgins each of Devas, sages, Siddhas and serpents were brought for the auspicious ceremony. With a delightful mind, he called Visnu from Vaikuntha. Siva rejoiced at the perfect devotion of Visnu.

In an auspicious hour, the great Lord made Visnu sit on the exquisite throne and delightedly decorated him in every way. A beautiful coronet was fixed on Visnu and the auspicious holy thread was tied to his waist. He was then crowned by Lord Siva in the Cosmic Hall. Siva eulogised Visnu. He then spoke to Brahma the creator of all worlds.

Lord Siva said: —

May you all hear. From now onwards, at my bidding, this Visnu has become worthy of my respect and that of all devas. Dear one, you too bow to him. May all the Vedas extol him at my bidding as they extol me.

Rama said: —

So saying, Rudra himself bowed to Visnu. Then Visnu was duly revered by Brahma followed by devas, sages, Siddhas and others. Then the delighted Lord Siva bestowed great boons on Visnu and the other devas.

Lord Siva said: —

At my bidding you are now the creator, sustainer and destroyer of all the worlds. You are the bestower of virtue, wealth and love and the chastiser of people of evil predilection. You are the Lord of the universe. You are worthy of the worship of the universe. You will be invincible in battle anywhere, even against me. You will be endowed with great strength and valour.

Oh Visnu, you are my left hand, as Brahma is my right hand. You shall be his progenitor and sustainer too. While stationed here you protect the entire universe taking different incarnations and diverse ways of protection. Oh Visnu, I shall certainly see the various incarnations of yours on the earth and shall be delighted by your devotion to me.

Rama said: —

After conferring thus unlimited prosperity on Visnu, Siva, freely sported about at Kailasa along with his attendants. Thenceforth Lord of Laksmi assumed the guise of a cowherd. The Lord of cowherds, cowherdesses and the cows wandered there with pleasure. Now he has taken a fourfold incarnation at the bidding of Siva. I, who am Rama, and my brothers Bharata, Laksmana and Shatrughna are his incarnations.

Oh Goddess Sati, at the bidding of my father I have come to the forest. Unfortunately I have fallen into deep distress. My wife Sita has been abducted by a demon. I am now seeking my beloved, separated from her and devoid of my kinsmen. By your blessings

I shall have the fortune of acquiring Sita after killing the demon of evil intention who is the cause of trouble. It is my good fortune that both of you have taken pity on me.

Brahma said: —

After speaking thus and bowing in diverse ways to Sati, Rama roamed in the forest with her permission. On hearing these words of Rama of pious rites, Sati was delighted. She praised him in her heart for his devotion to Siva. Remembering her own action she was very distressed.

She returned to Siva, pale in face and gloomy in spirit. While returning, the Goddess frequently mused— 'I did not accept Siva's explanation. I entertained a senseless thought against Rama. After going to Siva what reply shall I give?' Thinking thus, she began to repent in many ways.

Approaching Siva, she mentally bowed to him, with a pallid face and stricken with grief. On seeing her distressed, Siva enquired of her health and asked — 'Oh, have you finished your test?' On hearing Siva's words, she bent her head as a mark of respect but did not say anything. Agitated with grief she stood aghast.

After meditating for a while, Siva could understand everything about Sati. He remembered the promise that he himself had made on being requested by Visnu when he was angry with the latter. The Lord and the protector of righteousness, thought within himself.

Shiva thought to himself: —

'If I were to maintain my love towards Sati at the level as before, my promise will be broken — even if I follow the conventions of the world.'

Brahma said: —

Thus pondering within himself in diverse ways, he mentally discarded Sati but did not break his promise as the protector of Vedic virtue. Then after forsaking Sati mentally, the Lord returned to his abode. He did not at all reveal the promise. While they were on their way, an unembodied speech rose in the sky, telling him within the hearing of everyone particularly of Sati, Daksa's daughter.

The celestial voice said: —

Oh great Lord, you are blessed indeed. There is no other great Yogin or great Lord in the three worlds, on a par with you. No one else can maintain that promise.

Brahma said: —

On hearing the celestial voice, the goddess asked Siva — 'Oh Lord, please tell me, what is the promise that you made?'

Even when asked, the Lord who was benevolent to Sati, did not reveal the vow which he took in the presence of Visnu formerly. Then meditating on Siva, her own beloved husband, Sati understood the matter which meant the abandonment of her own self. After realising the abandonment of herself by him, the daughter of Daksa was grieved.

But the Lord Siva kept the fact of his vow a secret from her and narrated many a tale to her. Thus, narrating tales to her on the way, he reached Kailasa along with her. There Siva entered a trance and meditated upon his real form. Sati stayed in the abode, overwhelmed by grief. Great time elapsed even as the Lord and the Goddess followed the conventions of the world.

Then Siva stopped his meditation. On coming to know of it, Sati came there. The Goddess bowed to him with a moaning heart. The benevolent Siva offered her a seat in front of himself. He narrated several interesting tales to her. By these divine sports, he tried to entertain her and make her mind free from grief. She regained her previous happiness. He too did not forsake his vow.

But oh sage, some ignorant Pandits thus narrate the story of Siva and Siva and their separation. But how can there be a real separation between the two? Who knows the true life and conduct of Siva and Siva. They sport of their own accord and make their own lives. Sati and Siva are united together like words and their meanings. Only if they wish, can their separation be even imagined.

The Cause of Estrangement Between Daksa and Siva

Brahma said: —

Formerly, a great sacrifice was performed by the sages and noble souls who assembled at Prayaga. Siddhas, Sanaka and others, the celestial sages, devas with Prajapatis and men of perfect knowledge who had realised the Brahman attended the function. I too attended the same along with my followers. Oh sage, in the meantime, Lord Siva, accompanied by his attendants and Sati came there. The Lord conferred benefit on the three worlds and offered them protection. On seeing the Lord, everyone eulogised him with great devotion. I joined them too.

At the bidding of Siva they sat in their respective places. They were excessively delighted to see the Lord. They explained to Him the various activities they were engaged in. In the meantime, the Lord Daksa came there. After saluting me, Daksa sat there with my consent.

Daksa was a bit arrogant though worthy of honour, as he had no deep insight into reality. But Lord Siva sat firmly and did not bow to him. Seeing Siva not bowing to him, my son became displeased. Daksa, the patriarch, was furious with Siva. Haughty and devoid of perfect knowledge, Daksa looked cruelly at Siva and spoke aloud.

Daksa said: —

All these Suras and Asuras, brahmins and sages bow to me. How is it that this gentleman, who is always surrounded by goblins and ghosts, behaves like a wicked man? How is it that this shameless man does not bow to me now? How can he be honourable when he is always engrossed in the love of his wife? Hence I am going to curse him.

Brahma said: —

After saying thus the furious rogue spoke to Siva thus.

Daksa said: —

May all these brahmins and devas listen. May all of you deem him worthy of being killed by me. I expel him from my sacrifices.

Brahma said: —

On hearing these words of Daksa, Bhrgu and others reproached Siva. After duly saluting Siva along with the devas, Nandin, the attendant of Siva, was very furious and rolled his eyes. With an intention to curse him, he immediately spoke to Daksa.

Nandisvara said: —

Oh foolish Daksa, how is it that you have expelled my Lord Siva from sacrifice? How is it that you cursed him whose thought makes all sacrifices fruitful and all sacred places holy?

Censured and rebuked thus by Nandin, Daksa the patriarch who was still furious cursed Nandin too.

Daksa said: —

You all, the attendants of Siva, are expelled from Vedic rites. You will be abandoned by the followers of the Vedic path as well as by great sages. You will indulge in drinking wine. Matted hair, ashes and bones will be your embellishments.

Brahma said: —

Thus, Siva's attendants were cursed by Daksa. On hearing that, Nandin, the favourite of Siva became furious.

Nandisvara said: —

With the power of Siva (backing me) I now heap curses on these brahmins here who are against Siva and hence wicked like you. May these brahmins prattle that there is nothing else. May these brahmins indulging in lust, heavenly pleasures, anger, and pride be shameless beggars. They will be perpetually poor and eager to receive monetary gifts. Due to their acceptance of monetary gifts from undeserving persons they will fall into hell.

Oh Daksa, some of them will become brahminical Raksasas. Daksa will become goat-faced. He will be indulging in vulgar worldly lustful pleasures, and evil strategics. His bright, pleasing face will disappear. He will become an individual soul strayed from his ultimate goal.

Brahma said: —

When the brahmins were cursed by the furious Nandin and Siva was cursed by Daksa there was a great hue and cry. On hearing that, I, the creator of the Vedas and the knower of the principles of Siva, rebuked everyone. On hearing the words of Nandin, the Lord Sadasiva laughed and spoke sweetly to him, enlightening him further.

Sadasiva said: —

Oh Nandin of great intellect, listen. Do not get angry. You have cursed the brahmins in vain, erroneously thinking that I have been cursed. Do not angrily curse the knowers of the Veda. The Vedas shall not be cursed by anyone, not even by the evil-minded. I have not been cursed. You please understand the factual position. In vain did you curse the brahmins. Now, be free from anger and other emotions.

Brahma said: —

Thus exhorted by Siva, Nandikesvara became calm and free from anger. After enlightening him and also his favourite Ganas, Siva returned to his abode with delight. Seething with fury and malice against Siva, Daksa went to his abode along with the brahmins.

Thus, I have narrated the crooked intellect of Daksa. Now, hear about his evil intentions and thoughts. I shall tell you further.

The Inauguration of Daksa's Sacrifice

Brahma said: —

Once a great sacrifice was started by Daksa. To partake in that sacrifice, the celestial and terrestrial sages and devas were invited by Siva and they reached the place being deluded by Siva's Maya. Everyone was invited. Many arrived with their sons and wives at Daksa's sacrifice.

I was duly lauded and taken there along with my sons, followers and the embodied forms of the Vedas. Vishnu too was brought to the place of the sacrifice. Daksa received everyone with honour.

The sacrificial fire evinced its diverse forms in a thousand ways, during the sacrificial festivities, in order to receive the sacrificial offerings of Daksa. He followed all the rituals and rules of the sacrifice with utmost precision. With the proper initiation, tying of the holy thread around his wrist and Svastyayana rites duly performed, Daksa along with his wife, shone well.

But he did not invite Siva for that sacrifice, deciding that he was not worthy of taking part in the sacrifice. In view of the fact that Sati was the wife of Kapalin, she was not invited, though she was his beloved daughter.

While the great festivities in the sacrifice of Daksa were being celebrated Dadhici, a devotee of Siva, realised that Lord Siva was not there. He became dispirited and spoke thus.

Dadhici said: —

Oh ye all! Why has not Siva taken part in the festivities of this sacrifice? Of course, the chiefs of devas, the great sages and the guardians of the quarters have all come. Yet the sacrifice cannot be perfect and complete without the noble-soued Siva. Oh Daksa, if accepted by Triyambaka, all inauspicious things become auspicious. If your sacrifice is to be accepted, Siva has to be here. Hence the invitation to the great Siva shall be extended by you immediately or by Brahma or by Visnu.

All of you shall go where he is stationed. Immediately bring Siva along with Sati. If Siva comes here, the sacrifice will become sanctified, or it will remain incomplete and imperfect. I am telling you the truth.

Daksa said: —

Visnu, who is the prime cause of all deities and in whom eternal virtue resides, is here beside me. What is it that the sacrificial rite lacks? Brahma, the grandfather of the worlds, is also here. So are the sages and kings. Whoever is worthy of being included in the sacrifice and deserves honour has come.

Of what avail is Siva to us in this place? Oh brahmin, of course I have given my daughter to him but that was because I was persuaded by Brahma. Oh brahmin, this Siva is not a man of nobility. He has neither father nor mother. He is the Lord of goblins, ghosts and spirits and is incorrigible. He is unworthy of this sacred rite. Hence he is not invited by me.

Dadhici said: —

This sacrifice has become 'on-sacrifice' without the presence of Siva. Indeed your destruction is imminent in this very sacrifice.

Brahma said: —

After Dadhici left for his hermitage, some important devotees of Siva, who were present there, cursed Daksa and returned to their respective abodes. The evil-minded Daksa then mocked those who left.

Daksa said: —

Gone is that brahmin favourite of Siva named Dadhici and others too of his ilk have gone out of my sacrifice. This has become good. I always approve of this. They are slow-witted and senseless. They are rogues indulging in false deliberations and discussions. They are out of the Vedic circle.

These men of evil conduct shall be eschewed from sacrificial rites. You all, brahmins, sages and devas, with Visnu at the head shall make my sacrifice fruitful.

Brahma said: —

On hearing these words, the celestial sages, deluded by Siva's Maya, performed the worship of the deities in that sacrifice. Oh great sage, I have thus explained how the sacrifice had been cursed. Now I shall explain how the sacrifice was destroyed.

Sati's Journey

Brahma said: —

In the meantime when the celestial sages were on their way to Daksa's sacrifice, Sati was engrossed in diverse sports, surrounded by her friends. While she was thus gaily sportive, Sati saw the moon in the company of Rohini going to the sacrifice of Daksa. Sati asked Vijaya about it, who was her maiden-in-chief, her beloved friend.

Sati said: —

Oh beloved friend Vijaya, where does this moon go in a hurry in the company of Rohini after taking leave of us?

Brahma said: —

When Sati asked her, Vijaya went near the moon and asked him, 'Where are you going?' On hearing what Vijaya asked, the moon mentioned everything about the sacrificial festival of Daksa, with great respect.

Then Vijaya mentioned everything that the moon told her to Sati immediately. On hearing it, Sati was surprised. She thought over the possible reason, but not knowing it she mused like this.

Sati said: —

Daksa is my father. Virini is my mother. I am their beloved daughter Sati. Why did they not invite me? Have they forgotten their own beloved daughter? I shall ask Siva respectfully the reason for the same.

Brahma said: —

Making her maiden-in-chief Vijaya wait there, Sati immediately went near Siva. She saw him in the middle of the council-chamber surrounded by hosts of his attendants— Nandin and others of great valour. After seeing Siva, she went to him quickly to ask him the reason. Lovingly Siva took his beloved on his lap and delighted her with pleasing words.

Siva said: —

Oh slender-waisted lady, why did you come here in the council-chamber and that too in a state of surprise? Please tell me the reason.

Sati said: —

I have heard that my father is performing a great sacrifice. Great festivities are being conducted there. The celestial sages have assembled too. Does his great sacrifice not appeal to you? Why won't you take part in your friend's (Daksa) sacrificial ceremony? Please tell me the reason. Come with me to my father's sacrificial hall.

Brahma said: —

The words of Sati wounded Lord Siva's heart. He didn't know he was not invited.

Lord Siva said: —

Daksa is very well your father, dear. But he is my particular enemy. I was not invited by him. Those who go to another man's house uninvited, attains disrespect. Hence you and I particularly shall not go to Daksa's sacrifice. Oh beloved, I have told you the truth.

Brahma said: —

Thus advised by the noble-souled Siva, Sati was angry and spoke thus to Siva, the foremost of fluent speakers.

Sati said: —

Oh Siva, Lord of all, you by whom sacrifice becomes fruitful have not been invited by my father, thus he has committed a foul deed. I wish to know the thoughts of the evil-minded Daksa and those wicked sages. I wish to go to the sacrifice. Oh Lord Siva, grant me the permission now.

Siva said: —

Oh goddess, if this is what you wish, if you think it needful to go, Oh righteous one, you can immediately start for your father's sacrifice with my willing permission.

Brahma said: —

Sati, after getting Siva's permission, sat on the bull, bedecked herself and started for her father's abode. Sixty thousand attendants of Siva went with her.

Sati's Statement

Brahma said: —

Sati reached the place where the colourful sacrifice was in progress. The Goddess stopped at the gate and descended from Nandin, the bull. She went all alone inside the place of sacrifice. She was greeted respectfully by her mother and sisters. But Daksa did not show any sign of respect or love. The others, however, did not receive her out of fear of Daksa.

In that sacrifice, Sati saw the shares allotted to the deities, Visnu, and others but not to Siva. She then fell into a great fury. She aimed her fiery look and gazed with blazing eyes at Daksa and spoke to him.

Sati said: —

How is it that Siva, who is highly auspicious, has not been invited by you? What is that sacrifice without Siva? Every rite performed without him will be impure but with him or by the mere remembrance of him becomes pure. Did you disrespect him, considering him on a par with ordinary devas? You have become senseless and mean though you are my father. How did Visnu, Brahma, other devas and the sages happen to be present at your sacrifice without their Lord Siva?

Brahma said: —

After saying this, Sati addressed Visnu and others severally, taunting them.

Sati said: —

Oh Visnu, don't you know the real nature of Siva, whom the Vedas speak of as both full and devoid of attributes? How can you partake in a sacrifice to which Siva was not invited? Oh Brahma, you had five faces formerly. When you exhibited your haughtiness against Siva, he made you four-faced. It is surprising that you have forgotten it.

Oh Indra, don't you know the valour of the great Lord? Siva had once ruthlessly reduced your thunderbolt to ashes. All of you, Visnu, Brahma, gods, sages and others have turned foolish since you have assembled here without Siva.

Brahma said: —

Thus, the infuriated Sati spoke many words with her heart in distress. Visnu, gods, and sages kept silent on hearing her words, though their minds were distressed on account of Siva. Then, Daksa spoke to his daughter.

Daksa said: —

Gentle lady, nothing shall be gained by your speaking so much here. You can go or stay. Why did you come anyway? Your husband Siva is known to the wise as inauspicious. He is not of a noble lineage. Knowing Siva to be of indecent dress and features, my dear daughter I did not invite him to the sacrifice in the presence of gods and sages.

Induced by Brahma, I gave you in marriage to the wicked haughty Siva, who does not know customs. I have been a sinner and slow-witted. Hence leave off your anger. Calm yourself. Having come (all the way) to this sacrifice you can take your own share.

Brahma said: —

The daughter Sati on being addressed thus, became very angry to see her father full of contempt. She mused to herself—"How can I return to Siva?" Of course I am desirous of seeing Siva but what reply shall I give when He were to ask me? Sati, the mother of the three worlds, heaving sighs of wrath told her father Daksa, the evil-minded.

Sati said: —

He who reproaches Siva and he who hears such reproaches, both of them go to hell and stay there as long as the moon and the sun exist. I shall cast off my body and enter the fire. Oh father, of what avail is this life unto me who am unfortunate enough to hear contemptuous remarks about my Lord?

Brahma said: —

After stating this, she remembered the advice of Siva and repented (her hasty arrival) with a grief-stricken heart. Then inciting the fury of Daksa further, she said to Visnu and all other devas and sages unhesitatingly.

Sati said: —

Dear father, hating Siva now you are sure to repent later. After experiencing a lot of agony here, you are sure to experience further torture. The syllables Si and Va even uttered once casually can quell all sins. It is surprising that you are so wicked as to harbour ill feelings against Siva who is the Lord of all and who is the holiest of the holy. You are certainly an enemy of Siva.

Have the scholarly people, Brahma and others, Sanaka and sages, except you, considered Siva unholy? Why say more? You are wicked in every respect. You are evil-minded. I have nothing further to do with this body born of you. This body born of your limbs I shall cast off as a corpse. It is worthy of contempt. I shall abandon it and gain happiness.

Brahma said: —

Having said this to Daksa and others present in the sacrifice, Sati stopped. After thinking upon her dear Lord she desisted from her speech.

Description of Sati's Casting Off of Her Body and the Subsequent Disorder

Narada said: —

What happened after Sati became silent? Oh Brahma, please tell me.

Brahma said: —

Silently she remembered her Lord with great respect, Sati the Goddess, calmed down and sat on the ground. Having sipped water duly, covering up her body entirely with her cloth, she closed her eyes and remembered her Lord. She then entered the yogic trance. She desired to cast-off her body due to her anger with Daksa. She desired to burn off the body and retain the pure wind by yogic means.

In this posture she remembered the feet of her Lord and nothing else. Her body, divested of its sins, fell in the yogic fire and was reduced to ashes, in accordance with her own wish. The loud shouts and cries of those who witnessed it spread everywhere on the earth. Everything was surprisingly wonderful and terrifying to the devas and others.

Devas said: —

Alas, Sati, Siva's most beloved, has cast-off her life. Who is that wicked person who angered her? This patriarch of a hardened heart, inimical to the Brahman, will definitely become infamous in the whole world. Since he refused to comply with the request of his own daughter he will be falling into a terrible hell after death due to his own guilt.

Brahma said: —

Seeing Sati engulfed by the fire, the sixty thousand attendants of Siva who were waiting by the door, rose up with weapons in fury. Consulting one another, some of them, excessively stricken with grief, cut off their limbs with their weapons, some their heads, some their faces, with the sharp lethal weapons they had. Thus about twenty thousand of those attendants courted death along with Sati. It was very surprising.

Some of the attendants of the noble-souled Siva who survived, jumped up with their weapons to kill the furious Daksa. The holy sage Bhrgu offered the Yajur mantra in the fire to quell the obstructors of sacrifice. While the sage Bhrgu was pouring the offerings, thousands of powerful demons—Rbhus rose up. Oh excellent sage, a terrible fight ensued between Siva's attendants and the demons who had firebrands for their weapons. Their hair stood on end when people heard the uproar.

The attendants were killed by the Rbhus of powerful valour and favoured with Brahminical splendour. It had been the desire of Siva that the attendants were killed and routed quickly. It was a wonderful scene. Such was the obstacle to the sacrifice of Daksa who rivalled Siva, who was wicked and who professed to be a kinsman of Brahma.

The Celestial Voice

Brahma said: —

Oh excellent sage, in the meantime a celestial voice arose, even as Daksa, the devas and others were listening.

The celestial voice said: —

Oh Daksa, of evil conduct, of haughty disposition, what is it that you have foolishly done now, this misdeed bringing in many an unhappy calamity in its wake? You never gave any credence to the words of Dadhici, the king of devotees of Siva. Oh fool, if it had been carried out, everything would have been auspicious and pleasing.

How is it that you did not honour Sati, your daughter, the auspicious lady who herself came to your house? Oh you are weak in knowledge, how is it that you did not worship Sati and Siva? You are actually deluded. Siva indeed is the great Lord, the Lord of all, the greatest of the great, worthy of being served by Visnu, Brahma and others. Since you have not duly respected Siva's sakti, this sacrifice will definitely be destroyed.

Do you feel proud enough to suppose that you can attain welfare without worshipping Siva? That haughty pride will be quashed today. I do not see anyone among these devas who will come to your assistance. Let all the devas, sages, Nagas and everyone else depart quickly from this sacrificial altar. Otherwise you all will perish today without an escape.

Brahma said: —

After saying this to those who had gathered in the sacrificial hall, the celestial voice stopped. Oh dear one, on hearing the astral voice Vispu and other devas were surprised. The sages too were wonder-struck.

Virabhadra Is Born and Siva Advises Him

Narada said: —

On hearing the ethereal voice, what did the unwise Daksa do? What happened after that? Oh Lord, tell me please.

Brahma said: —

The remaining attendants of Siva, who were defeated and routed by the power of Bhrgu's mantras, fled and sought refuge in Siva. Bowing with great respect to Siva of immeasurable splendour they narrated everything that transpired there.

Ganas said: —

Oh Lord of Devas, save us who have sought refuge in you. Please listen with condescension to the detailed description of the events connected with Sati.

Brahma said: —

The attendants described everything to Siva in detail. They didn't leave anything out. On hearing the words of his attendants, the Lord remembered you, Narada, in order to know their activities. Endowed with divine vision, you reached the place and after bowing to Siva with devotion you waited there, with palms joined in reverence. After praising you, the Lord asked you about Sati's news at the sacrifice of Daksa and the incidents there. You told him everything that he asked.

Oh sage, on hearing the words spoken by you, Siva became furious in a trice. Then Rudra, the destroyer of the world, plucked out a cluster of his matted hair and struck the top of the mountain with it. The first half of that cluster of matted hair rose up the powerful Virabhadra, the leader of Ganas.

From the furious breath of Siva, the great Rudra, hundred fevers and thirteen humours came out. From the other half of the cluster of matted hair, Mahakali was born. Oh dear one, she was very terrible and was surrounded by crores of goblins. Then the heroic Virabhadra, eloquent in speech, addressed him.

Virabhadra said: —

Oh Rudra of terrific appearance, with the moon, what am I to do? Oh Lord, command me quickly. Am I to burn the universe into ashes? Am I to tear down mountains? Tell me. It is by your blessing that I am qualified for this task. Oh Siva, without your blessing and favour, none will have that power and efficiency.

Lord Siva said: —

Oh dear Virabhadra, listen to my words attentively. You must carry them out quickly. It will then delight me. Daksa, the wicked son of Brahma, has made arrangements to perform a sacrifice. He is particularly inimical to me. He is unwise and conceited now.

Destroy the sacrifice with all your might and then return to my abode quickly. Even if there are devas, Gandharvas, Yaksas or others, reduce them to ashes quickly.

Let there be Visnu, Brahma, Indra or Yama. Fell them to the ground now itself with strenuous efforts. Transgressing my injunctions, many haughty people are lingering there.

They are also my enemies. So burn them with a series of blazing fires. After reducing them to ashes, along with their wives, and all the paraphernalia at the sacrifice of Daksa, you shall return quickly.

It is possible that when you go there, devas and others may praise you. Still you shall burn them in the flames. Burn the devas too who have committed offence, in the blazing fire, after meditating on me, your protector.

Brahma said: —

After saying this to Virabhadra, Siva the Lord of all, stopped talking with his eyes still resembling copper (due to anger).

Destruction of Daksa's Sacrifice

Mentally meditating on Siva, the powerful Virabhadra took up all the great miraculous weapons for his fight with Visnu and roared like a lion. Vispu, the powerful, loudly blew his conch delighting his own people.

On hearing the sound of the conch, the devas who had fled before, returned quickly. The guardians of the quarters, including Indra, roared like lions and fought forcefully with the Ganas of Virabhadra. A noisy terrible fight ensued between the Ganas and the guardians of the quarters, both roaring like lions.

Indra fought with Nandin; the fire-god with Asman and the powerful Kubera fought with Kusmandapati. Nandin was hit hard by Indra with the thunderbolt that had a hundred spikes. Indra was hurt in the middle of his chest by Nandin with the trident.

The infuriated fire-god hit Asman with his spear. He too hit back the fire-god with his trident of very sharp point. Mahaloka, the heroic chieftain of the Ganas, remembered Lord Siva with joy and fought with Yaraa. Meditating on Lord Siva in his heart, the strong and heroic Kusmandapati clashed with Kubera and fought terribly.

Splitting up all the Devas, the great leader of Bhairavi, in collaboration with the circle of Yoginis, drank much of their blood. Desirous of gobbling up the leading devas, Kali split them and drank their blood. Ksetrapala too did the same.

Then Visnu, the slayer of enemies and who was excessively brilliant, hurled his discus and fought with them. The discus seemed to burn the ten directions. Ksetrapala saw the discus coming on. He ran to the place and bravely caught hold of it. On seeing the discus held in his mouth, Visnu caught hold of his throat and made him spit out the discus.

Visnu fought a great battle with them by hurling many weapons and evincing boisterous display of his terrific exploits. Bhairava and others displayed their strength furiously by hurling several weapons and by fighting with him. Virabhadra saw their battle with Visnu of unequalled splendour, returned and clashed with him in a great battle.

Then Visnu lifted up his discus and fought with Virabhadra. Visnu created some extremely strong warriors through his Yogic mantras. These warriors were as powerful as Visnu and Virabhadra. They then attacked Virabhadra.

Remembering Siva, his Lord and hitting them, he reduced them to ashes. The most powerful Virabhadra struck Visnu in the chest playfully with his trident in the course of the battle. Oh sage, hit suddenly by that blow, Visnu Purusottama, fell unconscious on the ground. Then that glorious Lord, with eyes red by anger, got up again. The best of beings lifted up his discus and stood ready to strike.

Thanks to the power of Siva, the great Lord controlling Maya, the Cakra held in the hand of Visnu became stunned and motionless. He himself stood stunned and motionless. Visnu then repeated formulas for redemption from torpidity and broke free from that state. He then took up his bow and arrows. But Virabhadra split his arrows in three parts. Then Visnu was enlightened by the great voice that the great Ganas were invincible. He therefore thought of vanishing from the scene.

On seeing the disorder and utter destruction of the great sacrifice, the sacrifice itself being afraid assumed the form of a deer and fled. Virabhadra seized it as it was fleeing up the sky in the form of a deer and beheaded it. Then Virabhadra caught hold of everyone who fought against Siva's army and split them apart one by one.

With the tip of his fingers he cut off the tip of the nose of Sarasvati and of Aditi the mother of devas. Vlrabhadra showed his exploits thus. The Ganas furiously showered filth and rubbish on the sacrificial fire. The heroic Ganas made the sacrifice inexpressibly impure.

After coming to know that Daksa had hidden himself behind the altar due to his fright, Virabhadra dragged him out with force. He was caught by his cheeks, his head and was struck with the sword. Due to the yogic power of Daksa it could not be split. Thinking that his head could not be pierced or cut with weapons he kicked his chest with the foot and wrestled the head with his hand. Virabhadra then threw the head of the wicked Daksa, the enemy of Siva, into the fire pit. Seeing Daksa and others entirely burnt, he laughed boisterously filling the three worlds with the sound. On seeing Virabhadra who had fulfilled his task, Lord Siva was pleased and he made him the presiding officer of his Ganas.

Journey to Kailasa and the Vision of Siva

Narada said: —

Oh Brahma of great intellect, tell me more. After destroying the sacrifice of Dakasa when the heroic Virabhadra went to Kailasa, what happened there?

Brahma said: —

Defeated and mutilated by Siva's armies, the gods and the sages came to my region. After making obeisance to me and eulogising me in various ways, they explained their distress entirely.

On hearing that, I was extremely pained for my son Daksa. In that mental anguish I thought to myself, 'What step shall I take to please the devas, whereby Daksa can be restored to life and whereby the sacrifice also be completed?'

After thinking a lot, I remembered Lord Visnu and knew what to do. Then I went to the world of Visnu along with the gods and the sages. I eulogised him, I poured my heart out. I asked Visnu to make arrangements so that the sacrifice was complete.

On hearing my words, the Lord of Laksmi, with his soul set on Siva and mind free from distress, replied after duly remembering Siva.

Visnu said: —

An aggression against a powerful person neither befits a weak aggressor nor leads to his welfare. Thus, Oh Brahman, the gods have committed sin and offended Siva, since they had partaken of his share in the sacrifice.

You shall propitiate Siva by falling at his feet, with pure mind. If Siva is pleased, resuscitation is certain and immediate. That Lord has been wounded in the heart by the wicked Daksa by harsh words. Crave the forgiveness of that Lord who has lost his beloved now.

I too have offended Siva. I shall also come, Oh Brahma, to Siva's abode along with you all and crave the forgiveness of Siva.

Brahma said: —

After commanding thus, Vishnu, the gods, and I desired to go to his mountain along with the devas. We all went to Kailasa then. On seeing this mountain named Kailasa, Visnu and other devas were surprised along with the excellent sages. Near it, the gods saw Alaka, the beautiful and divine city of Kubera—a friend of Rudra.

After going beyond Alaka, they saw the fig-tree of Siva. It was the place where Siva practised Yoga. It was divine. It was resorted to by other Yogins. Beneath that Vata of yogic potentialities, Visnu and other devas saw Siva seated. He was being attended upon by his friend Kubera, the Lord of Guhyakas and Raksas and particularly by his attendants and kinsmen.

Oh sage (Narada), (you were present there and while) you were asking him questions, he was explaining wise and excellent things to you, whereas the other saintly men were listening. On seeing Siva like this, Visnu and other devas humbly bowed to him immediately after joining their palms.

Lord Siva, stood up and approached Visnu who had gone there along with me. He performed obeisance with his head. Visnu and the devas made obeisance at his feet as Visnu would bow to Kasyapa. Everyone then eulogised him and sang hymns.

The Removal of Daksa's Misery

Brahma said: —

Lord Siva was delighted by the eulogy and conciliated. Consoling Visnu and other devas and laughing, the merciful Lord Siva blessed them and spoke.

Lord Siva said: —

Oh excellent devas, both of you listen with attention. Oh dear ones, I shall state the truth. I do not take into account the sin committed by my children. I have inflicted punishment on those who are afflicted by my illusion.

The destruction of the sacrifice of Daksa was not done by me. If a person hates another, ultimately it recoils on him alone. Let the head (the sacrificial head) of Daksa be that of a goat. Bhrgu who opposed me shall become goat-bearded. The gods who tried to uproot me shall have their physical bodies.

Brahma said: —

Saying thus, the lord Siva though merciful, yet of imperial nature, the lord of the mobile and immobile and the follower of Vedic injunctions, stopped. On hearing his speech, Visnu and other gods were delighted and sent out cries of approbation. Then at the invitation of Visnu and other gods, Siva went to Kanakhala at the sacrificial altar of Daksa. The celestial sages and I too accompanied him there. Then Rudra saw the extent of destruction carried out by Virabhadra, of the sacrifice and of the celestial sages. On seeing this destruction of the sacrifice, he called the chieftain of Ganas, Virabhadra spoke to him.

Siva said: —

Oh Virabhadra what is it that you have done? Oh dear, in your hurry you have inflicted very severe punishment on the celestial sages and others. Bring Daksa here quickly. Oh dear, he performed a sacrifice contrary to rules, whence this result arose.

Brahma said: —

Thus commanded by Siva, Virabhadra, hastened to bring the headless body of Daksa which he threw in front of Siva. On seeing the headless body, Siva said laughingly to Virabhadra — 'Where is the head of Daksa?' Virabhadra replied — 'Oh Lord Siva, at that time itself, the head was consigned to fire by me.'

On hearing the words of Virabhadra, Siva commanded the gods. After doing in accordance with what Lord Siva had said, Visnu, the gods and I acquainted Bhrgu with the same quickly. At the bidding of Siva, they immediately joined the head of the sacrificial animal, the goat, with the body of Daksa.

When the head was joined and Siva looked at it, Daksa regained his life and awoke as if from sleep. On waking up he saw Siva in front of him. Daksa stood there happy and joyful.

He wanted to eulogise Siva but could not do so because of his affection, emotional disturbance and anxiety for his deceased daughter. Then, he finally mustered the courage and addressed Siva.

Daksa said: —

Oh Lord, Lord of Devas, be merciful. Obeisance to thee. Oh Siva, the storehouse of mercy, forgive my faults. You have blessed me under the pretext of punishing me. Oh Lord, I have been wicked and foolish. Today I have realised the truth. You are above all. You are the supreme god. The great Lord has been wounded by my piercing harsh words. I have made everyone dejected. I seek forgiveness from all. Be so kind as to forgive me.

Brahma said: —

Having thus eulogised Lord Siva, Daksa stopped. Then Visnu also eulogised Lord Siva. I then addressed the supreme Lord. I said, 'Oh Siva, blessing has been conferred on my son in granting him a body. You have forgiven us all for the offence. Will you also resuscitate the sacrifice of Daksa?'Oh Lord of gods, be pleased. Remove all curses.' After thus eulogising Lord Siva, I joined my palms in reverence and bent my head in humility. After this, Indra, all the sages, gods, Nagas and the brahmins also eulogised Siva.

The Arrangement in Daksa's Sacrifice

Brahma said: —

Thus eulogised by Visnu, by me, by the gods, sages and others, the great lord became delighted. After consoling Brahma, Visnu, the sages and the gods by His benign glance, Siva spoke to Daksa.

Lord Siva said: —

Oh Daksa, listen. I am delighted. Although I am an independent Lord of all, I am always subservient to my devotees. Deluded men engrossed in rituals alone cannot attain me through the Vedas, sacrifices, gifts or austerities.

You wished to cross the ocean of worldly existence by observance of rituals alone. That was why I became angry and caused the destruction of the sacrifice.

Hereafter, think upon me as the great Lord and give more importance to knowledge you carry on rituals with care and attention. Oh patriarch, listen to another statement of mine with a clear conscience.

Without devotion to Brahma one cannot have devotion to Visnu; without devotion to Visnu none will have devotion towards me. If a devotee of Visnu hates me or if a devotee of Siva hates Visnu, both will incur curses and never realise reality.

Brahma said: —

With great joy, Daksa, his family and the gods realised Siva as the Lord of all and was engrossed in devotion to Siva. Lord Siva granted boons to all. Permitted by Siva and with his blessings, Daksa, with a delighted heart, completed his sacrifice.

He allotted full share to Siva and gave the gods their shares too. He also gave gifts to Brahmins and secured good blessings of Siva. Thus the sacrifice of Daksa was completed, thanks to the grace of Siva.

After this, everyone returned to their abodes. Lovingly honoured by Daksa, the great Lord Siva, returned to Kailasa along with his Ganas. After returning to his mountain, Siva remembered his beloved Sati and mentioned her story to the most important of his Ganas. Narrating her story, Lord Siva passed many days.

After forsaking her body thus, Sati was born as the daughter of Mena, the wife of Himavat. This is well known. Then Sati attained Siva as Parvati. Thus I have described the fascinating story of Siva and Sati to you.

The Goddess (Durga) Consoles the Gods

(The gods eulogise Sati after Himacala's marriage to Mena. They wish to see Sati and pray for a reincarnation.)

Brahma said: —

The gods eulogised Goddess Durga and she appeared in front of them. She was seated in a wonderful divine gem-set chariot over which a soft cushion had been spread and which was decorated with tinkling ornaments. She was shining with the brilliance of her limbs that surpassed even the lustre of a crore of suns. She was the supreme illusion, the beautiful wife of Sadasiva.

The gods said: —

Oh mother of the universe, we gods bow to you, the destroyer of all distress. Oh great Goddess listen to our submission which we, your slaves forever, are going to explain. Formerly you were born as the daughter of Daksa and were married to Siva. Being disrespected by your father, you cast off your body in accordance with your vow. You then went to your own world and Siva became miserable. Oh great Goddess, the purpose of the gods has not been completely carried out. Hence we, Gods, have sought refuge in you.

Please fulfil the desire of the god. Oh Goddess, incarnating again on the earth please be the wife of Rudra (Siva) again. Carry on your sports in a fitting manner and let the Gods be happy. Oh Goddess, may Rudra too, the resident of Kailasa be happy. Let all become happy. Let misery perish entirely.

Brahma said: —

Saying so, Visnu and the other gods, full of loving devotion, remained waiting silently and humbly. Remembering her Lord Siva, the compassionate Uma addressed the gods smilingly.

Uma said: —

Oh Visnu, Oh Brahma, Oh Gods and sages, listen to my words. I am undoubtedly delighted. The delusion of Daksa and other things were carried out by me alone. I shall take a full incarnation on the earth. There is no doubt in this. There are many reasons for the same. I shall mention them with respect.

Himacala and Sati rendered service to me as Sati. I shall become their daughter. Just as you, Rudra too, desires my incarnation in the abode of Himavat. Hence I shall incarnate. That shall be the end of misery in the world. All of you return to your abodes. You shall be happy for a long time.

After incarnating I shall give Mena full happiness. I shall become Siva's wife. I shall end his sadness that I brought on him when I cast off my body as Sati. In order to propitiate Rudra, I shall incarnate as the daughter of Mena and Himacala. Then I will perform severe penance as Siva's devotee. I bless you all. Now return to your abodes. You shall all be happy.

Brahma said: —

Oh dear, even as the gods were watching, Siva, the mother of the universe, vanished after saying this and returned immediately to her world.

Mena Obtains the Boon

Narada said: —

Oh dear, how did Mena and the Lord of the mountains perform the great penance? How did he beget a daughter of Mena. Please narrate.

Brahma said: —

Oh great Brahmin, listen to the story. I shall explain everything in detail.

When Visnu and other gods returned after instructing him, the Lord of the mountains and Mena performed a great penance. Meditating on Siva and Siva day and night with devout mind, the couple worshipped them continuously. Desirous of obtaining a child, she worshipped Siva everyday for twenty-seven years beginning in the month of March-April. She made clay idols of the Goddess and worshipped her by offering various things on the banks of Ganga.

Mena passed twenty seven years with pleasure and brilliant lustre, focusing on Siva. At the end of twenty-seven years, Uma, the beloved of Siva, the mother of the world, became highly delighted. She appeared in front of Mena and blessed her.

The Goddess said: —

Oh beloved of the mountain, I am delighted by your penance. Tell me what you desire in your mind. I shall grant you whatever you wish for and whenever you wish for it.

Mena said: —

Oh great goddess, if you consider me worthy of a boon, I shall choose one. Oh mother of the universe, at first let me have a hundred sons endowed with longevity, heroism, prosperity and accomplishments. After that let me have a daughter of comely features and good qualities who will delight both the families and who will be revered by the three worlds. Oh Siva, be my daughter for fulfilling the needs of the gods. Be Rudra's wife and indulge in divine sports with the Lord.

The Goddess said: —

May hundred heroic sons be born to you. One of them will be very strong, the first born. I shall be born as your daughter since I am delighted by your devotion. Since I have been served by the gods, I shall fulfil their desire and carry out their activities.

Brahma said: —

Saying so, the Goddess Siva vanished from there even as Mena was watching. Mena then gave the news to her husband. On hearing the words of Mena, the Lord of mountains became delighted. He praised his wife who was devoted to Siva lovingly. Oh sage, when their mutual sexual intercourse took place, Mena conceived and the child in the womb gradually grew up.

She gave birth to a beautiful son Mainaka who later on became the worthy recipient of the love of Naga ladies and entered into an alliance with the Lord of the ocean. He had neat strength and prowess. He was the most important of all the mountains born of him. He too became the Lord of mountains.

Parvati's Birth

Brahma said: —

Then the couple, with great devotion, remembered the goddess for her birth in order to carry out the work of the gods. The wife of the mountain, by the grace of the goddess, conceived.

The beloved of the mountain, Mena, shone all the more by the presence of the goddess who bore the entire universe. She appeared as if she was in a brilliant sphere. Mena bore the characteristic signs of pregnancy which almost indicated the imminent rise in pleasure of her Lord.

However, the weakness of her body did not allow her to wear ornaments. Her face became pale. She resembled the night when there are very few stars and the moon is in a waning state.

Kissing her face, emitting the fragrance of the earth in the course of his secret dalliance, the Lord of the mountains, was not satiated. His love increased.

Himacala asked her friends the things Mena desired but couldn't say to him out of bashfulness. Whatever she wanted was brought to her. There was nothing that Himacala couldn't get for her. Surmounting the difficulties of the early days of pregnancy, she grew more plump in her limbs.

Mena then shone like a tender creeper putting forth more leaves and flowers. At the proper time, he saw his wife Mena about to deliver the child. She felt very brilliant with the mother of the universe in her womb. In the meantime, Visnu, and other gods as well as the sages came there and eulogised Siva who was in the womb.

Brahma said: —

Thus eulogising, in many ways, the great goddess stationed in the womb, the gods returned to their abodes, highly delighted in their minds. When the nine months were completed she was born at midnight.

Coming out of the belly of Mena at the proper time in her real form, she resembled Laksmi coming out of the ocean. When she was born, Siva was glad. A slow, fragrant and auspicious wind blew favourably. Along with the rain there was a shower of flowers. Fires calmly glowed and the clouds rumbled. At the time of her birth, riches and prosperity flourished in the city of Himavat. All miseries perished.

Visnu and other gods reached there in time and saw the mother of the universe. They were delighted and happy. They eulogised Siva, the mother of the universe, of divine features and resident of Siva's region.

Brahma said: —

After eulogising Siva thus, Visnu and other gods bowed to her again delightedly and returned to their abodes praising her great divine ways. Mena's happiness knew no bounds. She started talking to Uma, who was now born in her arms.

Mena said: —

Great favour has been shown by you, Oh Goddess, Oh mother of the universe as you have manifested yourself in front of me brilliantly. Be pleased. Remain in my meditation in this form, but have the form of my daughter in public view.

Brahma said: —

After hearing Mena's words, the Goddess was delighted. Even as the mother was watching with pleasure, she assumed the body of a daughter by her power of illusion.

The Childhood Sports of Parvati

Brahma said: —

The goddess of great brilliance assumed the form of her baby child in front of Mena and began to cry in accordance with the ways of the world. She then grew up to be of great beauty and intellect. The child was fondly attached to every member of the family. Hence the kinsmen called her Parvati, a name befitting her family. The girl had all the qualities of good conduct and behaviour.

During her childhood, the goddess played frequently on the sandy banks of the Ganga in the middle of her playmates with balls and dolls. When the suitable time for her education arrived, she learnt all the lessons from a good preceptor, with a concentrated mind and great pleasure.

Oh sage, thus I have described one of the divine sports of Siva. I shall narrate another one of her divine sports. Please listen to it lovingly.

Narada-Himalaya Conversation

Brahma said: —

Once, induced by Siva, you went to the abode of Himacala lovingly. Oh sage Narada, on seeing you, the Lord of the mountains bowed to you and worshipped you. He called his daughter and asked her to fall at your feet.

Himavat said: —

Oh sage Narada, of good knowledge, you are omniscient. You are sympathetic. Please read the horoscope of my daughter and tell me about her good and bad fortune. Whose beloved wife will my fortunate daughter be?

Brahma said: —

O excellent sage, being thus requested by Himavat the lord of mountains, you looked at Kali's palm and limbs. O dear, you are wise. You know many facts. You are eloquent in speech. You then spoke.

Narada said: —

Oh Mena, oh king of mountains, your daughter has all the auspicious signs. She will delight her husband, and heighten the glory of her parents. She will be a great chaste lady. She will always grant bliss to everyone. I see all good signs in the palm of your daughter, except one.

There is an abnormal line also. Listen to the indication thereof. Her husband will be a naked Yogin, without any qualities. He will be free from lust. He will have neither mother nor father. He will be indifferent to honours. His dress and manners will be inauspicious.

Brahma said: —

On hearing your words the couple thought them true. Both Mena and Himavat were very distressed. Though Parvati was overjoyed as she understood all the signs of her future husband were that of Siva.

Himavat said: —

Oh Narada, Oh sage, what is the way out? What shall I do? A great misery has befallen us.

Narada said: —

Oh Lord of mountains, listen to my words with affability. They are true. The lines in the palm are the lines of Brahma. You now hear what I have to say. You will be very happy.

There is a bridegroom like that. He is Lord Siva who has sportively assumed a physical form. In him all bad characteristics are equal to good characteristics. Hence you give your daughter in marriage to Siva. That will be a wise step. By performing penance, Siva can be propitiated quickly and he will accept her undoubtedly.

Oh Lord of mountains, she will be the wife of Siva and will remain his favourite always. Performing a penance she will fascinate Siva's mind towards herself. He too will marry none else except her. A love akin to this pair will not be found anywhere. Not in the past, present or future.

Oh best of mountains, Siva will become Ardhanarisvara (half male and half female). Their meeting once again will be delightful. After propitiating Lord Siva by the power of her penance, your daughter will take away half the body of Siva. Oh excellent mountain, you shall not give her to anyone else. This is a secret of the gods. This shall not be revealed to anyone else.

Himavat said: —

Oh sage Narada, I have one submission to make. Please listen to it lovingly and make us delighted Lord Siva is ever busy with his penance and meditation. How can I bring him out of that pious state? Siva had also entered into a contract with Sati, he vowed to take no one else as wife except her, then how will he take Parvati?

Narada said: —

Oh Lord of mountains, you need not worry. This daughter of yours, Parvati, was formerly the daughter of Daksa. She was Sati. Being dishonoured at the sacrifice of her father, and being the witness of Siva's dishonour, she was furious and she cast off her body. She herself is now born to you as Parvati. Hence, by all means, Siva will take her as his wife.

Brahma said: —

On hearing the story from Narada, Parvati bent down her head in bashfulness but her smile heightened the beauty of her face. On hearing the story, the Lord of mountains stroked her fondly, kissed her on the head and placed her on his seat.

Parents Advice Parvati to Propitiate Siva.
Siva Appears before Parvati in a Dream

Narada said: —

Oh Brahma, what happened after I went to my abode? Please tell me.

Brahma said: —

After you had gone to heaven, some time passed. Once, Mena approached the Lord of mountains and bowed to him. She spoke to him.

Mena said: —

The words of the sage have not been understood by me well. (I think it is better) that you perform the marriage of our daughter with a handsome bridegroom. Let the bridegroom of Parvati be born of a good family endowed with good characteristic signs. In every respect that marriage will yield an unprecedented happiness.

Himacala said: —

Oh gentle lady Menaka, listen. I shall tell you the truth. The sage's statement will never be false. If you feel affectionate towards your daughter, zealously instruct your daughter. Let her perform the penance with Siva as the object, devotedly and steadily. If Siva is delighted, he will marry her. Everything shall be auspicious. The inauspicious features indicated by Narada will perish. Hence, immediately teach your daughter to hasten to perform the penance for attaining Siva.

Brahma said: —

On hearing these words of the Lord of mountains, Mena was greatly delighted. She approached her daughter to advise her to take interest in penance. But on seeing the tender limbs of her daughter, Menaka was greatly distressed. Her eyes welled up in tears immediately. She was unable to advise Parvati to perform the penance. Parvati understood her mother's predicament and spoke to her thus.

Parvati said: —

Oh mother, listen. At night I had a dream I shall tell you. Be pleased. A brahmin sage advised me lovingly and compassionately to perform the penance of Siva.

Brahma said: —

On hearing that, Menaka called her husband there and told him the dream as seen by her daughter. He then spoke to his wife thus.

The Lord of the mountains said: —

Oh dear, I too had a dream. Please listen to it lovingly. A great saint of exquisite limbs, as mentioned by Narada, arrived near my city to perform penance there. I took Parvati there with me. He was recognised as Lord Siva, the bridegroom as mentioned by Narada. Advising our daughter to render service to that saint, I requested him to approve of it but he didn't. A great discussion took place between her and Siva. Thereafter at his bidding my daughter stayed there. She served him with devotion. This is the dream I had.

Brahma said: —

Himacala and Menaka thus watched everything unfold. When a few days passed by, Lord Siva came to Himacala's place with few of his Gana's to perform penance. The Lord was completely agitated due to Sati's love and separation from her. While he performed his penance, Parvati engaged herself in his service continuously.

Although the gods sent Kama to hit Siva with his arrows of love, Siva was not swayed at all. Siva became angry and burned Kama with his fiery eyes. He then vanished from the scene. After sometime Lord Siva quelled the pride of Parvati but he was propitiated by her through her great penance. Following the conventions of the world, the Lord married Parvati after being sponsored by Visnu. Then everything auspicious ensued.

Mars is Born and Is Raised to the Status of a Planet by Siva's Grace

Narada said: —

Oh Brahma, the fortunate disciple of Visnu, please answer some more of my questions. When did Siva go to the ridge of Himavat to perform penance? How did the discussion between Siva and Siva take place? How did Parvati attain Siva by performing penance?

Brahma said: —

Oh celestial sage, listen to Siva's glory.

Returning to his mountain, Siva in his excitement caused by his separation from his beloved, remembered Sati. He talked about her to his Ganas, narrating her qualities and heightening his love. Then he roamed around the universe after casting off his dress. He searched for her everywhere but couldn't find her. To break his misery, he returned to his mountain and entered into a trance. Thereupon he saw his imperishable form. Then he gave up his trance. Many years elapsed. What happened thereafter, I shall now recount to you.

The drops of sweat caused by exhaustion fell on the Earth from the Lord's forehead and took the shape of a child immediately. The child was tawny-coloured and had four arms. He was comely in features. His brilliance was supermundane and unbearable to others. Like a common child, he cried in front of the great Lord who was engaged in worldly activities. Afraid of Siva, the Earth pondered deeply over it and appeared before him in the guise of a good lady.

She lifted up the child immediately and held him to her chest. Lovingly she suckled the child with her excellent breast milk that flowed in her body. She kissed the child's face lovingly and petted him smilingly. In the absence of Sati she herself acted as his mother in the interest of Lord Siva. Siva knew that she was the Earth. Siva, on seeing her activities became content and eagerly said to her laughingly.

Siva said: —

Oh Earth, you are blessed. Keep this child of mine lovingly, born of my glittering drops of sweat over you. Although the child is born from my sweat, he shall be famous after your name. This boy of yours will be a bestower of lands and will have good qualities. He will make me happy. Accept him with pleasure.

Brahma said: —

After saying this he stopped. He was a bit relieved of his pangs of separation. The child acquired the name Bhauma (son of the Earth).

He attained youth immediately. He worshipped Lord Siva in Kasi for a long time. By the grace of Siva, the child acquired the status of a planet. He went to the heavenly sphere beyond the region of Venus. By the grace of Lord Siva, the son of the Earth, acquired the status of a planet. He went to the heavenly sphere beyond the region of Venus.

Siva and Himavat Meet Together

Brahma said: —

Oh Narada, the daughter of The Mountain, was brought up in the palace of Himacala. When she was eight years old, Siva, distressed by Sati's separation, came to know of her birth. Keeping her wonderful memory within his heart he rejoiced much. In the meantime, Siva wished to perform penance in order to concentrate his mind properly.

Taking some quiet natured Ganas, Nandin and others, he went to the Himalaya ridge. Taking some important Ganas of quiet nature, Nandin and others, with him, he went to the excellent Himalayan ridge—Gangavatara. Siva began his penance there. He concentrated entirely on himself.

Some of the Ganas rendered service to Siva, and some became gatekeepers. They observed silence and did not shout. On discovering that Siva had come, Himavat too went there. He bowed to Siva and eulogised him.

Himavat said: —

Oh great god, obeisance to Thee. Oh Lord, you have come here because my fortune is in its ascendancy. Today my life has borne fruit, in fact everything connected with me has become fruitful since you have come here. I am your slave, you can freely command me. I shall serve you with great pleasure.

Brahma said: —

On hearing these words Himavat, Lord Siva slightly opened his eyes and cast a glance on the Lord of mountains who was accompanied by his attendants. He then addressed Lord Himavat.

Lord Siva said: —

I have come to perform penance in secret on your top. Make arrangements so that none should be able to come near me. Oh king of mountains, delighted in resorting to you, I am going to perform penance here at Gangavataran. Please ensure that my penance can be conducted without obstacles. This alone is the greatest service that you can render. Please arrange for it with due effort. Please return to your abode with your mind full of pleasure.

Himacala said: —

Oh great Lord, there is none more fortunate than me; there is none more meritorious than me, since you have come to perform penance on my summit. I shall ensure you are not disturbed. I shall do all service to you.

Brahma said: —

After saying this, the Lord of the mountains returned at once to his abode and enthusiastically narrated everything to his beloved wife. He then called all his attendants and said emphatically.

Himacala said: —

From now onwards, none of you shall go to the ridge of mine, called Gangavataran. This is my command. If anyone goes there I shall punish that rogue particularly. This is the truth I am speaking.

Siva-Himavat Dialogue

Brahma said: —

Then, the delighted Lord of the mountains, took some fresh flowers and fruits to Siva. He brought his daughter along. He stood in front of Siva, bowing to him and mentally dedicated his daughter to him. He then spoke to Siva in soft words.

Himacala said: —

Oh Lord, my daughter is eager to serve you, I have brought here with a desire to propitiate you. Let her and her two maids be of service to you.

Brahma said: —

Then Siva looked at her in the first flush of her youth. Her complexion resembled the full blown blue lotus petals. Her face appeared as the full moon. Her features were the repositories of all graceful charms.

Her eyes were wide and her ears shone exquisitely. Her two breasts resembling lotus-buds were stout, plump and firm. Her waist was slender and the curly locks of her hair shone well. She was a crest-jewel of all the maidens in the world.

On seeing her in that exquisite form, his pleasure and love increased. He then closed his eyes and meditated upon his real form.

Himacala said: —

Oh great Lord of the gods, O Siva, open your eyes and look at me who have sought refuge in you. Please listen to my entreaty with a long heart. I am your slave. Oh dear Lord, in humility I shall explain the same to you. By your favour I feel most fortunate. I shall be visiting you daily along with my daughter. Oh Lord, be pleased to command me accordingly.

Lord Siva said: —

Oh mountain, you shall come every day to see me, leaving your daughter in your abode. Otherwise I cannot be seen.

Himacala said: —

Oh Lord, please explain to me why this girl cannot accompany me here. Is she unworthy of your service? I don't know why.

Siva said: —

This auspicious slender-bodied maiden of comely hips and moon-like face should not be brought near me. I forbid you again and again. A woman can be very distracting. I cannot be distracted thus. A woman is the reason for all worldly attachments. If she is here I will not be able to perform my penance.

Brahma said: —

On hearing the ruthless words of Siva, the Lord of the mountain was distressed and agitated. However, he kept quiet.

Siva-Parvati Dialogue

Parvati said: —

Oh Yogin, wise and clever, please listen to the reply to what you said to the Lord of mountains. Oh Siva, you perform this great penance because you possess the energy of penance. This penance is Prakrti, the cause of all activities. Without Prakrti how can the great Lord of the phallic form exist? You are worthy of the worship, respect and meditation of all living beings forever. Thinking of this in your heart, please reply.

The great Lord said: —

I am destroying the Prakrti with my great penance. I remain in reality without Prakrti. Indeed Prakrti should not be taken in by good people. They should remain unaffected, eschewing all worldly conduct.

Parvati said: —

Oh Lord Siva, based on what you said, how can that Prakrti cease to exist and how can you be considered beyond that Prakrti? You shall ponder over this and say with reference to the facts as they are.

Everything in the universe is bound by Prakrti continuously. Hence you shall not say anything, not do anything. Know that speaking, doing is a Prakrta activity. Everything that you do, hear or eat, are the activities of Prakrti. To say that it is unreal is meaningless.

Oh Lord, if you are greater than Prakrti, then why do you perform penance? If I am a distraction, then it is also Prakrta. Though you say you are beyond Prakrti. If you are really superior to Prakrti, if what you say is true, you need not be afraid to be near me, oh Siva.

Lord Siva said: —

Oh Parvati, if you say so, you render me unforbidden service every day. If I am the Brahman, unsullied by illusion, comprehensible through spiritual knowledge and the master of illusion, what will you do then?

Siva continued: —

Oh Lord of mountains, I shall perform my penance showing to the world my real blissful form and nature. Please give me permission to perform penance on your ridge. Without your permission it is not possible for me to perform any penance here.

Himavat said: —

The entire universe consisting of gods, Asuras and human beings, is yours. Oh great god, though insignificant, I blabber something to you.

Brahma said: —

Thus addressed by Himavat, Siva, the benefactor of the worlds, laughingly permitted him to go. Himavat then returned to his abode with Parvati. He wanted to visit him daily. Parvati, without her father, accompanied by her maids, approached Siva to serve him. On Siva's commands, none of the gatekeepers prevented Parvati from doing so.

Then, the Lord of mountains, returned to his city and rejoiced in the company of his wife, the sages and attendants. Parvati, along with her maids, continued her daily service to the moon-crested Lord, coming and going without any hindrance. She washed Siva's feet and drank that holy water. With a cloth heated in fire she wiped his body.

Sometimes Siva thought to himself, 'I shall take her only when the last seed of ego goes away from her; when she herself performs a penance.' As for Parvati, she served him everyday with great devotion.

In the meantime Indra, other gods and the sages eagerly sent Kama there at the bidding of Brahma. They had been harassed by the demon Taraka, the demon of great strength. Hence they wanted to unite Parvati and Siva in love. After reaching there Kama tried all his tricks but Siva was not at all agitated. He reduced Kama to ashes. Parvati too was divested of her ego. At his bidding she performed a penance and obtained him as her husband. Parvati and Siva were very happy. Engrossed in helping others they carried out the work of the gods.

Description of the Perturbation Caused by Kama

Brahma said: —

After going there, the haughty Kama, deluded by Siva's magic power, stationed himself. The enchanting influence of Spring spread everywhere. The vast diffusion of Spring caused the display of emotions of love. It was unbearable to the forest dwelling sages.

On seeing the untimely display of Spring, Siva the Lord, who had assumed a physical body, thought it surprising. But he still continued his penance with full concentration. When spring spread everywhere, Kama accompanied by Rati, stood on his left side, with the arrow of mango blossom taken out and kept in readiness. Then they initiated their dalliance. The sentiment of love too accompanied by coquettish gestures and emotions reached the vicinity of Lord Siva along with his attendants.

When Kama realised that he would not be able to enchant Lord Siva, he started thinking to himself. He thought, 'Who could gain access to Siva in meditation, who could fix an eye in his forehead that resembled fire by shooting blazing flames?' At that time, Parvati came to Siva to offer her devotion and service. Siva also came out of his meditation for a short while when Parvati visited. Parvati reached the place near Siva with emotions of love and accompanied by Spring. It was at that moment that Kama discharged his flowery arrow on him.

As was her usual practice she approached Siva, bowed to him, worshipped him and stood in front of him. Siva stared at Parvati while she was laying bare some of the limbs bashfully, as is natural to women in such circumstances. Lord Siva began to describe her limbs joyfully.

Siva said: —

Is this your face or the moon? Are these your eyes or lotus petals? These two eyebrows are the bows of Kama, a noble soul. Is this your lower lip or Bimba fruit? Is this your nose or the beak of a parrot? Do I hear your voice or the cooing of the cuckoo? Is this your slender waist or the sacrificial altar? There is no other woman equal to your beauty in the three worlds.

Brahma said: —

After describing her beauty again and again, Siva stopped. He then put his hand within her garment and moved it. She bashfully withdrew and kept aloof. But she soon laid bare some parts of her body and cast graceful glances at him with pleasure. On seeing these movements and gestures, Siva became fascinated. He said to her then.

Siva said: —

I feel great pleasure in merely seeing her. What pleasure shall I derive by embracing her?

Brahma said: —

Thinking thus only for a moment, the enlightened Siva became detached, honoured Parvati and spoke.

How wonderful and mysterious is the situation that has arisen! How is it that I have been deluded and fascinated? Though I am the Lord and master, I have been perturbed by Kama. If I am so affected by Kama's magic, what can other incompetent and insignificant creatures do to me?

Kama's Destruction by Siva

Brahma said: —

Oh dear one, hear the story of what happened thereafter. On seeing the dissipation of his courage, Lord Siva thought within himself.

Siva said: —

How can obstacles come my way when I am performing a great penance? Who is that wicked person who made my mind highly perturbed? I have contravened rules of virtue and transgressed the bounds of the Vedas.

Brahma said: —

Lord Siva got suspicious and started looking for the person responsible. He saw Kama stationed with his bow fully drawn and ready to discharge the arrow. On seeing this, Lord Siva was instantly angered. He saw the arrow coming towards him. The weapon, however, did not affect Siva.

Kama was frightened when he saw his weapon fail. He trembled at the sight of Lord Siva. He then called upon Indra and other gods who put him to this task. They all arrived and eulogised Siva. During the eulogy, a great flame of fire sprang up from Lord Siva's third eye. The fire kept blazing higher and higher.

After shooting up in the sky, it fell on the ground and rolled over the earth. Kama was reduced to ashes instantly. The gods didn't even get the chance to ask for mercy and forgiveness for him.

Due to the misery on account of the death of her husband, Rati fell down unconscious. When she woke up, Rati, in her great agitation, lamented loudly.

Rati said: —

What shall I do? Where can I go? What have the gods done by making my husband a victim? They called him here and destroyed him. Oh Kama, oh dear, what has happened here? Ha, Ha, my dear, my dear!

Brahma said: —

Lamenting thus and crying out various piteous words she beat with her hands, kicked with her legs and plucked her hairs. In the meantime Indra and other gods remembered Lord Siva and consoled Rati.

The gods said: —

Take some ashes and preserve them. The Lord will resuscitate your lover. You will regain your lover again. All enjoy and experience the fruit of what they do. In vain do you curse the gods.

Brahma said: —

After consoling Rati thus, all the gods approached Siva and propitiated him.

The gods said: —

Oh Lord, Oh great god, be pleased to ponder over the action of Kama. He didn't do anything out of selfishness. He was asked to do this by all the gods after being harassed by the wicked Taraka. Oh Lord, the chaste Rati is lonely and miserable now. She is in great lamentation, please *console* her. Please remove her distress.

Siva said: —

Oh gods, Oh sages, all of you listen attentively. What has happened cannot be altered. The Lord Kama, husband of Rati, shall remain bodiless till Visnu incarnates as Krisna on earth and marries Rukmini. Krisna will have Kama with Rukmini as their child when they go to Dvaraka to procreate. His name will be Pradyumna.

The demon Sambara will abduct the boy at the time of his very birth. The great demon, Sambara, will throw him in the sea. The foolish fellow will take him for dead and will return to his city.

Oh Rati, you shall stay in his city till then. There alone you will get back your husband Pradyumna. Kama in the name of Pradyumna will regain his wife after killing Sambara in a battle. Oh gods, he will be happy thereafter.

The gods said: —

Oh great god, the ocean of mercy, please resuscitate Kama quickly. Oh Siva, save the life of Rati.

Siva said: —

Oh gods, I am delighted. I shall resuscitate Kama within myself. He will be one of my Ganas and will always sport about. Oh gods, this story should not be narrated in the presence of any one. All of you return to your abodes. I shall destroy all miseries.

Brahma said: —

After saying this Rudra vanished even as the gods were eulogising him. Abiding by the directions of Siva and consoling Rati, the gods returned to their respective places. Then Rati went to the city and waited for the time mentioned by Siva.

Narada instructs Parvati

Narada said: —

Oh dear Brama, what happened after Kama was reduced to ashes and the fire from Siva's third eye was deposited in the ocean? What did Parvati do?

Brahma said: —

Oh dear, I shall now tell you what happened next. A loud sound arose when the fire issuing from Siva's eye burnt Kama. On hearing that sound, Parvati was terrified.

When Siva vanished, she returned to her abode along with her maids. Himavat was also surprised. He started worrying about his daughter Parvati after hearing that sound. Then he saw Parvati approach him. She was distressed from being separated from Siva and crying. He wiped off her tears and consoled her.

Parvati was extremely agitated due to her separation from Siva. She did not attain any peace or pleasure anywhere. She returned to her father's abode and cursed her own beauty. No one could console her. She lamented her own beauty and always muttered Siva's name.

Then, employed by Indra, you came to Himalaya mountain roaming here and there as you pleased. The Lord of the mountain worshipped you on your arrival. He then told you the story of Siva and Parvati's separation after Lord Siva burnt Kama. On hearing that, you told the Lord of the mountains to worship Lord Siva. You then hastened to meet Parvati. You spoke to her respectfully. Your words were true.

Narada said: —

Oh Parvati, listen. I am sympathetic to you. I shall speak truly. The great god has been served by you without austerities. You had some pride which he eradicated by vanishing. Hence you shall now propitiate him by performing a great penance. Siva will take you as his wife, after you have been sanctified by austerities. Oh goddess, you will not take any one other than Siva as your husband.

Parvati said: —

Oh sage, please tell me a formula for the propitiation of Lord Siva.

Brahma said: —

On hearing these words of Parvati, you taught her the five-syllable mantra of Siva in accordance with the sacred law. Generating her faith you told her the supreme efficacy of the great formula thus.

Narada said: —

Oh goddess, listen to the wonderful efficacy of this formula. This formula is the king of all formulas. It yields all cherished desires, bestows all worldly pleasures and salvation, and appeals much to Siva. Repeating this formula you shall propitiate Siva. He will certainly appear before you. Meditate on his form, observing all restraints. Repeat the five-syllable mantra. Siva will be pleased quickly. Oh chaste lady, perform the penance thus.

Brahma said: —

Oh Narada, on hearing your words and securing the excellent five-syllable mantra, Parvati was extremely pleased.

Description of Parvati's penance

Brahma said: —

After your departure, Parvati decided to perform the penance with utmost devotion. She took her maids Jaya and Vijaya into confidence and through them made her parents acquainted. She asked her maids to address her father first.

The maids said: —

Oh Himavat, let the words of your daughter be heard through us. She wishes to make her body, beauty and family fruitful. This can be achieved through penance and not otherwise. She wishes you to give her permission to go to the forest and perform penance there.

Himacala said: —

This appeals to me. If it appeals to Mena as it ought to be, what else can be a better course? This will bring happiness to my daughter and our house. If her mother also likes this, what can be more auspicious?

Brahma said: —

After securing Himacala's permission, the maids approached Parvati's mother with due respect. They repeated the same words to her, making her aware of her daughter's desire. After listening to the maids, Mena became distressed. She did not accept the proposal. Then Parvati herself spoke to her mother with humility and devotion.

Parvati said: —

Oh mother, I shall be going in the morning to perform penance to achieve Siva. Please permit me to go.

Mena said: —

Oh daughter, if you are distressed, if you wish to perform penance, you can do it at home. Oh Parvati, do not go out. Where do you wish to go to perform penance? All the deities are in my house. All the holy centres and the different temples too are here. Do not be stubborn. You shall not go out of your home. What did you achieve when you went out previously? What are you going to achieve now? Dear child, slender is your body and hard is the penance. Hence you shall perform penance here. You shall not go out.

Brahma said: —

Thus, in various ways, the daughter was dissuaded by her mother. But she did not find any pleasure except in propitiating Siva. Parvati acquired the name Uma since she was prevented from going to forest by Mena and forbidden to perform penance. However, on realising that Parvati was quite dejected, Mena permitted her to perform penance.

On getting permission from her mother, Parvati was delighted. Discarding all the fine clothes of her taste, she wore tree-barks and the fine girdle of Munja grass.

Parvati got herself initiated for the observance of ritualistic activities. Suppressing her sense-organs with her mind, she started the great penance in a place within the proximity. She kept performing her penance in all the seasons. Even in the blazing hot summers, rain and chilling winds of the winters, she kept muttering the five-syllable mantra. Fixing her mind in Siva alone she remained firm and steady.

After the first few years, she did not eat any food at all. She was engrossed in the penance. Then Parvati performed great penance standing on one leg and remembering Siva, she continued muttering the five-syllable mantra. Parvati thus spent three thousand years in the penance-grove performing penance and meditating on Lord Siva.

She performed penance difficult to be performed even by the sages. Everyone came to witness her penance. They were all surprised to witness such an event. They praised Parvati and considered themselves blessed. Then they all returned to their abodes. Her penance resulted in auspicious things in the forest. The forests soon became as beautiful as Kailasa.

Attempt of Himavat to Dissuade Parvati; Gods Go to Meet Siva

Brahma said: —

Oh excellent sage, Siva did not appear in front of Parvati even after her penance. Then Himavat came to meet Parvati along with Mena and his sons.

Himavat said: —

Oh Parvati, do not torture yourself by this penance. Dear girl, Siva is not to be seen. Certainly he is detached. You are a young woman of tender limbs. You will be overpowered and exhausted by this penance. There is no doubt about it. Hence please come back to our house.

Brahma said: —

The same thing was said by Mena, and all others who had come to visit Parvati. When she was thus addressed by all of them, she spoke to Himavat with a broad smile.

Parvati said: —

Have all of you forgotten what I had said before? Then listen to me again. I shall perform my penance as long as needed. I shall propitiate him by means of my penance. Hence I request all of you to go back to your abodes. He will be pleased, do not worry.

Brahma said: —

Thus addressed by Parvati, the Lord of mountains and the other mountains went back the way they came, surprised within and praising her. She then continued her penance.

Due to this penance, the three worlds became heated. Everyone had scorched bodies and did not understand why. They then took refuge in me. They came to me and eulogised. Before speaking their mind.

The gods said: —

Oh Lord, you have created these worlds. Then why is it scorched so much? We do not understand. Oh Brahma, you shall protect us, the gods whose bodies have been scorched. There is none else to protect us.

Brahma said: —

On hearing their words, I realised that the universe was scorched as a result of Parvati's penance. Accompanied by them, I hastened to inform Visnu about it. I pleaded to Visnu to save us all.

Visnu said: —

The entire reason has been known to me. It is caused by Parvati's penance. I shall now go to Lord Siva accompanied by all of you. We shall request Lord Siva to approach Parvati and marry her for the welfare of all the worlds.

The gods said: —

We dare not go near the great Lord Siva who is very terrifying and who has the burning brilliance of the deadly fire of dissolution. Undoubtedly he will burn us all in his anger.

Visnu said: —

Oh gods, the Lord will not consume you in fire. Considering Siva to be benevolent you shall shrewdly seek refuge in him. We shall all seek refuge in him.

Brahma said: —

Thus urged by the great Lord Visnu they set out to see Lord Siva. After reaching there the gods sent you (Narada) in, and stood at a distance from Siva. They were watching. Oh Narada, you, the fearless devotee of Siva, approached Siva and saw the Lord extremely pleased. You then came back to us and took us all inside to see him.

Siva Consents to Marry Parvati

Brahma said: —

After the god eulogised Siva, Nandikesvara was greatly moved. He began to inform Siva of his opinion.

Nandikesvara said: —

Oh Lord Siva, all of them eulogise you in order to see you. They are being threatened by Asuras. Hence they seek some remedy and resort to thy feet. Hence please protect them all.

Siva said: —

Oh great gods, Visnu, Brahma and others, why have you come near me? Mention the reason for the same.

Visnu said: —

Oh Siva, all the gods have come here to submit to you their misery perpetrated mysteriously by Taraka. Only your self-begotten son can kill Taraka. Hence we have come here to ask you to marry Paravati. Only then can we be free from suffering at the hands of Taraka. Hence, Oh Lord Siva, accept her hand as offered in marriage by the Lord of mountains. She is full of noble attributes.

Siva said: —

If goddess Parvati, the most beautiful lady were to be accepted by me, she will be able to resuscitate Kama on account of the marriage. Then all the gods, sages and ascetics will become lusty and incompetent due to Kama's doings. I ask you all to ponder upon why I burnt Kama. It was to keep myself and everyone else free from lust and distraction.

Brahma said: —

After saying this, Siva became quiet to meditate. On seeing Siva again engaged in meditation, all the dwellers of heaven, Visnu, Indra and others, humbly told Nandin.

The gods said: —

What shall we do now? Siva has become detached and has gone on meditation. You are a companion of Siva and pure assistant. You are omniscient. Please guide us. What is the remedy by which Siva can be propitiated?

Nandisvara said: —

Oh god, Oh Visnu and Brahma, pay heed to my words now. If you still wish to convince Siva to marry Parvati, you shall eulogise him with respect.

Brahma said: —

Thus the gods eulogised Siva with many piteous entreaties. They cried loudly, agitated by their devotion. Visnu accompanied by me spoke out many piteous words, remembering Siva with great devotion. Then Siva opened his eyes and ceased his meditation.

Siva said: —

Oh Visnu, Oh Brahma, Oh Indra and other gods, why have you all collectively come here in my presence? Tell me the truth.

Visnu said: —

Oh great Lord, you are omniscient, you must already know. Many kinds of miseries have befallen us due to the demon Taraka. It is for that that you have been propitiated by the gods. The demon's death can only be at the hands of your son who will be born after your marriage to Parvati. At the instance of Narada, she is performing a great penance. Oh Lord Siva, please go and grant Siva the boon. Destroy our misery and bestow happiness on us.

Siva said: —

All of you please hear with attention. I am going to say a specific thing in a suitable manner. Marrying is not a proper thing for men. Marriage is a great fetter that binds firmly. Indulging in a dalliance keeps a man away from salvation. Although I know and realise all these, yet I shall accede to your request and make it fruitful. I know the sufferings you undergo from the demon Taraka. I shall remove them. Although I am not interested at all in dalliance I shall marry Parvati for begetting a son. You may all go back to your abodes now. Fear not, I will achieve your task.

Parvati-Jatila Dialogue

Brahma continues to narrate the story after the seven celestial sages test Parvati and she passes all of them.

Brahma said: —

When the sages returned to their abodes, Lord Siva wanted to test the penance of the goddess. Under the pretext of testing, Siva wanted to see her. With a delighted mind, he assumed the form of a Jatila (an ascetic with matted hair) and went to the forest of penance of Parvati.

He took the form of a very old man with the body of a brahmin. He had an umbrella and a staff (to support him). He then saw the goddess and approached her. On seeing that brahmin, goddess Parvati worshipped him with all the articles of worship. Thereafter Parvati enquired after the health of the brahmin with respect.

Parvati said: —

Who are you and whence have you come in the guise of a Brahmacarin? You are making this forest shine with your presence. Please tell me.

The brahmin said: —

I am an aged brahmin roaming about as I please. I am an intelligent ascetic bestowing happiness and helping others. Now tell me who are you? Why do you perform this penance? This penance cannot be surpassed even by the greatest of sages. You appear to be an auspicious young woman. How is it that you are performing this penance even when you are unmarried? Tell me who your parents are. Are you the mother of the Vedas? Are you Laksmi or Sarasvati?

Parvati said: —

Oh brahmin, I am not the mother of the Vedas, nor Laksmi nor Sarasvati. I am the daughter of Himacala and my name is Parvati. Previously I had been born as Sati, the daughter of Daksa. By Yogic means I cast off my body since my husband was insulted by my father. Even in this life, Siva came to me but due to ill luck, he reduced Kama to ashes, left me and went away.

Then I came out of my father's house to perform penance. Even after so many years of penance I could not attain Siva. I was just going to step in fire but on seeing you, I stopped for a while. Now you can go. I shall enter fire as Siva still doesn't accept me. Wherever I take birth I shall woo only Siva.

Brahma said: —

After saying so, Parvati jumped into the fire although she was forbidden by the brahmin again and again. Even as she jumped into the fire, it became as cool as sandal paste due to her ascetic power. The brahmin stopped her as she was trying to go away and asked her laughingly.

The Brahmin said: —

Oh gentle lady, I cannot understand anything. Your penance is wonderful. Your body is not charred by the fire. Still your desire remains unsatiated so far. Tell me your desire.

Please tell me everything truly and methodically. Since we have become friends nothing should be kept a secret from me. Whom do you wish to have as your husband? You have cast off everything beautiful in your possession to perform this penance. Now you must tell me the reason for this penance.

Brahma said: —

Thus asked by him, Parvati urged her maid to narrate everything on her behalf. Vijaya then spoke to the ascetic. She told the Brahmin about Parvati's family and that she wishes to attain Siva as her husband. The maid also tells the Brahmin that sage Narada had advised her to perform penance to propitiate Siva.

Brahma said: —

On hearing Vijaya tell him about Parvati's journey so far, Siva, who came disguised as an ascetic, said laughingly.

The ascetic said: —

The maid has said something, but I deduce only a huge joke therefrom. If it is true, let the gentle lady herself speak out.

Description of the Fraudulent
Words of the Brahmacarin

Parvati said: —

Oh great brahmin, I am telling you the truth. Siva has been wooed by me, by mind, speech and action as well as by means of ascetic feelings. I know that it is an inaccessible object. How can I attain it? Still out of my eagerness I am performing this penance.

The brahmin said: —

So long I had been desirous of knowing why you perform this penance. I have now known it through your own words. I am now going away from this place. You can do as you please.

Parvati said: —

Oh excellent brahmin, why do you go? Stay and give me wholesome advice.

The brahmin said: —

If you are stopping me with devotion, truly desirous of hearing then I shall explain everything. The great Lord is bull-bannered. His body is smeared with ashes. His hair is matted. His caste is unknown and he resides in a forest.

You have everything. Your father is the Lord of the mountains. You have a palace and all the good things one can desire. You can get anyone else as your husband then why do you desire Siva? He left you behind and insulted you after burning Kama, then why do you still perform penance for such a man? He is nothing compared to your beauty and elegance. Then why do you still wish for him? I do not like your resolution. You can do whatever you please.

Brahma said: —

On hearing these words of that brahmin, Parvati was extremely angry at the brahmin who discredited Siva.

Parvati Sees Siva's Real Form

Parvati said: —

So long I have been thinking that someone else has come. Now everything has become clear. You are a person who cannot be killed. What has been said by you is known. Sometimes Lord Siva is seen in that guise. But he is the supreme Brahman who, out of his own accord, takes up bodies in his own sports.

You have now come in the form of a student ascetic for the sake of deceiving me. Using false arguments, you have spoken fraudulent words. I know Siva's real form very particularly. I shall therefore explain Siva's reality in the proper perspective.

Brahma said: —

Parvati goes on to explain the real form of Siva. Siva who is devoid of all attributes. She tells the brahmin everything ever known about Siva. In doing so, she eulogises Siva without knowing.

Parvati said: —

You have censured Siva of immeasurable splendour and I have worshipped you, hence I have become sinful. Oh wicked one, you profess knowledge of Siva. But you should know that the eternal Siva is not known at all. Whatever may be the form or feature of Siva, he is multiformed. Still he is my favourite.

Brahma said: —

After saying this, Parvati, the daughter of the mountain, stopped and meditated on Siva with an unaffected mind. On hearing the words of the goddess, the brahmin began to say something. Parvati instantly stopped him by addressing Vijaya, her maid.

Parvati said: —

This base brahmin must be prevented strenuously. He is inclined to say something again. He will surely censure Siva. A person who disparages Siva is definitely worthy of being killed by Siva's attendants. Since he is a brahmin, he is not to be killed. He shall be abandoned. He shall not be seen at all. Let us leave this place at once and go elsewhere. Let there be no more talk with this ignorant man.

Brahma said: —

Saying this, as Parvati was about to step ahead, the brahmin manifested as Siva, clasped his beloved. After assuming the handsome form in the manner Parvati had meditated upon, Siva addressed her while she stood with her lowered head.

Siva said: —

Where will you go, leaving me? You are not to be discarded again by me. I am delighted. Tell me what boon shall I grant you. There is nothing that cannot be given to you. From today I am your slave bought by you by performing penance. I have been bought by your beauty. Even a moment appears like a Yuga. Oh Parvati, you are my eternal wife. Let this shyness be eschewed. You please ponder with your keen intellect. I am your bridegroom. I shall immediately go to my abode along with you.

Brahma said: —

When the Lord of the gods spoke in this way, Parvati rejoiced. Whatever distress she had felt during penance she cast off as something old.

Siva-Siva Dialogue

Narada said: —

Oh Brahma, what happened thereafter? Please narrate the glory of Parvati to me.

Brahma said: —

Oh celestial sage, on hearing the words of Siva and on seeing his pleasant form and features, Parvati was delighted. Goddess Parvati replied to the Lord with great pleasure and face beaming with love.

Parvati said: —

Oh Lord, you are my husband. I am born of Mena for the achievement of the task of the gods terrified to the quick by Taraka. If you are delighted, if you are sympathetic, become my husband. With your permission I am going to my father's abode. Oh Lord, you will please go to Himavat. Please ask for my hand from my father. He will be delighted. Hence, Oh Lord, you will celebrate our marriage. The customary procedures of the marriage shall certainly be followed. Let Himavat know that an auspicious penance has been performed well by his daughter.

Siva said: —

Oh great Goddess, listen to my important statement. See that our marriage rites are performed in the proper manner without deficiency. Oh daughter of the mountain, I will not go up to Himavat your father. I will not beg him for you. A weighty person becomes meaningless when he utters the words 'Please give me'. Hence I shall not say this to your father. Knowing this, oh benevolent lady, what do you wish to do now?

Parvati said: —

Oh Lord Siva, with effort, you will please do as per my request. Oh Siva, beg of Himavat for me. You will bestow a fortune on him. Oh great Lord, be sympathetic. I am your devotee forever. I am your wife for ever in every birth. Take pity on me.

Brahma said: —

Thus addressed by her, Siva decided to follow the conventions of the world. Being desirous of doing so he rejoiced. Then Siva vanished. With great delight he went to Kailasa but at his separation from Parvati his mind was distressed.

After reaching there, he mentioned the news to Nandin and others. He was very much delighted. Everyone from then on became overjoyed. All misery was at an end. Siva too was in a pleasant mood.

The Celebration of Parvati's Return

Narada said: —

Oh Brahma, when Siva returned to his mountain, what did Parvati do and where did she go? Please tell me.

Brahma said: —

Oh dear, listen with pleasure to what happened thereafter.

Accompanied by her maids and assuming a meaningful dress she returned to her father's house. On hearing that Parvati was returning, Mena and Himavat, excessively delighted, went ahead seated in a divine vehicle. In the meantime Parvati reached the outskirts of the city. Entering the city she saw her parents.

On seeing the parents rushing towards her, she gladly bowed to them along with her maids. They gave her their blessings and embraced her. Saying, 'Oh darling', they shed tears in their excitement of love. They also lauded her for finishing her penance and getting Siva's attention.

The Lord of the mountains gave monetary gifts to brahmins and Lords. The happy and delighted Himavat, honoured everyone. Then he went to the Ganga for his bath.

In the meantime, Siva assumed the guise of a dancer and approached Menaka. In the guise of a dancer with the skill of dancing and singing, he danced well and sang many songs in a sweet voice. All the citizens assembled there to witness the performance.

Parvati, upon seeing him, became unconscious. In her visions, she saw Siva in his splendid form. He asked her to choose a boon. Parvati, mentally replied, 'Be my husband'. Then she regained her consciousness.

Mena, who was greatly delighted, took gems and jewels in order to give them to him. But the dancer did not accept the gifts. He requested for the hand of Parvati and began to dance and sing again. Mena was furious and rebuked him. She wished for him to be thrown out. Himavat also came there just then. After hearing the daring words of the dancer, he ordered his men to drive the dancer out.

But none of them could push him out as he was hot to the touch like a blazing fire. Siva decided to delude Himavat then. He took the form of Visnu and recited the Vedic hymns. Then he formed the sun. Then he showed the wonderful form of Siva with Parvati, smiling at him.

Then the dancer begged Himavat and Mena for the hand of Parvati. The Lord of mountains, deluded by Siva's magic, did not accede to this request. The dancer then vanished from the scene. Then Himavat and Mena realised that Siva had deceived them and went to his abode.

Description of Siva's Magic

Brahma said: —

On knowing their undistracted great devotion to Siva, Oh Narada, Indra and other gods started thinking.

The gods said: —

If the mountain were to give his daughter to Siva with single minded devotion, he would attain salvation immediately and would disappear from Bharata. If he were to leave off the Earth and go, the name of the Earth—Ratnagarbha (having gems in the womb) —shall be a misnomer. He will cast off his immobile aspect and assume a divine form.

Brahma said: —

Thinking like this and consulting one another they, in their bewilderment, decided to send god Brhaspati there. So Indra and the other gods went to Brhaspati quickly. They bowed to him and gave him every detail.

The gods said: —

Oh god Brahspati, please go to the abode of Himavat for the fulfilment of our task. After going there, you shall make disparaging remarks about Lord Siva. Let the Lord of the mountain give away his daughter without complete devotion towards Siva. This way, he will not attain salvation and stay on earth longer.

Brhaspati said furiously: —

All of you gods seem to be selfish in nature. You want to destroy other's interests. Indeed I will go to hell by disparaging Siva. The solution to this is also simple. Go to the Lord of the mountain and tell him your desire. Let him stay in Bharata after giving his daughter without willingness. It is certain he will attain salvation if he gives his daughter with devotion. Afterwards the seven celestial sages will properly persuade the mountain. If you do not wish to do so, go to Brahma, he will get your work done.

Brahma said: —

The gods came to my assembly. After duly bowing to me they informed me about the details. On hearing their suggestion to censure Siva, I was furious. I told them to go to Kailasa and propitiate Siva. Then they must ask Siva to go to Himavat and make disparaging remarks about himself.

On hearing my words, all the gods joyously bowed to me and went to Kailasa. The gods eulogised Siva. Eulogising Lord Siva thus, Indra and other gods respectfully submitted all the details. On hearing the words of the gods, Lord Siva agreed to the proposal. He made the gods return after assuring them smilingly. Hastening to their abodes, the gods rejoiced much, considering their work fully fulfilled and praising Sadasiva.

Then the Lord Siva went to Himavat. He went to him in the guise of a saintly brahmin. He was repeating the name of Visnu with devotion. On seeing that extraordinary guest, Himavat with his attendants stood up and greeted him with devotion. Parvati bowed with devotion to her dear lover in the guise of a brahmin. On realising him mentally, the goddess eulogised him with great joy.

Then the Lord of mountains asked him, 'Who are you, please?' Immediately the chief of brahmins spoke to the Lord of mountains thus.

The chief of brahmins said: —

Oh foremost among mountains, I am a brahmin, devotee of Visnu, and a great scholar. My occupation is that of a match-maker. I roam about on the earth. I have come to know that you desire to give your daughter to Siva, this daughter who is tender like a lotus flower and endowed with all accomplishments. To Siva—who has no support, who is devoid of associations, who is deformed. He does not deserve your daughter. Oh foremost among the wise, learn sense. He has not a single kinsman. You are the storehouse of great gems and jewels. He has no assets at all. So I urge you to reconsider this arrangement.

Brahma said: —

Saying this, the brahmin stopped. He took food and left the place with pleasure for his abode.

The Seven Celestial Sages Arrive

Brahma said: —

On hearing the words of the brahmin, Mena spoke to Himavat with tears welling up in her eyes.

Mena said: —

Oh Lord of mountains, please listen to my words. Please consult important devotees of Siva regarding what has been mentioned by the brahmin. On hearing these words, my mind is dejected. I shall not give my daughter to Siva with ugly features, ignoble conduct and defiled name. If you do not accede to my request, I shall die. I will immediately leave this house or swallow poison. With a rope, I shall tie Parvati around my neck and go to a thick forest. I would rather drown than give my daughter to him.

Brahma said: —

In the meantime, all those seven celestial sages were remembered by Siva whose mind was agitated by the pangs of separation from Parvati. They came to Siva almost immediately. Arundhati too came there. After eulogising Siva, they spoke to him.

The sages said: —

Oh Lord of all the worlds, how can our fortune be so excellent? Oh Sadasiva, we have become the most excellent of all people as you have remembered us. By seeing you today we have become the most respectable sages worthy of the worship of all the worlds. Please command us to do whatever you please.

Siva said: —

Oh brahmins, it was for a specific reason that you have been summoned here. Whatever I am doing is for the benefit of the universe. I have agreed to marry Parvati and I shall only marry her. However, if Himavat were to give his daughter to me with full devotion to me, he would attain salvation instantly and vanish from Earth. In order to prevent this from happening, the gods suggested that I go to Himavat and Mena in disguise and rebuke myself. This way their devotion will reduce and Himavat would stay on Earth. After doing so, they refused to give Parvati's hand to me. Hence you all go to the abode of Himavat and urge the excellent mountain and his wife. Do whatever necessary to straighten this out. Convince Himavat and his dear wife to proceed with the marriage.

Brahma said: —

On hearing these words, the seven sages became delighted and immediately went away to carry out Siva's request. On seeing that city of heavenly splendour, the sages were surprised. They spoke among themselves.

The sages said: —

We are really blessed and meritorious to see this city. It is extraordinary and magnificent. Men are eager to go to heaven only because they have not seen this city. Oh brahmins, what is the use of heaven in front of this city?

Brahma said: —

Describing the city, they all went towards Himavat's palace. Himavat was surprised to see them approach and spoke humbly.

Himavat said: —

These sages shall be worshipped by me now. We householders are really blessed, to whom great men like these, bestowing happiness on all, pay their visit.

Brahma said: —

In the meantime they descended to the ground from the sky. On seeing them Himavat advanced to welcome them. He eulogised them and offered them seats. Then he spoke to them.

Himavat said: —

I am blessed. I am content. My life is fruitful. I am the best person worthy of being seen in the three worlds. I am your servant. Some tasks may be entrusted to me. Mercifully may it be spoken out. May my life be fruitful.

The Appeasement of Himavat

The sages said: —

Siva is the father of the universe. Parvati is the mother of the universe. Hence your daughter shall be given to Siva, the supreme soul. By this activity your life will be fruitful.

Himavat said: —

Oh ye seven sages, what you just said has already been cherished by me. But now a certain brahmin professing Vaisnava cult came here and spoke very critically about Siva. Ever since, the mother Parvati has gone out of sense. Hence she does not wish for her daughter's marriage with Siva.

She has entered the chamber of anger. She is aggrieved and her clothes have become dirty. I too am, you can say, out of sense. I do not wish to give my daughter to Siva who is apparently a mendicant.

Brahma said: —

Oh sage, after saying these words, Himavat became silent. The sages then sent Arundhati to Menaka. Arundhati went and found Mena lying in her grief, Parvati sitting with her. She spoke to Mena then.

Arundhati said: —

Oh Menaka, get up. I, Arundhati, have come to your house. The seven sages of sympathetic nature have also come.

Mena said: —

Ha, what a meritorious thing this is! We are blessed. Arundhati, the wife of Vasistha, has come here. Oh gentle lady, what is the purpose of your visit? My daughter and I are your slaves. Be merciful to us.

Brahma said: —

Arundhati thus addressed, advised Mena in various ways and returned to the place where the sages were seated. Then they began to advise the Lord of the mountains. They were clever in speech and they spoke respectfully.

The sages said: —

Oh Lord of the mountains, hear us now. Give Parvati to Siva. Become the father-in-law of the world-destroyer. For the destruction of Taraka, formerly Brahma requested Siva to strive for this alliance. Siva was not eager to marry. But since requested by Brahma, the Lord agreed to take your daughter. Parvati performed a penance and the Lord promised her. Thus, for these two reasons the Lord of Yogins wishes to marry her.

Himavat said: —

I do not see any royal paraphernalia with Siva. He has none to support him. He has no assets. He has no kinsman. I do not wish to give my daughter to a Yogin who is extremely detached. Out of my own free will, I will not give her to the trident-bearing Siva. Oh sages, whatever arrangement is befitting here, may kindly be carried out.

Vasistha said: —

Oh Lord of mountains, listen to my words. They are true and shall bring about your joy here and hereafter. The brahman that came to you was a devotee of Visnu. Vishnu was born out of Siva. So was Brahma. The entire universe is Siva's then how can he be without any assets? The greatest of gods, Visnu and Brahma are his kinsman so how can Siva be without any kinsman?

Your daughter Parvati was formerly Sati, born out of the womb of Daksa's wife. Daksa gave her to Siva. She was married and vowed to be Siva's wife in every lifetime. Now, she is born out of Mena's womb. Hence, Parvati (Sati) only belongs to Siva, in every birth. Hence, you give your daughter to Siva out of your own free will. Otherwise she will herself go and surrender herself as his beloved wife. Your daughter was granted this boon, she shall get it by any means.

Brahma said: —

When Himavat was still doubtful, Vasistha gave the example of Anaranya, who gave his daughter to a brahmin in order to save his assets and his people. Himavat then enquired about Anaranya's daughter Padma. He wished to know what Padma did after marrying Pippalada.

Vasistha then narrated the story of Padma and Pippalada. Padma was loyal to her husband even when Dharma disguised as a beautiful man to test her loyalty. When she did not give in, Dharma blessed her for her loyalty to her husband. He also blessed Pippalada with comely looks and sexual vigour. After that Padma and Pippalada lived happily with great riches and pleasure.

The Statements of the Seven Sages

Brahma said: —

On hearing the stories narrated by Vasistha, Himavat and his wife were very surprised.

Himacala said: —

All of you mountains, please listen to me. Vasistha has asked me to consider. It is to be considered what I shall do now. You consider well, decide and let me know.

The mountains said: —

Parvati is born only for the purpose of the gods. She is the reincarnated form of form. Siva has been propitiated by her and Siva has also spoken to her. Hence, there is no need for any other discussion.

Brahma said: —

On hearing the words of Meru and other mountains, Himacala was greatly pleased and Parvatl laughed within herself. Arundhati also convinced Mena with reasoned statements and examples from various mythological legends. Then the chief of mountains, freed from wrong notions and grown wise, spoke.

Himacala said: —

Oh fortunate sages, please listen to my words. Everything that I possess, my body, wife, Mena, sons, daughter, assets and achievements and other things belong to Siva and not otherwise.

The sages said: —

Oh mountain, since the course of your summits is befitting, you are blessed, you are the chief of all mountains, you are great in every respect.

Brahma said: —

After saying thus, the sages of pure mind offered their blessings to the girl— 'Be pleasing to Siva. Everything will be well with you. As the moon is in the bright half of the month, may your qualities increase.' After saying this, the sages made Himacala believe that the alliance was a settled fact.

After fixing the auspicious Lagna for the marriage and congratulating and complementing one another, the sages came to Siva's abode on the fourth day. After reaching the place, Vasistha and other sages bowed to Siva and eulogised him. They then spoke to Lord Siva.

The sages said: —

Oh Lord Siva, Lord of the gods, please listen lovingly to the narration of what we, your attendants, have done. We used different examples from mythological legends to convince them. Undoubtedly, they were enlightened. Parvati has been betrothed to you by the Lord of mountains. Now please prepare for the marriage with your attendants and gods. Go to Himacala's abode and marry Parvati with all the customs for the sake of a son.

Lord Siva said: —

Oh fortunate one, a marriage ceremony has never been witnessed nor even heard of by me before. The details of the same shall be mentioned by you all, specifically.

The sages said: —

Please invite and summon Visnu with his retinue, Brahma with his sons, Lord Indra, all the sages, Yaksas, Gandharvas, Kinnaras, Siddhas, Vidyadharas, heavenly nymphs and others. All of them will jointly accomplish everything for you. There is no doubt about it.

Brahma said: —

Saying this and taking his permission, the seven sages joyfully returned to their abodes praising the way of Siva.

The Letter of Betrothal Is Despatched, the Requisites for the Celebration Are Gathered and the Mountain Invitees Arrive

Narada said: —

Dear wise father, when the seven sages returned, what did Himacala do? Please tell me.

Brahma replied: —

Oh great sage, I shall tell you what Himacala did. After the sages left, Himacala rejoiced in the company of his sons and wife. He got his priest Garga to write the letter of betrothal.

He dispatched the letter to Siva along with some articles to pay homage. The people who took the letter to Siva were honoured by the great Lord. Himavat was delighted. Himavat then sent invitations to his other kinsmen who were stationed in different places. He ensured to invite everyone to the wedding of Lord Siva and Parvati.

After the invitations were sent, other wedding preparation commenced. Food, jewels, gems and other riches were stacked in huge numbers. Everyone invited was to be honoured duly. The invitees came there along with their wives, children and attendants. All the mountains came to the wedding. The brilliant rivers Ganga, Sonabhadra, Godavari, Yamuna, Brahmastri and Venika also attended the wedding assuming a divine form. Himavat welcomed everyone and seated them all honourably.

The Gods Arrive at Kailasa on Invitation and Siva Prepares to start

Narada said: —

Oh dear father, what did Lord Siva do on receiving the auspicious letter of betrothal? Please narrate that story of Siva.

Brahma replied: —

On reading the auspicious letter with joy, Siva laughed in delight. The Lord honoured the messengers duly. He told the sages, 'Everything is auspicious and well done. All of you shall grace the celebration of my marriage. The marriage proposal has been accepted by me.' On hearing these words of Siva, they were delighted. Then Lord Siva remembered you, oh sage. You went to Siva immediately and bowed humbly. Lord Siva then spoke to you.

'Oh excellent sage, at your bidding, a great penance has been performed by Parvati. I have granted her the boon of being her husband. I shall marry her in seven days from today. I shall make a grand festival of the same', said Siva.

Brahma said: —

Oh sage, you were delighted to hear Siva's words. You replied to him humbly.

Narada said: —

Oh Lord, a task befitting my capacity must be mentioned by you. Consider me your own servant. Command me as you please.

Siva said: —

Oh sage, on my behalf, invite all the gods beginning with Visnu, and sages, Siddhas and others. I wish everyone to attend the wedding with their wives and children. Those who do not take part in my celebration will not be my people.'

Brahma said: —

Oh sage, you then invited everyone on Siva's behalf. After carrying out your duties as his emissary, you returned to Siva and stayed with him.

Visnu came there with his wife and attendants, dressed suitably. I too went to Kailasa soon after. Indra also arrived at Kailasa along with other gods, sages, Nagas. Lord Siva received them with due respect. Then the great festival was celebrated in Kailasa. Everyone arrived and they eulogised Siva, said Brahma.

All of them said: —

Oh Lord, please start your journey for the wedding now. Let us all accompany you in this journey.

Thus requested by everyone, Lord Siva started following the sacred rites as written in the Vedas.

Authorised by him, I performed all the rites conducive to prosperity, assisted by the sages. All of them who had mastered the Vedas performed the safety rites for Siva and tied the auspicious thread round his wrist.

After all the rituals were performed, Siva started his journey. Everyone was happy and excited, singing and dancing, said Brahma.

The Marriage Procession of Siva

Brahma said: —

Then Siva called Nandin and other Ganas and ordered them to accompany him. The Lord of Ganas as ordered, took their armies and started joyously. In the marriage procession of Siva, Nandin and other leaders of Ganas went surrounded by hundreds and twenties of crores of Ganas. Thus, Lord Siva, accompanied by his Ganas, gods and others, went to the city of Himagiri for the celebration of his marriage.

Oh great sage, listen to another incident that happened when Siva, the Lord of all, went for his marriage along with the gods and others.

Rudra's sister Candi, assuming a great festive mood, came there with great pleasure but inspiring terror in others. She was riding on a ghost. She was bedecked in the ornaments of serpents. A gold pot filled (with water) shone over her head. Her attendants were with her. The divine Bhuta attendants were crores and crores in number. They shone in diverse forms. Accompanied by them, Candi of deformed face went ahead gladly and enthusiastically. She was equally competent to please and to harass.

All the Ganas of Siva numbering to eleven crores, terrible but favourites of Siva were kept by her far behind.

The loud sounds of Damarus, the Jhankara sound of the Bheris pervade all the three worlds. Visnu was also there, shining vibrantly amongst the group. I too shone well in my vehicle. I was eager to render service to Siva.

Seated on the elephant Airavata in the midst of his armies, Indra shone well, fully decorated in various ways. Many other sages enthusiastic about the marriage of Siva shone well on their way.

Lord Siva was seated on his bull of crystal purity and beauty—the bull who is called Dharma by the Vedas, Sastras, Siddhas and sages. Siva was being served by the gods and sages on his way. He shone well. Accompanied by all of us, Lord Siva was going to the abode of the mountain Himalaya for the marriage with Parvati.

Description of the Altar-structure

Brahma said: —

Then after mutual consultation and getting Siva's permission, Visnu sent you ahead to the abode of the mountain. Oh sage, after going there, you saw your own image made by Visvakarman and were surprised. You were a bit ashamed too. Then you saw the images of all the other gods and Lords. You entered the great altar of Himavat, studded with various gems and decorated with gold pots and stumps of plantain trees. You spoke to the Lord of mountains thus.

Oh Lord of mountains, tell me the truth. Has Lord Siva come already for the marriage? Have the gods with Visnu and others, the sages, the Siddhas and the secondary gods come already? Narada enquired.

Himavat said: —

Oh Narada, Siva with the marriage party has not come till now for the purpose of marrying Parvati. Please know that all these things have been portrayed by Visvakarman. Oh celestial sage, shake off your bewilderment. Be calm. Showing kindness to me, you take your food and rest for a while. Then go to Lord Siva accompanied by these mountains and bring him here.

Brahma said: —

You accepted the suggestion noble-heartedly and performed the duties there. Then, accompanied by the sons of the mountain and others, you went to Siva's presence. Upon seeing you and the sons of Himavat, everyone was surprised. They asked you about this.

The gods asked, 'Oh Narada, you appear to be bewildered. Have you been duly honoured by Himavat or not? Tell us in detail. Why have these excellent mountains come here? Does the mountain intend to give his daughter to Siva or not? What is it that is taking place in the abode of Himavat now? Please tell us and clear our suspicions.'

Brahma continued: —

On hearing these words of the heaven-dwellers, you who have been fascinated by the magic of Visvakarman, spoke to them.

The distorted portrayal of heaven-dwellers is something enchanting. He desires to delude the gods in a loving but cunning manner. I have been fascinated by my shining portrait made by Visvakarman. Visnu, Brahma and Indra have been realistically portrayed by him. He has made artificial prototypes of all the gods. No one, not a single detail, has been left out. It is for the purpose of particularly enchanting the gods that this spell has been employed by him through this caricature, said Narada.

Lord Indra said: —

Oh Lord of gods, Visvakarman who is agitated due to the grief over his son will surely kill me under this pretext and not otherwise.

Brahma said: —

On hearing this, Visnu laughingly consoled Indra by saying this.

Visnu said, 'Oh Indra, Siva will undoubtedly look to our welfare. Fear not, nothing shall go wrong in this marriage procession.'

Siva said: —

Oh Visnu, what are you speaking to each other? Oh Narada, what does the great mountain say? Tell me the truth with details. You must not keep any secret. Does the mountain want to give his daughter or not? Tell me that quickly. On going there, what did you see?

Narada replied: —

Oh great Lord, the Lord of mountains will surely give his daughter to you. These mountains have come to take you there. Visvakarman has created a wonderful illusion of the altar that is filled with surprising things. It is only to fascinate everyone with the magic. On seeing it I was deluded by his skill and was struck with surprise.

Oh Visnu, if the mountain Himavat gives his daughter to me, what have I to do with this spell? Oh Brahma, Oh Indra, Oh sages, Oh gods, speak truly. What have I to do with the spell if the mountain gives his daughter? Go ahead, hasten, and seek the answer, Siva asked the Gods.

Brahma said: —

At the bidding of Siva, Visnu and other gods, kept you and the mountains at the head and started for the abode of Himavat. They were surprised to see the wonderful abode. The delighted Siva reached the outskirts of the city accompanied by Visnu and others as well as his delighted Ganas.

Description of the Meeting of
the Lord and the Mountain

Brahma continued: —

Himavat learned that Siva was very near to his city. He was overjoyed. He went to personally welcome Siva along with the other mountains and brahmins. On seeing the army of the gods, Himavat was struck with wonder. Considering himself blessed he appeared in front of them. Meeting each other, the gods and the mountains considered themselves blessed. They were greatly delighted.

Seeing Siva in front, Himavat and everyone else bowed to him. The beauty of his divine person illuminated the quarters. His body shone in the delicate silken garments. His crown was lustrous with the gems set in it. He was smiling, shedding pure brilliance everywhere. Visnu, the others and I were right with him. The mountain, on seeing us, great favourites of Siva forever, bowed to us. He then bowed to everyone who was accompanying Lord Siva.

At the bidding of Siva, the mountain went ahead to his city. Behind him went Visnu, me, the sages and the gods. Everyone praised the city of Himavat. Then Himavat welcomed all and performed the customs. He gave gifts and offered auspicious things. Then he sent his sons to Siva accompanied by all his attendants and followers, Visnu and others. After meeting Siva, the sons of the mountain came back to their abode with his permission and informed Himavat gladly that the bridegroom and the party were on their way there.

In the meantime, Mena desired to see Siva. Oh sage, through her Lord, you were requisitioned there. Urged by the Lord who desired to fulfil the task of Siva you went there. After bowing to you, Mena told you that she wanted to see the real form of Lord Siva that dispels haughtiness.

Description of Siva's Wonderful Sport

Mena said: —

Oh sage, I shall first see the bridegroom of Parvati. Let me have an idea of the form and features of Siva for which she performed the great penance.

Brahma said: —

Thus she went to the terrace along with you to see Siva. Then Siva, realising her false pride in herself, spoke to Visnu and I as a part of his wonderful sport.

Siva said: —

At my bidding, both of you go one by one accompanied by the gods to the threshold of the mountain. I shall follow afterwards.

Brahma said: —

On hearing it, Visnu called all, and told them of his suggestion. The gods then walked in accordance with that suggestion enthusiastically. Lord Siva let Mena stand on the terrace and see the procession along with you in order to make her mind confused. Oh sage, Mena became delighted as usual. She saw Vasu, the Lord of Vasus and exclaimed, 'Oh this is Siva.' Then you told her that these were only the attendants of Siva. The bridegroom is yet to come.

On hearing this, Mena started thinking, 'A person greater than this! Ha, how will he be!' Like this, many attendants of Siva, all in their extraordinary glory, passed by. Mena was convinced either of them was Lord Siva. But you, Oh Narada, kept telling her that they were not Siva. Even when Indra and Visnu came, Mena thought they were Siva. But again, you told her the truth.

Narada said: —

The bridegroom Siva is better than Visnu, Brahma and all the other gods that you just saw. Oh Mena, it is impossible for me to describe his beauty. He is the Lord of the entire universe, the Lord of all, the Self-Emperor.

Brahma said: —

On hearing your words, Mena thought that her daughter was auspicious, rich, fortunate and a harbinger of happiness for the three families. Her face was beaming with pleasure and her heart was delighted. Frequently congratulating herself on her good luck, she said to herself–

'By the birth of Parvati, I have become blessed in every respect. The Lord of mountains too is blessed. Everything connected with me is blessed. Her would-be-husband is the Lord of these leaders of great lustre whom I have seen now. How can I describe her good luck even in a hundred years? It is impossible!'

Brahma said: —

Thus spoke Mena with her mind full of love and hope. By that time Siva came that way. He showed himself in his real form free from change of illusion. Oh dear, the Ganas of wonderful forms proved to be the dispeller of Mena's pride. Oh sage Narada, on seeing him come, you lovingly pointed him out to her as the bridegroom of Siva and spoke to her.

Narada said: —

This is Siva himself, Oh Lady, see. It was for him that Parvati performed a great penance in the forest.

Brahma said: —

Thus addressed by you, the delighted Mena stared at the Lord with joy. Immediately the army of Siva came there consisting of wonderful arrays of Bhutas, Pretas and Ganas. Some were in the form of violent gusts of wind. Some had no faces. Some had distorted and deformed faces. Some had many faces. Some had no hands. Others had deformed hands. Some of them had many hands.

Oh sage, on seeing the innumerable Ganas, Bhutas and Pretas, Menaka was terribly frightened instantaneously. On seeing Siva in their midst, the mother of Parvati trembled. She then saw Siva. He was seated on the Bull. He had five faces and three eyes. He had ashes smeared over the body. He had matted hair and ten hands with the skull in one of them. His upper cloth was a tiger's hide. He had odd eyes, ugly features utterly dishevelled and untidy. He wore the hide of an elephant.

She was stunned, tremulous, agitated and confused. You said to her, 'This is Siva,' and pointed him out to her. On hearing your words she fell on the ground like a tender creeper blown by the wind. Mena the chaste lady was grief-stricken.

'What is this? I have been deceived for being too ambitious. Of what use is it to see this deformity?' asked Mena.

Brahma said: —

Mena fell on the floor unconscious. She gradually gained her consciousness.

Mena Regains Consciousness

Brahma continued: —

On regaining consciousness, Mena started to rebuke everyone, including her sons and Parvati. Then she spoke to you.

Mena said: —

Oh sage, formerly it was mentioned by you that Parvati would marry Siva. My daughter even performed a penance that was difficult to even look at. Nobody could have done what she did. But what is the fruit of all that? It was all meaningless. What shall I do? My family has been deceived. How can I let my daughter marry Siva now?

Oh wretched daughter, what have you done? This is extremely painful to me. How can you cast aside great Lords like Visnu and Brahma and perform penance for someone like Siva? Fie on you. Fie on your intellect. Fie on your beauty and conduct.

Do not let the Lord of the mountains come near me or the seven celestial sages. I shall not see anyone's face. I shall cut off your head, oh daughter. But what will I do after that? Oh what will I do?

Brahma said: —

After saying this Mena fell unconscious on the ground. Agitated by grief and anger she did not go near her husband. The gods came near her. I too came myself. On seeing me, O excellent sage, you spoke to her.

Narada said: —

The real handsome form of Siva is not known by you. This form is assumed by Siva in a sportive mood. It is not the real form. Hence, Oh chaste lady, cast off anger. Be calm. Do what is proper to be done. Give Parvati to Siva.

Mena replied: —

Oh wicked one, get up and go away. I do not want to hear anything.

The Gods said: —

Oh Mena, this Siva is the Supreme Lord himself, the bestower of the greatest happiness. On seeing your daughter's severe penance he had appeared before her and granted her the boon.

Brahma continued: —

Mena cried aloud frequently and spoke to the gods—'My daughter will not be given to Siva of fierce features. Why have you all conspired together to render her beauty futile?'

Oh excellent sages, when she uttered thus, the seven sages, Vasistha and others spoke then.

The seven sages responded: —

Oh dear Mena, we have come here to achieve a purpose. In this important affair how can we entertain opposite views? Siva is at your doorstep to marry Parvati. You must not turn him away.

Mena said: — —

I would rather slay her with weapons than give her to Siva. All of you go away. You shall never come near me.

Then Himacala came there and lovingly spoke to her.

Himacala said: — —

Oh beloved Mena, how is it that you have become dispirited? Why are you insulting so many important people? You do not know Siva. Siva has many names and many forms. Seeing a peculiar distorted form you have become excited. He has been realised by me. He is the protector of everyone. He is worthy of worship and he can bless and countermand. Let me remind you of a former incident when Siva came to our place in a hideous form and exhibited his sports. But on seeing his greatness we both consented to give our daughter in marriage to him. Oh beloved, keep that promise.

Mena said: — —

Oh Lord, let my words be heard. You can carry out what I say. I shall not give Parvati to Siva. You can tie her up and cast her down or drown her. But she will not be married to Siva. If that happens, I will leave this mortal frame, Mena replied.

Parvati said: — —

Oh mother, your noble intellect has become perverted. This Siva has no one else greater than him. He is the Lord of all and the creator and protector of everyone. Why do you not see this? Please get up. Endeavour to make your life fruitful. Give me to Siva. Make my effort meaningful. I shall not marry anyone else.

Brahma said: — —

On hearing these words of Parvati, Mena became angry. She caught hold of Parvati and thrashed her with fists, elbows gnashing her teeth. She was greatly agitated and furious. You and other sages who were there, separated her from the mother and took her far off. Mena then rebuked them again and again. She hurled harsh repulsive words at all of them.

Mena said: — —

See what I will do to Parvati of evil inclination. I will give her poison or drown her or push her down a height. Then I will cast off my own body. But I will not give her to Siva, the wicked bridegroom. What a repulsive body he has! What does he have that can tempt me? No. Nothing at all!

Brahma said: — —

I went to Mena quickly and narrated to her the principles of Siva. I requested her to realise Siva's greatness and give Parvati away to him.

Oh Brahma, why do you render her excellent beauty futile? Why don't you kill her yourself? Do not tell me this again. I will not give my daughter, dearer than my own life, to Siva, said Mena.

Oh great sage, when she expressed such sentiments, Vishnu rushed to her. He attempted to change her opinions.

Visnu said: — —

Oh Mena, listen to my reason. Siva created me and Brahma, who you find good looking and has all the riches and ornaments. You feel we are more suited for Parvati for we have looks that Siva is not showing you in himself. But oh Mena, Siva is the one who gave us these looks. He created us, he created the Vedas and everyone. Then how can he have a deformed face? If he is capable of making us beautiful, can you not understand how beautiful he himself is? So I thus request you to worship Siva. All pain will be quelled.

Mena said: —

Oh Visnu, I hear you. There is but one way that I can agree with you. Let Siva assume a lovely form and body. Only then will I give my daughter to him. Otherwise I will not. This is my firm decision.

Siva's Comely Form and the Jubilation of the Citizens

Brahma said: —

In the meantime, Oh sage, you went immediately to Siva. After reaching there you pleaded with Siva to heed to Mena's request. You eulogised him thereafter. On hearing your words Siva joyously assumed a divine form and showed his mercifulness. On seeing this you were delighted and went to Mena. You spoke to her about it.

Narada said: —

Oh Mena, see the excellent features of Siva. The merciful Siva has taken great pity on us.

Brahma continued: —

Mena looked at the divine form of Siva. Every part of the body was exquisite. He was embellished with different ornaments. He was smiling with great delight. His comeliness was highly pleasing. He was fair-complexioned and lustrous. He wore the best of the garments.

Visnu, Indra, the other gods and I bedecked our bodies and dresses and accompanied Siva. Thus everyone was very jubilant and in the company of their wives they eulogised Siva. On seeing him in that form, Mena stood stunned as though drawn in a picture for a moment. She then spoke.

Mena exclaimed: —

Oh great Lord, my daughter is indeed blessed, she by whom the great penance was performed. Oh Lord of Parvati, be pleased now. Pardon me for the heap of repulsive words I showered on Siva.

Brahma said: —

After saying this and eulogising the moon-crested Lord, Mena bowed to him with palms joined in reverence and stood shy. By then all the ladies of the city left their important work to see Siva. That was the only thing important to them at that moment.

Thus the ladies forsook their activities, left their houses and came out. On seeing the exquisite form of Siva they were greatly fascinated. They cherished him and described him thus.

The ladies announced: —

The eyes of the residents of this town have become fruitful. The life of the people who have seen this comely form has become meaningful. Parvati has accomplished everything when she performed penance for Siva. She is blessed, she is content in securing Siva as her husband. This is well done. The excellent pair has been united. Everything has become meaningful in every activity. All of us, men and women, are blessed—we who see Siva, the Lord of all, the husband of Parvati.

Brahma said: —

Saying thus, they worshipped Siva with sandalwood paste and raw rice grains. They showered him with fried grains respectfully. The Lord became delighted by being treated this way.

The Arrival of the Bridegroom

Brahma said: —

Siva was welcomed by Himavat and Mena. For the customary Nirajana (waving of lights) rites of Siva, Mena came to the entrance with her womenfolk. Mena saw with pleasure Lord Siva, the bridegroom of Parvati.

Siva had the complexion of the colour of the champaka flower. He had only one face but retained the three eyes. The face was beaming with a simple smile. He was bedecked in gems and gold. He wore brilliant necklaces. He was decked in bangles and bracelets of fine workmanship. He was shining well with the two clothes of great value, fine texture and unrivalled beauty and purified in fire. He was extremely beautiful. He appeared to be very young. Seeing the Lord as her son-in-law, Mena forgot all her grief. She was glad.

The delighted Himacala also carried out the customary rites of reception at the entrance. Mena also jubilantly took part in the same along with all the womenfolk. She made formal inquiries about the health of the bridegroom and gladly went into the house. Siva went to the apartments assigned to him along with the Ganas and the Gods. In the meantime the servant-maids in the harem of the mountain took Parvati out in order to worship the tutelar family deity.

The Gods saw the winkless eyes of the dark complexioned bride, fully bedecked in ornaments. With a side glance she was respectfully looking at the three-eyed Lord avoiding the eyes of others. With a gentle smile playing on her face she appeared very beautiful.

On seeing the primordial deity, the Gods and others bowed down their heads with great devotion. The three-eyed deity saw her with the corner of an eye and was glad. On seeing the shapely body of Sati he forgot the pangs of separation. With his eyes riveted to her, he forgot everything else. Then Parvati went out of the city, worshipped the family goddess and returned to her parental abode along with the brahmin women. The marriage was about to begin.

Description of Marriage

Brahma narrated the wedding scene: —

Himavat started the marriage rites as asked by the priest Garga. The brahmins were requested by Himavat, 'May the rite be formally started after narrating the Tithi.' The brahmins proclaimed the auspicious time as asked. Then Himacala, with a smile, spoke to Siva. He said, 'Oh Siva, please do not delay. Please mention your genealogy, saintly lineage, family name and your Veda along with your branch of the Vedas. You must also mention your Gotra.' On hearing these words of Himavat, Siva was unable to answer.

At that moment, you (Narada) did something laughable. Siva mentally urged you and you played your Vina even when all of us had forbidden you. Even the Lord of the mountains asked you not to play, 'Do not play the Vina now', he said. But you only listened to Siva mentally and thus spoke.

Narada said: —

You have been utterly deluded. You do not know anything about Siva of whom you speak. You have no inner vision. He has created everyone, then how can he have a family? He is the start of everything in this universe. Hence he has no Gotra, family or name. He is independent. At his will he assumes bodies taking many names. Oh father of Parvati, have no doubt. Siva does not need any of these.

Oh great mountain, listen to my words. After hearing them, give your daughter to Siva. Know that the divine sound alone is the gotra, and family of Siva in his divine form, who assumes forms in his divine sport.

Brahma said: —

Oh sage, on hearing your words, Himavat was satisfied and the bewilderment in his mind vanished. Then Meru, and all the excellent mountains, became angry to see that Himavat still had doubts. They spoke to Himavat thus.

Oh Lord of the mountains, be firm and stand by your decision. If you say No, you stand to lose. We speak the truth. Do not hesitate. Let the girl be given to Siva, the mountains said.

Brahma continued: —

On hearing the words of his friends, Himavat, urged by Brahma, gave his daughter to Siva. Himavat repeated the mantra, 'Tasmai Rudraya Mahate'. Placing the hand of Parvati in the hand of Siva the mountain rejoiced mentally.

Siva grasped the lotus-like hand of Parvati in his hand repeating the Vedic mantras. Lord Siva was greatly delighted. Touching the ground and showing the worldly course of action, Siva recited the mantra 'Kamasya Kodat'.

Visnu, Indra, the gods and I were delighted. Himavat then gave some articles in dowry to Siva. Thus Himavat attained perfect satisfaction after giving his daughter Parvati to Siva, the great Lord, in accordance with the rules. Then the Lord of mountains joined his palms in reverence and eulogised Lord Siva joyously.

The Delusion of Brahma

Brahma said: —

Siva poured offerings into the fire with mantras. Parvati's brother Mainaka offered handfuls of fried grains. Then according to the worldly convention, Parvati and Siva performed the circumambulation around the fire.

On that occasion, deluded by Siva's power of illusion, I stared at the feet of the goddess as well as the crescent shaped nails. On seeing them, I became overwhelmed by passion. Deluded by the cupid, I stared at her limbs frequently. Then, immediately after staring at them, my semen dropped on the ground. I, the grandfather, was ashamed by the emission of my semen. I pressed the penis secretly with my feet. Oh Narada, on coming to know of it, the great god Siva became furious. He wanted to kill me immediately because I was overwhelmed by lust. Everyone trembled by Siva's anger, even Visnu was terrified. Then Visnu and the gods eulogised Siva to calm him down.

On hearing their words, Lord Siva was delighted. Favourably disposed to his devotees, he offered me freedom from fear. Oh dear, then Visnu, the other gods and the sages began to smile and became merry. Oh dear, my semen pressed very frequently, turned into several sparkling drops. Thousands of sages called Valakhilyas sprang up from the sparkling drops. Then those sages gathered near me with great pleasure and said, 'Oh father Oh father.' They were then sternly told by you, urged by Siva's wish. The Valakhilyas were rebuked angrily by you.

Narada ordered the Valakhilyas: —

All of you together go to the mountain Gandhamadana. You shall not stay here. No purpose shall be served by your staying here. Perform penance there. After this you will become great sages and disciples of the sun. This is Siva's command.

Brahma said: —

Thus addressed, all the Valakhilyas went immediately to the mountain Gandhamadana after bowing to Siva. I was able to breathe fearlessly, thanks to Visnu and others, the noble souls urged by Lord Siva. Then I eulogised Siva and asked for his forgiveness. Visnu and the other gods also joined me in the eulogy. Siva was delighted and everyone was happy again.

Description of Fun and Frolic

Brahma said: —

Oh Narada, thereafter at the bidding of Siva, I carried out the concluding ceremonies of the wedding of Siva and Parvati joyously. At the behest of the brahmins, Siva applied Sindoor on the head of Parvati. The lustre of Parvati at that time was beyond description and very wondrous.

When the sacrificial rites in the marriage ceremony were thus concluded duly, Lord Siva gave the Purnapatra to me. Siva then made the gift of cows to the presiding priest. Other gifts of auspicious nature were also made.

Visnu accompanied me, while all the gods and sages took leave of the mountain and returned to their abodes. The ladies in the city of the mountain then took Siva and Parvati to the abode of Kubera. Several customs and conventions were followed there. Then the bride and the groom were taken to their bed chamber. The room was exquisitely decorated.

Then the sixteen celestial ladies arrived there and saw the couple with great respect. They were Sarasvati, Laksmi, Savitri, Jahnavi, Aditi, Saci, Lopamudra, Arundhati, Ahalya, Tulasi, Svaha, Rohini, Vasundhara, Satarupa, Samjna and Rati. A throne was offered to Siva who sat on it joyously. The celestial ladies made these sweet witty remarks to him one by one.

Sarasvati remarked: —

Oh great Lord, Sati who was more than your life to you has now joyously rejoined you. Oh lover, seeing the face of your beloved of moonlike splendour, cast off the heat of your distress. Spend your time in the close embrace of Sati. Thanks to my fervent wish, there will be no separation at any time between you both.

Lakshi said: —

Oh Lord of gods, leave off your shyness. Take Sati to your bosom and stand close to her. Why do you feel shy of her without whom your vital airs may go off?

Savitri said: —

Oh Siva, give the sweets to Sati and eat them yourself. Do not be in a flutter. Perform Acamana and offer her betel leaves along with camphor.

Jahnavi said: —

Take hold of the hand of your beloved wife glittering with gold and stroke her hair. There is no higher pleasure than at the hands of a lover.

Aditi said: —

At the conclusion of the meal, for the purity of the mouth, please give water. The love of this pair is very rare to be seen.

Saci said: —

Why should you be shy of your beloved for whom you lamented and roamed here and there, always keeping her in your heart?

Lopamudra said: —

Oh Siva, a duty shall be performed by women in the bedchamber after the meal. Hence give Tambula (betel leaves with spices) to Siva and go to bed.

Arundhati said: —

This lady was not intended at first to be given to you. But it is after my efforts that she has been given to you. Hence you must have a good dalliance with her.

Ahalya said: —

Leave off your old age. Be extremely youthful so that Mena whose mind is fixed in her daughter may approve of you.

Tulasi said: —

Sati was formerly abandoned by you. Kama too was burnt. Then Oh Lord, how is it that Vasistha is sent as an emissary now?

Sudha said: —

Now, be steady in the words of women. There is a duty for women after marriage, maturity and loftiness of demeanour.

Rohini said: —

Oh Lord, expert in erotic science and technique, fulfil the desire of Parvati. Loving that you are, try to cross the ocean of the love of your beloved.

Vasundhara said: —

Oh Lord, the knower of innermost thoughts, you know the emotions of love-oppressed maidens. It is not only the husband that she cherishes in her heart but she keeps the supreme Lord there forever.

Satarupa said: —

A hungry person will not be satisfied until he partakes of a sweet hearty meal. Oh Siva do everything whereby the woman will be satiated.

Samjna said: —

Now please send Siva along with Parvati to a secluded spot after making the bed, giving them betal and keeping the gem-bedecked lamp ready nearby.

Brahma said: —

Siva heard the women. Being free from aberrations and the great Yogin, he exclaimed.

Siva said: —

Oh dignified ladies, do not utter such words to me. You are the chaste mothers of the worlds, how do you speak so trivially in regard to your son?

Brahma said: —

On hearing the words of Siva, the celestial ladies were ashamed. In their excitement they became motionless like dolls in a picture. Eating the sweets and performing Acamana, Lord Siva was very delighted. In the company of his wife he chewed the betal with camphor.

The Resuscitation of Kama

Rati said: —

Why did you reduce my beloved husband to ashes when all he wanted to do was bring you closer to Parvati? He was my only fortunate possession, very rare to get. Give me back my husband. Remove my distress caused by separation. Oh Lord Siva, in the great festival of your marriage, everyone is happy but me. Without my husband, how can I be happy? Please resuscitate my husband quickly.

Brahma said: —

After saying this she gave him the ashes of the cupid along with the bag in which they had been contained. On hearing the lamentation of Rati, Sarasvati and other celestial ladies wept bitterly and spoke in piteous tones.

The celestial ladies said: —

Obeisance to you, Oh Lord. You are a friend of the distressed, storehouse of mercy. Resuscitate the cupid. Make Rati jubilant.

Brahma said: —

On hearing their words, Lord Siva was touched. The Lord glanced compassionately. Thanks to the nectarine glance of Siva, Kama came out of the ashes, a comely wonder inspiring body with splendid dress and features.

On seeing her husband in the same form as before, wielding the bow and the arrows, Rati bowed to Lord Siva. She and Kama then eulogised Siva over and over again.

Siva said: —

Oh Kama, I am delighted by your eulogy in the company of your wife. Tell me the boon you desire. I shall grant it.

Kama pleaded: —

Oh Lord of gods, please forgive my faults. Please grant me great affection towards my people and devotion to your feet.

Oh Kama, I am delighted. Oh intelligent one, do not fear. Go near Visnu and wait outside, Siva answered.

Brahma said: —

Kama then bowed to Siva and went outside. He met Visnu and all the gods. They all were delighted to see him. They congratulated Kama and blessed him. Then they spoke.

Oh Kama, you are blessed. Burnt by Siva you have been blessed by him. The Lord of all has resuscitated you by means of his sympathetic glance, the Sattvika part, said the gods.

Brahma said: —

After saying this, the gods happily honoured him. Visnu and other gods who had realised their desire stayed there with pleasure.

At the bed-chamber Siva placed Parvati on his left side and fed her with sweets. She too delightedly fed him with sweets in return. Then, after performing customary rites, Siva took Mena's leave and came to the audience hall. Then he saluted everyone, including Visnu and me. Then the gods and us eulogised Siva.

After the eulogy, Visnu and others joyously served Lord Siva, the husband of Parvati. Then Siva, the Lord granted boons and honour to all present there. After that, everyone took his leave and returned to their places.

Siva Returns to Kailasa

After a brahmin lady instructs Parvati on the duties of a chaste wife, Parvati and Siva get ready to go to Kailasa.

Brahma narrated: —

After the chaste brahmin ladies instructions to Parvati, Mena starts preparing to see off her daughter and son-in-law. Embracing Parvati in her arms, Mena cries profusely. Parvati too starts crying uncontrollably. Everyone present there started crying too.

In the meantime, Himavat came hurriedly along with his sons. He held his daughter to his bosom and cried. As happy as he was for Siva and Parvati, he was unable to let his beloved daughter go. After a while, he finally separated from his daughter.

Then the brahmins respectfully intimated them the auspicious hour for the starting of the journey and consoled them. Himavat and Mena composed themselves and asked the palanquin to be brought for Parvati to sit in. Everyone blessed Parvati as she was getting inside. Mena and the Lord of mountains gave her a royal send-off with various auspicious rare presents. Himavat, the sensible affectionate father with his sons accompanied her as far as the place where the Lord was waiting joyously along with the gods.

Everyone was jubilant and jolly with love. They bowed to the Lord with devotion. Praising him they returned to Kailasa. Then Siva told something to Parvati.

Siva said to her: —

I am reminding you although you know the previous birth. If you remember, speak out. In my divine sport you are always my beloved.

Oh dear Lord, I remember everything as well as the fact that you became a silent ascetic. Obeisance to you. Please do everything necessary now befitting the occasion, Parvati replied.

On hearing her words as pleasing as the steady flow of nectar, Siva rejoiced much. He followed all the customs of departure. He fed the gods including Visnu and others with various pleasant things. He fed all the others who had attended his marriage with juicy cooked food of various sorts.

Brahma said: —

After taking food the gods and the Ganas, with their womenfolk bowed to the moon-crested Lord. They eulogised him and praised the marriage. Then they returned to their abodes. Siva then bowed to Visnu and I and Kasyapa to offer his respects. We bowed to him in return and then went back to our abodes. Siva and Parvati thus returned to Kailasa.

RUDRA-SAMHITA
Kumara Khanda

The Dalliance of Siva

Narada asked: —

Oh Brahma, after marrying Parvati and returning to his mountain, what did Siva do? Please narrate it to me.

Suta said: —

On hearing these words of Narada, Brahma was highly delighted and he replied after thinking of Siva.

Brahma narrated: —

Oh Narada, I shall narrate the story of Guha's birth and the slaying of the demon Taraka.

Returning to Kailasa after marrying Parvati, Siva attained added lustre. He thought over the task of the gods and the pain of the people involved in the fulfilment of that task. When Siva returned to Kailasa, there was great jubilation there. The gods returned to their realms with their minds full of joy.

Then taking Parvati, with him, Siva went to a delightful brilliant isolated place. Making a wonderful bed conducive to good sexual pleasure, Lord Siva indulged in dalliance with Parvati for a thousand years of god.

In that divine sport at the mere contact with each other, both Siva and Parvati lapsed into unconsciousness. They neither knew the day nor the night. The pleasure of the love and dalliance was so high that a great length of time passed by without their realisation. Then, Indra and the gods gathered together on the mountain Meru, began their mutual discussion.

The gods asked: —

It has been a long time now but no son has been born yet. We do not understand why. What can be done?

Brahma said: —

In the meantime, from Narada, the gods came to know the extent of the enjoyment of the couple engaged in dalliance. They then spoke to me and we all went to Visnu and narrated the details. For a thousand years according to the calculation of the gods, Siva the Yogin has been engaged in sexual dalliance. He does not desist from it.

Visnu said: —

Oh creator of the universe, there is nothing to worry about. Everything will be well. The interruption to amorous dalliance will take place at the proper time, not now. If the enjoyment is desired by Siva, who can check it? When another thousand years are completed, he will desist from it, out of his own will.

Oh gods, Siva's act of enjoyment will extend to a thousand years of celestial calculation. After that period is over, you can go there and do such things as will necessitate the fall of the semen on the ground. The son of the Lord named Skanda will be born of that. You may all return to your abodes now. Let Siva carry on enjoyment in the isolated place in the company of Parvati.

Brahma said: —

After saying this, the Lord of Laksmi immediately returned to his harem and so did all the gods. On account of the dalliance of Siva and Parvati, the earth quaked with the weight of Sesa (the serpent) and Kacchapa (the tortoise).

By the weight of Kacchapa, the cosmic air was stunned and the three worlds became terrified and agitated. Then the gods along with me sought refuge in Visnu.

The gods exclaimed: —

Oh Visnu, the vital air of the three worlds is stunned. We do not know wherefore. We all are frightened.

Brahma said: —

On hearing those words, Visnu took us all immediately to the mountain Kailasa. We all desired to see Siva. Unable to see him there, Visnu and the gods became surprised. With humility he asked the Ganas of Siva about it.

Visnu asked: —

Oh Ganas of Siva, where has Siva, the Lord of all gone?

The Ganas of Siva replied: —

Oh Visnu, please listen. Siva, the Lord of all, had gone into the apartment of Parvati after stationing us here with love. He is an expert in indulging in divine sports. Many years have gone by. We do not know what Siva, the great Lord, is doing within her apartment.

Brahma said: —

On hearing their words, we immediately went and stood at the doorway of Siva's apartment. Visnu then spoke to Siva.

Visnu asked: —

Oh great Lord, what are you doing there inside? Save us who are harassed by Taraka and who have sought refuge in you.

The Birth of Siva's Son

Brahma said: —

On hearing that, the great Lord did not emit the semen, fearing to offend Parvati. He came to the door, near the gods distressed by the demon. On seeing Lord Siva, we became delighted and eulogised him.

The gods said: —

Oh Lord, carry out the task of the gods. Save us. Slay Taraka and other demons and take pity on us.

Oh Lords, what has happened has already happened. Now listen to what is relevant to the context. Let him who will take up this discharged semen, Siva said.

Brahma said: —

After saying this, he let his semen fall on the ground. Urged by the gods, Agni became a dove and swallowed it with his beak. In the meantime Parvati came there. On coming to know of the incident she became very furious.

Parvati said: —

Oh gods, you are wicked, selfish and for that purpose you give pain to others. For the sake of realising your self-interests you all propitiated the Lord and spoilt my dalliance. I have become a barren woman therefore. Oh gods, after offending me none can be happy. Hence you will remain unhappy. From now on let the wives of the gods be utterly barren and let the gods who offended me be unhappy.

Brahma said: —

Cursing Visnu and other gods, Parvatl furiously told Agni, who had swallowed Siva's semen.

Parvati continued: —

Oh Agni, be the devourer of everything and let your soul be afflicted. You are a fool. It is neither proper nor beneficent to you to have eaten up Siva's semen. You are a rogue, a wretched vile.

Brahma said: —

After cursing the fire thus, Parvati immediately returned to her apartment along with Siva, dissatisfied. Oh great sage, after returning she persistently pleaded with Siva and bore a son named Ganesa.

The details of that story I shall narrate to you later on. Now listen to the story of the birth of Guha which I am going to narrate.

The gods became pregnant after taking the food served in Siva's abode. Unable to endure the force of the semen they became afflicted. Visnu and other gods had already lost their sense at the curse of Parvati. Then Visnu and other gods were overwhelmed and scorched. In this state they sought refuge in Siva. They reached Siva and Parvati's abode once again and eulogised them.

Oh great Lord, what has happened now? We have become pregnant and also scorched by your semen. Oh Siva, take pity on us. Remove our miserable plight, said the gods.

Brahma said: —

On hearing the eulogy of the gods, Siva immediately came to the threshold where the gods stood waiting.

Siva said: —

Oh Visnu, O Brahma, O gods, all of you listen to my words with attention. You will be happy. Be careful. At my behest you shall vomit this semen virile of mine. You will be happy.

The gods said: —

Accepting this command, Visnu and the other gods immediately vomited it out. The semen of Siva, lustrous and golden in colour falling on the ground, seemed to touch heaven as it was as huge as a mountain. Everyone was free from their misery and happy. Only Agni did not become happy. Siva then gave a separate hint to him.

Agni pleaded: —

Oh Lord of gods, I am a stupid and deluded servant of yours. Forgive me my fault. Please remove my burning sensation.

Siva replied: —

An improper action has been committed by you in swallowing my semen. Hence your sin has become formidable at my bidding and the burning sensation has not been cured. But now that you have sought refuge in me you are sure to be happy. All your misery will be dissolved. Deposit carefully that semen in the womb of some good woman. You will become happy and particularly relieved of the burning sensation.

Agni said: —

Oh Lord Siva, this splendour of yours is inaccessible and unbearable. There is no woman in the three worlds except Parvati to hold it in her womb.

(Narada came there just in time after Siva remembered him)

Narada said: —

Oh Agni, listen to my words that will dispel your burning sensation. You shall deposit this semen of Siva in the bodies of the ladies who take their morning baths in the month of Magha.

Brahma said: —

Meanwhile the wives of the seven celestial sages came there desirous of taking their early morning bath in the month of Magha. After the bath, six of them were distressed by the chillness and were desirous of going near the flame of fire. Arundhati saw them deluded and dissuaded them at the behest of Siva. But the six ladies stubbornly insisted on going there. Immediately the particles of the semen entered their bodies through the pores of hairs. Agni was relieved of the burning sensation. Then Agni vanished.

The women became pregnant and were distressed by the burning sensation. They went home. Arundhati was displeased with fire. The husbands of the six wife were furious by this and they discarded their wives. On seeing their own state, the six ladies felt very miserable and distressed. The wives of the sages cast off their semen in the form of a foetus at the top of Himavat. They felt then relieved of their burning sensation.

Unable to bear that semen of Siva and trembling much, Himavat became scorched by it and hurled it in the Ganga. The intolerable semen was then deposited by Ganga in the forest of Sara grass. The semen that fell was turned into a handsome, good-featured boy, full of glory and splendour. He increased everyone's pleasure. This is how Siva's son was born. Learning of this, Siva and Parvati became very happy.

Out of joy, milk exuded from the breasts of Parvati. On reaching the spot everyone felt very happy. All the miseries came to an end.

Search for Karttikeya and His Conversation with Nandin

After Karttikeya is born, he grows up to be a mischievous boy. The six ladies named Krittikas, take Kartikeya with them after being enchanted by his divine sports. Karttikeya is nurtured by them.

Brahma said: —

Oh sage, after the son of Siva had been taken over by the Krttikas, some time elapsed but Parvati had no knowledge of the same. Meanwhile Parvati talked to her husband Siva.

Parvati said: —

Oh Lord of the gods, listen to my auspicious words. My dalliance with you was interrupted in the middle by the gods. Your semen fell on the ground and not in my womb. Where did it go? Among the gods by whom could it have been concealed? Your semen is infallible, how can it be fruitless? Or has it developed into a child somewhere?

Brahma said: —

Oh great sage, on hearing the words of Parvati, the Lord of the universe called the gods and the sages and laughingly said to them.

Siva said: —

Oh gods, listen to my words. Has Parvati's statement been heard by you? Where has my unfailing semen gone? By whom has it been concealed? If he, out of fear, falls at my feet quickly he may not be punished.

Brahma said: —

Everyone who was called told Siva that they did not know where the semen went or if it developed into a child. Then Siva threatened Dharma and others, the cosmic witnesses of all activities.

Lord Siva said: —

The infallible semen of mine, has not been concealed by the gods. By whom could it then have been concealed? All of you are the witnesses of all actions. Has it been concealed by you? Have you come to know of it? Please narrate.

Brahma said: —

The infallible semen of Siva, infuriated at the intervention in the course of his sexual dalliance, fell on the ground. This was observed by me. Then Earth, Agni, Ganga, Vayu, Mountain, Sun, Moon, Water, Dusk and Dawn narrated what they observed. When the course of the events was narrated by each of them, the whereabouts of Kartikeya was finally known. On finding out about his son, Siva and Parvati became extremely happy.

Urged by the gods, sages and mountains, the Lord sent his Ganas as his emissaries to the place where his son was staying. All the emissaries of Siva went and haughtily encircled the abode of the Krttikas with various miraculous weapons in their hands. On seeing them the Krttikas were extremely terrified. They spoke to Karttikeya blazing with divine splendour.

Krttikas said: —

Dear boy, innumerable soldiers have encircled the house. What shall be done? A great danger has beset us.

Oh mothers, cast off your fear for I am here. Although I am a boy I am invincible.

Brahma said: —

In the meantime, Nandisvara the commander-in-chief sat in front of Karttikeya and talked to him.

Nandisvara said: —

Oh brother, O mothers, listen to me please. I have been commissioned by Lord Siva, the annihilator. Goddess Parvati and Siva have come to know that you are residing with Krttikas and they have asked me to bring you back to Kailasa. The cosmic witness of the universe told us about your whereabouts.

Brahma said: —

Nandisvara then went on to narrate the events that followed after Siva's semen fell on the ground. Karttikeya listened patiently.

Nandisvara narrated: —

Now you shall come down to the Earth. Siva will be crowning you in the company of the gods. You will get miraculous weapons and will slay the demon Taraka. You are the son of the annihilator of the universe and these (Krttikas) are impatient to gain possession of you. But they cannot hold you. Being the son of Siva, you are the creator of the universe, you are the Lord. Your place is not among these. You are a mass of attributes and splendour as the soul of a Yogin. Please come with us now.

Karttikeya said: —

Oh brother, you know everything. You are perfectly wise possessing the knowledge of the past, present and future, since you are an attendant of Siva. Hence no praise of yours is specially called for. The Krttikas are wise women of Yogic practice. They have helped in nurturing me with their own breast milk. I am their foster son. They are my own part and parcel. So I shall always protect them. You have been sent by Siva. You are like a son to Siva. I am coming with you. I shall see the gods.

Karttikeya is Crowned

Brahma said: —

In the meantime he saw an excellent, lustrous and wonderful chariot, made by Visvakarman. It had been sent by Parvati and was surrounded by the excellent attendants of Siva. With an aching heart, Karttikeya got into it.

At the same time, the distressed grief-stricken Krttikas approached him with dishevelled hair and began to speak like mad women.

Krttikas said: —

Oh ocean of mercy, how is it that you ruthlessly leave us and go? You have been brought up by us affectionately. Hence you are our son in virtue of that. What shall we do? Where shall we go?

Brahma said: —

After saying this and closely embracing Karttikeya, the Krttikas fell unconscious due to the imminent separation from their son. Restoring them to consciousness and instructing them with spiritual utterances, he got into the chariot along with them and the Parsadas too.

Kumara (Karttikeya) reached the foot of Kailasa. He waited there delightedly. Then all the gods, sages, Visnu and I, announced his arrival. Siva went to see him with Visnu and I and other sages. Then in order to see him Siva, along with Visnu, Brahma, the gods, sages and others went there.

The entire Kailasa was decorated at the orders of Parvati. All the goddesses along with Parvati waited to see the son of Siva. When Siva and Parvati finally saw their son, they were overjoyed.

On seeing Parvati and Siva, Karttikeya got down from the chariot immediately and saluted them. Embracing him with love, Siva kissed Kumara on the head. Embracing him in great excitement and melting with love, Parvati suckled him at her breasts.

The Nirajana rite was performed by the delighted gods in the company of their wives. The sages adored Kumara with the Vedic chants, the musicians by singing songs, and others by playing musical instruments.

At the bidding of Siva, Kumara in the company of his Ganas came to Siva's abode. Kumara then sat on Siva's lap and played. He teased Vasuki around Siva's neck with his hands. Seeing the gentle smile of Kumara, Lord Siva and Parvati attained great joy.

Then Siva, the Lord of the universe, following the worldly convention delightedly placed Karttikeya on a beautiful gemset throne. Visnu gave him a crown, a coronet and bracelets moulded and set in gems. Siva gave him the trident, the bow Pinaka, the axe, the arrow Pasupata, the weapon of destruction and the greatest lore. I gave him the holy thread, the Vedas, the mantra Gayatri, the vessel Kamandalu, the arrow Brahmastra and the lore that destroys the enemy. Parvati gave him power and prosperity smilingly and joyously. She gave him longevity too with great pleasure. Then Siva spoke to us.

Siva said: —

Oh Visnu, Oh Brahma, Oh gods, you listen to my words. I am delighted in all respects. Please choose the boons you wish.

The gods said: —

Oh Lord, Taraka will certainly be killed by Kumara. It is for that purpose that he is born. Hence in our effort to kill him we shall start this very day. Please give your directions to Kumara. I let him slay Taraka for our happiness.

At the bidding of Siva, Brahma, Visnu and other gods jointly started from the mountain keeping Kumara in front. A divine, exquisite and brilliant house was built for Kumara. Tvastr then made an excellent throne for him.

Brahma said: —

The intelligent Visnu performed the auspicious ceremony of crowning Karttikeya in the company of the gods by means of waters from all holy centres. Bowing to Karttikeya with pleasure along with the gods and sages he eulogised the eternal form of Siva with various hymns.

The Miraculous Feat of Karttikeya

Brahma said: —

Kumara showed a miraculous feat. A certain brahmin Narada came there, seeking refuge in Kumara. He was glorious and had been performing a sacrifice. Approaching Kumara, the delighted brahmin related his tale.

The brahmin said: —

Oh Lord, relieve my distress. I seek refuge in you. I began a goat sacrifice. The goat got loose and strayed away from my house. I do not know where it has gone. I have searched for it here and there but have not found it. Hence this will cause a serious default in my sacrifice. Oh Lord, I eulogise you, please take pity on me.

Oh Lord, you are the cause of welfare, the destroyer of the sins of Kali age and a friend of Kubera. Your heart melts with pity. You are the protector of the three worlds, favourite of those who seek refuge in you. You are the performer and sustainer of sacrifices. You remove those who bring in obstacles.

Brahma said: —

On hearing his words, Siva's son sent his attendant Virabahu on that mission. At his bidding, the great hero Virabahu started to search for it. He searched throughout the universe but nowhere did he find the goat (although) he heard about the havoc done by it. Then he went to Vaikuntha where he saw the powerful goat creating havoc with the sacrificial stake tied to its neck.

The hero dragged it catching hold of its horns and brought it quickly before his Lord even as it was bleating loudly. On seeing it, Lord Karttikeya quickly rode on it.

Within a Muhurta, oh sage, the goat walked round the universe and without exhaustion returned to the same place. Then the Lord got down and resumed his seat. The goat stood there itself. Then the brahmin Narada told the Lord.

Narada said: —

Obeisance to you, Oh Lord of gods give the goat to me. Let me perform the sacrifice with pleasure. Please assist me as my friend.

Karttikeya said: —

Oh brahmin Narada, this goat does not deserve to be killed. Return home. May your sacrifice be complete. It has been so ordained in my favour.

Brahma said: —

On hearing the words of the Lord, the brahmin was delighted. He returned home after bestowing his excellent blessings.

Commencement of the War

Brahma said: —

On seeing that miraculous feat of Kumara, Visnu and other gods became delighted. They were convinced of his prowess. Keeping Kumara at the head, shouting and roaring, purified by Siva's splendour they started to attack Taraka. When Taraka heard about the preparation of the gods, he rushed to fight back the gods with a great army. On seeing the great army of Taraka approaching, the gods were surprised but roared like lions. Then a celestial voice, prompted by Siva, addressed Visnu and all other gods.

The celestial voice announced: —

Oh gods, keeping Kumara at the head you have entered the lists. Defeating the Asuras in the battle, you will be victorious.

Brahma said: —

On hearing the celestial voice, the gods became enthusiastic. Fearlessly they roared like heroes. With their fear subsided, and keeping Kumara ahead, the gods went to the confluence of the river Mahi and the ocean desirous of fighting.

Immediately Taraka, along with a great army, came to the place where the gods stood and was surrounded by them in a body. The Asuras in the company of Taraka roared and shook the ground with their thudding footsteps, leapings and bouncings. The gods too rose up to fight. Lord Indra seated Kumara on an elephant and rushed forward. Leaving the elephant, Kumara got into an aerial chariot and charged ahead. Everyone else joined him with their own divisions.

A terrific tumultuous fight between the gods and the Asuras ensued. Wounded and killed by great weapons, hundreds and thousands of heroic soldiers fell on the ground. The entire body of some was smashed by the maces. The chests and hearts of some were pounded by iron clubs. Blood flowed like streams in hundreds of places. In the meantime Taraka came there with a huge army to fight with the gods.

The Asura Taraka fought with Indra. Lord Varuna fought with Nairrta and Bala. Suvira, the king of Guhyas, fought with Vayu. Sambhu fought with Isana. Kumbha the Asura fought with the Moon. Kunjara, an expert in different kinds of battles, fought with Mihira. Thus the gods and the Asuras fought duels using their full strength with resolution.

The Battle Between the Gods and Asuras

Brahma said: —

Oh Narada, in the tumultuous fight, Lord Indra, struck by the great spear, fell from his elephant and became unconscious. In the same manner, the guardians of the quarters were defeated in battle by the Asuras. The other gods too lost. Unable to bear their ferocity they took to flight.

In the meantime Virabhadra reached the place along with his Ganas and approached Taraka. He faced Taraka all by himself. The Ganas also fought the Asuras.

Virabhadra hit Taraka with a trident and he fell unconscious on the ground. Then Taraka got up and hit Virabhadra with his spear. They hit each other with various weapons and missiles both being equally skillful in the art of warfare. On seeing the fight between him and Virabhadra, you, the favourite of Siva, went there and said to Virabhadra.

Narada said: —

Oh Virabhadra, please desist from this fight. Your killing him does not fit in properly.

Virabhadra replied: —

Oh excellent sage, listen to my weighty words. I will kill Taraka. See my exploit today. A soldier must never let his master fight on his behalf. Hence I will kill Taraka and free my master from this burden. I shall make the earth free of Taraka today even without bringing my master here.

Saying thus and taking up his trident, Virabhadra mentally meditated on Siva and fought with Taraka. Soon the Asuras were defeated by the Ganas. The battle outcome had changed. The Asuras started to flee from there. Seeing this, Taraka became furious and assumed ten thousand hands and rode a lion. He charged at the gods. Virabhadra became furious and picked up his trident to kill Taraka. Just then, his master stopped him. On his command, Virabhadra returned.

But Taraka did not stop. He charged and attacked the gods with all his might. Seeing the gods defeated, Visnu became furious and went there to fight Taraka. Taking discus, Sudarsana and other weapons with him, Lord Visnu rushed to meet the great Asura in the battle. A great fight ensued between Visnu and Taraka. It was very fierce. It caused horripilation to the onlookers.

Visnu and Taraka continued to attack each other. Then, Taraka hit Visnu with his spear and he immediately fell unconscious. But he got up again and charged Taraka with all his might. Like this, both the masters of the battle kept fighting each other with unabated strength, Brahma said.

The Boasting of Taraka and the Fight Between Him and Indra, Visnu, Virabhadra

Brahma said: —

Oh son of Siva and Parvati, the fight between Visnu and Taraka is futile. Vishnu cannot kill Taraka as he was given a boon by me. Only you, son of Siva and Parvati, can slay him. Oh Kumara, I request you to put an end to this battle and kill Taraka. Please have mercy on us. Make the three worlds happy.

'So be it,' Kumara said.

Brahma said: —

Resolving to kill the Asura, the great Lord, got down from the aerial chariot and stood on the ground. seizing his lustrous spear blazing like a meteor, the powerful warrior Kumara shone well.

On seeing the incomprehensible six-headed deity coming forward, Asura said to the gods, 'Oh this child will indeed slay the enemies. I will fight him single handed.' Saying thus, the powerful Asura rushed at Kumara to fight with him. Taraka seized his wonderful spear and spoke to the gods.

Taraka said: —

How is it that you all kept Kumara face to face with me? You gods are shameless especially Indra and Visnu. You both are sinful. Oh gods, you will never gain victory in the battle by relying on them. Why then did you foolishly come here to lose your lives?

These two impudent fellows are presumptuous enough to place a child in front of me. Why? I can kill the child too. But if you let the child leave from here, you will save his life. Oh Virabhadra, formerly in the sacrifice of Daksa, many brahmins had been killed by you, I shall show you the fruit thereof.

Brahma said: —

Saying this and dispossessing himself of his own merit by that act of censure, Taraka seized his wonderful spear. Indra, who was going ahead of Kumara, hit the demon Taraka forcibly with his thunderbolt as he was approaching the boy.

Taraka was shattered and split by that blow of the thunderbolt, his power being sapped up already by the act of censure. He fell on the ground. Though he fell down, he got up immediately and furiously hit Indra with his spear and felled him to the ground. He stamped on Indra with his foot after he fell down and seized his thunderbolt.

Vishnu, on witnessing this insult to Indra, rushed towards Taraka and hit him. Taraka fell on the ground but got up again. He hit Visnu on the chest and Visnu got injured. Seeing this, Virabhadra plunged towards Taraka with his trident that had the lustre of lightning and was blazing forth. The trident had a halo around, like that of the sun, the moon and the fire. When Virabhadra was about to hit Taraka with it, Kumara stopped him.

Jubilation of the Gods at the Death of Taraka

Brahma said: —

After preventing Virabhadra, the powerful Karttikeya of great splendour roared. Angrily he got ready for the fight. He was surrounded by a vast army. Shouts of victory were raised by the gods and the Ganas. He was eulogised by the celestial sages with pleasing words.

The fight between Taraka and Kumara was terrific and unbearable. They fought each other with spears and other weapons. Each was wounded in the heart by the other with the spear. Each tried to escape from the other's thrust. Both were equally strong like two lions. Both were fully equipped for the fight. Each wanted to kill the other. They utilised all their power. They continued the fight swaggering and vaunting with heroic words.

Then a celestial voice rose, appeasing the gods and onlookers— 'In this battle Kumara will kill the Asura Taraka. None of the gods need be anxious. For your welfare, Siva himself is standing here in the form of his son.' On hearing the auspicious words of the celestial voice, Kumara became happy.

The fight continued and both Kumara and Taraka kept attacking each other. Even as they both fell unconscious at a time, they got up again and fought. Both had the desire to gain the upper hand. Both fought on foot, had wonderful forms and features and were equally courageous.

In the meantime, Himalaya and other mountains anxious to see Kumara out of affection came there. They were extremely terrified.

Kumara said: —

Oh mountains, O fortunate sirs, do not be vexed, or worried. Even as you stand looking on, I will kill this sinner.

Possessing the brilliance of Siva, Kumara with his spear struck Taraka who had harassed the worlds. Immediately the Asura Taraka fell on the ground with all his limbs shattered.

The great warrior Taraka was slain by Kumara. Oh sage, even as all were looking on, he passed away. When the powerful Asura was slain, other Asuras were killed by gods and Ganas. Thousands of them fled to Patala for their life. Those who tried to flee were disappointed and put to distress.

Brahma said: —

Oh great sage, thus the entire army of the Asuras disappeared. None dared to remain there for fear of the gods and the Ganas.

When the wicked Asura was killed, Indra and other gods became happy. Thus when Kumara came out victorious the gods were happy. The three worlds attained great pleasure.

Then Siva and Parvati arrived after knowing that their son killed the vicious Taraka. Siva took his son to his lap and fondled him. Parvati also embraced Kumara and showered her love.

Then everyone eulogised Siva, Parvati and their son Karttikeya. Songs were sung and dances were performed. After the celebration on the battlefield, Siva and Parvati went back to their abode.

The Story of Siva and Parvati Including That of Karttikeya

Brahma said: —

On seeing Taraka killed, Visnu and other gods, with faces refulgent with pleasure, eulogised Karttikeya with devotion. Then, being pleased with the gods, Kumara granted them fresh boons.

Even the mountains eulogised the son of Siva and Parvati. He became pleased with them and spoke to them after granting boons.

Skanda said: —

All of you mountains will become worthy of being worshipped by the sages. Oh mountains, at my word you will be assuming the forms of phallic emblems, the special forms of Siva. My maternal grandfather, the excellent mountain Himavat, will become the fortunate bestower of fruits to ascetics.

The gods said: —

Oh Kumara, you have made us all very happy. Now you must go back to Kailasa and see your father and mother.

Brahma said: —

Then Visnu and other gods jubilantly went to that mountain along with Kumara. When the Lord Kumara started for Kailasa, sounds of victory arose indicating great auspiciousness. With great pleasure, Visnu and I accompanied Kumara.

Upon reaching Kailasa, Kumara descended from the aerial chariot in all humility and bowed joyously to Siva and Parvati seated on a throne. Then Siva and Parvati got up and kissed Kumara on his forehead. They placed him on their lap and showered him with love and affection.

There was great jubilation in the abode of Siva. Everywhere the sound of shouts of victory and obeisance rose up.

After eulogising Siva, Visnu and other gods stood before him after placing Skanda ahead. Then Siva addressed all of us.

Siva said: —

Oh Visnu, Oh Brahma, Oh gods, listen to my words with attention. I am merciful. I shall by all means protect you. Oh excellent gods, whenever you are faced with misery you shall worship me for your happiness.

Brahma said: —

Oh sage, thus ordered, Visnu, the other gods and the sages bowed to Siva, Parvati, and Kumara joyously, and returned to their abodes. Siva stayed on the mountain with Parvati and his Ganas.

The Birth of Ganesa

Narada said: —

Oh Lord of gods, now I wish to hear the excellent story of Ganesa, the details of his divine nativity, auspicious of the auspicious.

Suta said: —

On hearing the words of Narada, Brahma became delighted and replied to him remembering Siva.

Brahma said: —

Oh sage, I shall narrate the tale of Ganesa whose head was cut off by the merciful Siva. Listen to this tale and understand Siva's reasons.

A long time had lapsed after the marriage of Siva and his return to Kailasa that Ganesa was born. Once the friends Jaya and Vijaya conferred with Parvati and discussed. They advised her that it was now time for Parvati and Siva to create someone of their own. Goddess Parvati thought hard about it and then decided to do it.

So, one day when Parvati was taking her bath, Sadasiva rebuked Nandin and came into the inner apartment. She instantly stood up from her bath on seeing Siva. Her unclothed body made her shy in front of Siva. Then Parvati thought to herself, 'There must be a servant of my own who will be expert in his duties. He must not stray from my behest even a speck.' Thinking thus, she created a person from the first of her body.

He was spotless and handsome in every part of his body. He was huge in size and had all the brilliance, strength and valour. She gave him various clothes and ornaments. She blessed him with benediction and said — 'You are my son. You are my own. I have none else to call my own.' Thus addressed, the person bowed to her and spoke sweetly.

Ganesa said: —

What is your order? I shall accomplish what you command.

Parvati said: —

Oh dear, listen to my words. Work as my gatekeeper from today. You are my son. You are my own. It is not otherwise. There is none-else who belongs to me. Without my permission, no one, by any means, shall intrude my apartment. This is what I want.

Brahma said: —

Oh sage, saying this, she gave him a hard stick. On seeing his handsome features she was delighted. Out of love and mercy she embraced and kissed him. Then the son of the goddess stayed at the doorway armed with a staff with a desire to do what was good to her.

Thus, placing her son at the doorway, Parvati began to take a bath with her friends, unworried. It was at that moment that Siva arrived at the doorway. Not knowing that he was Lord Siva, Ganesa said to him, 'Oh sir, without my mother's permission you shall not go in now. My mother is taking a bath so no one shall enter. Please go away now.' Saying this, he took up his stick and threatened the Lord. When Siva refused to leave,

Ganesa beat him with his staff. Then Siva was infuriated and said to Ganesa.

Siva said: —

You are a fool. You do not know that I am Siva, the husband of Parvati. Oh boy, I can go inside my own house whenever I want. Why do you forbid me?

Brahma said: —

When Lord Siva tried to enter the house, Ganesa became infuriated, and struck him with his staff once again. Then Siva too became furious and enquired with his Ganas to know about him.

The Ganas Argue and Wrangle

Brahma said: —

The infuriated Ganas of Siva at his bidding went there and questioned the son of Parvati who stood at the gate.

Siva's Ganas said: —

Who are you? Where do you come from? What do you propose to do? If you have a desire to remain alive go away from here.

Ganesa said: —

Oh handsome fellows, who are you? Where have you come from? Go away. Why have you come here and why do you stand in opposition to me?

Siva's Ganas replied: —

Listen. We are the excellent Ganas of Siva. We are his doorkeepers. We have come here to throw you out at the bidding of Lord Siva. If you do not want to be killed, you better go away now.

Brahma said: —

Though warned thus, Ganesa, the son of Parvati, stood fearless. He did not leave his post at the door. He rebuked Siva's Ganas. Then the Ganas went back to Siva and told him about Ganesa's resolve.

Lord Siva said: —

Who is this fellow? What does he say? He is standing there haughtily as though he is our enemy. Certainly he wants to die. Let this new doorkeeper be thrown out.

Siva's Ganas said to Ganesa: —

Oh gatekeeper, who are you still standing here? Why have you been stationed here? Why don't you care for us? We can crush you at any moment. Oh fool, you will roar only as long as you do not feel the brunt of our attack.

Brahma said: —

Thus taunted by them, Ganesa became furious and took the staff with his hands and struck the Ganas even as they continued to speak harsh words. Then the fearless Ganesa rebuked the heroic Ganas of Siva and spoke to them.

The son of Parvati: —

Get away. Get away. Or I shall give you a foretaste of my fierce valour. You will be the laughing-stock of all.

Brahma said: —

Then the Ganas of Siva went to Siva who was standing at the distance of a Krosa from Kailasa and spoke to him. Siva ridiculed them then ordered them to beat Ganesa for insulting him. The Ganas went back and threatened Ganesa. Listening to that, Ganesa became unhappy.

In the meantime, Parvati heard the noises of this wrangle. She asked her friend to find out more about it. Parvati's friend returned soon after understanding the whole matter. She started to manipulate Parvati.

The friend told Parvati: —

Oh great Goddess, the heroic Ganas of Siva are taunting and rebuking our own Gana who is standing at the door. How can they and Siva enter your apartment without looking at your convenience? They are taunting our Gana which means they are taunting us. Hence you shall not abandon your prestige of high order.

Parvati muttered: —

Alas, he did not wait for a moment. Why should he force his way in? What shall be done now? Or shall I adopt a humble attitude. Oh well, what has happened has happened. I will take a stand now.

Brahma said: —

Parvati then told her friend to inform Ganesa of her resolve.

The friend told Ganesa: —

Oh gentle sir, well done. Let them not enter forcibly. What are these Ganas before you? Can they win against a person like you? Whether good or bad, let your duty be done. If you are conquered there will be no further enmity at all.

Ganesa said: —

I am the son of Parvati. You are the Ganas of Siva. Both of us are thus equal. Let your duty be done, as I am doing mine. I have to carry out the orders of Parvati faithfully. Hence, oh Ganas, you shall not enter forcibly or humbly.

Brahma said: —

The Ganas when decisively told by Ganesa became ashamed. They went to Siva and narrated every detail.

Siva said: —

Oh Ganas, hear you all. A battle may not be a proper course. You are all my own. He is Parvati's Gana. But if we are going to be humble, there is likely to be a rumour, 'Siva is subservient to his wife.' This is certainly derogatory to me.

What can a boy like him do to you? How can you shy away from a war? How can a woman be obdurate, especially with her husband? Parvati will certainly derive the fruit of what she has done. Hence, my heroic men, listen to my words with attention. This war has to be fought by all means. Let what is in store happen.

Ganesa's Battle

Brahma said: —

When Siva told them thus, they got ready for a war and went to Ganesa. On seeing the excellent Ganas, fully equipped for war, Ganesa spoke thus to them.

Ganesa said: —

Welcome to the leaders of Ganas, carrying out the behest of Siva. I am only one and that too a mere boy carrying out the directions of Parvati. Yet let the goddess see the strength of her son. Let Siva see the strength of his Ganas too. Even if I lose today, no shame will come to me. But if you Ganas, who have fought many battles, lose to me, great shame will befall on Siva. Oh leader of the Ganas, the war shall be fought after realising this. You shall look up to your Lord and I to my mother.

Brahma said: —

When thus taunted and rebuked they rushed towards him with big batons.

Nandin came first and caught hold of his leg. He pulled at it. Bhrngin then rushed at him and caught hold of his other leg. Immediately, Ganesa struck a blow at their hands and freed himself. Then seizing a big iron club and standing at the doorway he smashed the Ganas. Soon the army of Siva's Ganas was crushed. Some got their arms broken, some had their legs crushed and some had shattered their heads. The Ganas who were able to run, fled from there in thousands. Then Ganesa returned to the doorway and stood there. At this time, urged by Narada, all the gods including Visnu and Indra came there. They asked Siva about this matter at hand.

Oh excellent sage, on hearing their words and seeing the Ganas completely shattered, Lord Siva told them everything. Then Siva spoke to me specifically.

Siva said: —

Oh Brahma, listen. A boy is standing at the entrance to my house. He is very strong. He prevents me from entering the house. He strikes very dexterously. He has forcefully defeated my Ganas. Oh Brahma, now you go. Bring this strong boy under control.

Brahma said: —

On hearing the words of the Lord I went near Ganesa accompanied by the sages, not knowing the reality entirely. On seeing me approach, the powerful Ganesa came to me very furiously and plucked my moustache and beard.

I said to him, 'Forgive me I have not come for fighting. I am a brahmin and shall be blessed. I have come to make peace and I will cause no harm.' As I said this, Ganesa retrieved his iron club. Seeing that, I ran away. Ganesa struck the other sages who couldn't run away in time.

On seeing them in that plight, Siva became very angry. He ordered Indra and other gods to kill Ganesa. They immediately picked up their weapons and marched ahead.

On coming to know of this, Parvati created two Saktis to assist Ganesa in the battle. One Sakti assumed a very fierce form and stood there opening her mouth as wide as the cavern of a dark mountain. The other assumed the form of lightning. She wore many arms. She was a huge and terrible goddess ready to punish the wicked. The weapons hurled by the gods at Ganesa were caught in the mouth and hurled back at them. Then Ganesa struck Indra and other gods with his iron club. He defeated all of them single handedly.

Then the gods and Ganas started to discuss the matter amongst themselves.

The gods and Ganas said: —

What shall be done? Where should we go? The ten directions have become visible. He is whirling the iron club right and left.

Brahma said: —

When Siva came to know of this, he became even more angry. He took his entire army along with Visnu to defeat Ganesa. In the meantime, you, oh Narada, spoke to Siva.

Narada said: —

Oh Lord of the gods, by indulging in a great sport, the arrogance of the Ganas has been removed by you. O Sankara, the impudence of the gods too has been removed by giving this (Ganesa) much strength. Now, please do not treat him leisurely. Kill him in your play now.

The Head of Ganesa
Is Chopped Off During the Battle

Brahma said: —

Oh Narada, on hearing your words, the great Lord became desirous of fighting with the boy. He called Visnu and consulted him. Then with a great army and the gods, he stood face to face with him. First Visnu went ahead and fought with Ganesa with all his strength. Ganesa hit all the chief gods with his staff. He hit Visnu too as the hero had been conferred great strength by the Saktis.

Oh sage, after fighting for a long time along with the army and seeing him terrific, even Siva was greatly surprised. He started thinking to himself.

Siva muttered: —

He has to be killed only by deception and not otherwise.

Brahma said: —

Then Lord Siva assumed the attributive form and merged with the army. Seeing this, Visnu and other gods were delighted. Then Ganesa, the heroic son of Sakti, struck Visnu with his stick again. Then Visnu consulted with Siva mentally.

Visnu said: —

I shall cause him delusion. Then let him be killed by you, Oh Lord. Without deception he cannot be killed. He is of Tamasika nature and inaccessible.

Brahma said: —

With Siva's permission, Vishnu indulged in delusion. On seeing Visnu in that manner, the two Saktis handed their power to Ganesa and merged with him. Ganesa became stronger and took his iron club to hurl. At that moment, Siva took his trident and went to attack Ganesa. With Parvati's blessings, Ganesa, who had become more powerful, struck Siva on his arm. Then the trident fell from Siva's hand.

Then Siva took his bow Pinaka and attacked Ganesa. He fell on the ground. But Ganesa got up again and kept fighting. Seeing this, Visnu decided to intervene and distract Ganesa. The two of them fought again with weapons and their hands.

For a long time the two continued to fight. But, in one fine moment of opportunity, Siva picked up his trident while Ganesa fought Visnu and chopped off Ganesa's head. Oh Narada, when the head of Ganesa was cut off, the armies of the gods and the Ganas stood still.

Then you, Narada, went to Parvati and said, 'Oh proud woman, listen. You shall not cast off your pride and prestige.' Saying this, Oh Narada, you, who is fond of quarrels, vanished instantly, Brahma said.

The Resuscitation of Ganesa

Narada said: —

Oh Brahma, what happened after that? What did Parvati do?

Brahma said: —

Oh Narada, listen. When Ganesa was killed, the Ganas were very jubilant. But Siva was very sorry. Goddess Parvati became furious.

Parvati said: —

Oh what shall I do? Where shall I go? How can this misery be dispelled now? My son has been killed by all the gods and the Ganas. I shall destroy them all or create a deluge.

Brahma said: —

Lamenting thus, the great goddess of all the worlds angrily created hundreds and thousands of Saktis. The Saktis who were thus created, bowed to Parvati and asked to be commanded. Parvati ordered them to devour all the sages, gods, Yaksas, Raksasas and others.

On being commanded by her, the infuriated Saktis got ready to destroy the gods and others. They started devouring everyone in their sight. Wherever one looked, Saktis were present.

On seeing that, Siva, Brahma, Visnu, Indra, the other gods became worried. They started fearing what Parvati might do if she wasn't stopped.

All the gods said: —

Only when the goddess Parvati is pleased can there be a relief; not otherwise, even with our maximum efforts. Even Siva cannot calm her down now. Her powers and fury cannot be matched by anyone, not even Siva.

Brahma said: —

In the meantime, Oh sage Narada, you of divine vision came there for the happiness of the gods and Ganas. You all discussed that until Parvati favours us, this madness will not stop. So you and the other sages went to Parvati and eulogised her.

The great goddess Parvati thus eulogised by you and other sages glanced at them furiously. She did not say anything.

The sages said: —

Oh goddess, forgive us. The final dissolution seems near at hand. Please forgive our faults. Have mercy on us, give us peace now.

The goddess said: —

If my son regains life there may not be further annihilation. If you can arrange for him an honourable status and position among you as the chief presiding officer, there may be peace in the world. Otherwise you will never be happy.

Brahma said: —

Then Siva was told about this. Siva understood Parvati's plight and agreed to make corrections.

Siva said: —

It shall be done accordingly so that there may be peace over all the worlds. You shall go to the northern direction and whatever person you meet at first you cut off his head and fit it to this body.

Brahma said: —

Then they carried out Siva's behest and acted accordingly. They brought the headless body of Ganesa and washed it well. They paid homage to it and started towards the north. It was a single-tusked elephant that they met first.

They took the head and fitted it to the body. After joining it, the gods bowed to Siva, Visnu and Brahma and spoke—'What has been ordered by you has been carried out by us. Let the task left incomplete be performed now.'

Then, reciting Vedic mantras and sprinkling holy water on the body, they prayed for the resuscitation of Ganesa. As Siva willed, the boy woke up from a sleep. He was handsome, extremely comely. He had the face of an elephant. He was red-complexioned. He was delighted with face beaming. He was brilliant and had fine features.

Oh great sage, on seeing the son of Parvati resuscitated to life, they all rejoiced and their miseries came to an end. Goddess Parvati was delighted to see Ganesa and she made everything merry again.

Narada asked: —

Oh Lord, what happened then?

Brahma said: —

On being resuscitated, Siva and Parvati were both very happy. Parvati pulled Ganesa on her lap and kissed his divine face. Siva too showered his love and blessings. Then Siva crowned Ganesa as the chief of Ganas as he was extremely powerful even though he was a little boy.

Siva also laid down rules of Vrata that people would keep in Ganesa's name. He blessed everyone who would keep this Vrata and follow all the rituals. Then Siva crowned him as the presiding officer of all his Ganas. This is how Ganesa was honoured by Siva and Parvati.

Ganapati's Marriage

Narada said: —

Oh dear father, what happened after that? Please tell me more.

Brahma continued: —

Oh excellent sage, listen then. Both Parvati and Siva were delighted to witness the divine sports of both their sons. Their love increased everyday for the sons.

Then one day Siva and Parvati discussed the marriage of both their sons. As they had attained marriageable age, it was best to get them settled. Oh sage, coming to know of their parents' opinion, the sons too were eager to get married. In order to decide who would get married first, Siva and Parvati designed a contest.

Siva and Parvati said: —

Oh good sons, both of you are equal in our eyes hence we cannot decide by ourselves who will get married first. To ensure fairness, we have designed a contest. Listen sons carefully. The one who comes back to us first after going around the earth once will get married.

Brahma said: —

On hearing their words, the powerful Kumara immediately started from a fixed point to go around the earth quickly. Ganesa, however, stood there, thinking to himself. Siva and Parvati both knew of his intellect and hence were eager to see what Ganesa would do. Then Ganesa performed the ceremonial ablution and returned home. He then spoke to his father and mother.

Ganesa said: —

For your worship, I have placed two seats. Please be seated. Let my desire be fulfilled.

Brahma said: —

On hearing his words, Parvati and Siva sat on the seats for receiving worship. They were delighted. Ganesa worshipped them and circumambulated seven times around them. Then he bowed to them. Ganesa eulogised his parents and spoke to them.

Ganesa said: —

Oh mother, Oh father, you please listen to my weighty words. My auspicious marriage shall be celebrated quickly.

Siva and Parvati said: —

If you want to celebrate your marriage you must fulfil the task. Go around the earth and return as Kumara is doing.

Ganesa asked: —

Oh father, oh mother, I have circumambulated the earth seven times already. Why do you ask me to do it again?

Oh son, when was the great earth circumambulated by you, the earth consisting of seven continents, extending to the oceans and consisting of vast jungles? The parents said.

Ganesa replied: —

By worshipping you, Parvati and Siva, I have intelligently circumambulated the earth extending to the oceans. You are the creator of this universe and the earth. You are my universe, hence by going around you seven times I have achieved more than what was asked in the task. It is also mentioned in the Vedas that a son shall never leave his parents behind. He who does so, committed a sin. So I could not leave you and go against the Vedas for my own benefit.

Let my auspicious marriage be celebrated and that too very quickly. Otherwise let the Vedas and Sastras be declared false.

Brahma said: —

Hearing Ganesa's intellect, Parvati and Siva were surprised. They praised their son who was clever and intelligent and spoke to him who had spoken the truth.

Oh son, you are a supreme soul and your thoughts are pure. What you have said is true and not otherwise. We have honoured what you have done. Hence your marriage will be celebrated, said Siva and Parvati.

The Celebration of Ganesa's Marriage

Brahma said: —

In the meantime, Prajapati Visvarupa became delighted and happy on knowing their intention.

Prajapati Visvarupa had two daughters of divine features. They were famous as Siddhi and Buddhi. They were exquisite in every part of their body. Lord Siva and Parvati jubilantly celebrated the marriage of Ganesa with them. The delighted gods attended their marriage as desired by Siva and Parvati. Visvakarman made all arrangements for the marriage. The sages and the gods were full of great joy. Ganesa himself was overjoyed.

After some time, the noble Ganesa begot two sons, one from each of his wives. They were endowed with divine features. The son Ksema was born to Siddhi. The highly brilliant son Labha was born to Buddhi. While Ganesa was enjoying the inconceivable happiness, the second son returned after circumambulating the earth.

Thereupon he was addressed by Narada.

Narada said: —

Listen Kumara to the truth. After sending you off to go around the earth, your parents celebrated Ganesa's wedding. He has two wives and now he has two sons from each of his wives. Begetting two sons of auspicious features of his wives Ganesa is continuously enjoying happiness. Your parents have deceived you thus. They have not done well. Just ponder over it. I don't think their actions have been good.

Brahma said: —

Oh Narada, following the mental process of Lord Siva, you spoke these words to Kumara and then kept quiet.

After bowing to his father, the infuriated Skanda went to the Kraunca mountain though forbidden by his parents.

Karttikeya said: —

Oh parents, I shall not stay here even for a moment when deception has been practised on me, eschewing affection towards me.

Brahma said: —

Saying so, he went away. Even today he is staying at the mountain and removing the sins of people just by his vision. He has remained a bachelor since that day. Parvati became grief stricken by her son's separation. She urged Siva to accompany her to the mountain where Kumara was.

When Karttikeya found out that Siva and Parvati had come, he decided to leave that place. However, after being urged by the gods, he stayed there but lived three Yojanas away from them.

RUDRA-SAMHITA
Yuddha Khanda

Description of the Tripuras

Narada said: —

The excellent story of the householder Siva, has been heard by us. Now please tell us how Siva killed wicked people. How did the Lord burn three cities of the Asuras with a single arrow? What sort of an arrow was it? Please tell us everything.

Brahma said: —

When he was asked by Vyasa the same, the excellent sage Sanatkumara narrated the story. I will repeat the same.

Sanatkumara began the story: —

Oh Vyasa, listen to the story of Siva who burned three cities with a single arrow.

When Asura Taraka was killed byKumara, his three sons performed austerities. The eldest of them was Tarakaksa, the middle one Vidyunmali and the youngest Kamalaksa. All of them were of equal strength.

Eschewing all enjoyments captivating the mind, they went to the cavern of the mountain Meru and performed a wonderful penance. They kept performing the penance through all the seasons no matter how harsh they were.

They were not at all vexed or distressed thereby. They gradually increased the severity of their austerities. Thus the three excellent sons of Taraka performed penance with Brahma as the object of their worship.

Standing on the bare ground on a single foot, the strong Asuras performed the penance for a hundred years. Then they continued the penance for a thousand years. Satisfied by their penance, Brahma the supreme Lord of the gods and Asuras, appeared in front of them in order to grant them boons.

Brahma said: —

Oh great Asuras, I am now pleased with your penance. I shall grant you everything. Speak out the boons you wish to have.

Sanatkumdra said: —

On hearing his words they bowed to the grandfather, with their palms joined in reverence and spoke to him revealing their mind's desire slowly.

The Asuras said: —

Oh Lord of gods, if you are pleased, if boons are to be given to us, please grant us indestructibility at the hands of everyone, every living being. Let not old age and sickness befall us. Make us free from death. Let no one in the three worlds kill us.

Brahma said: —

Oh Asuras, there cannot be invariable indestructibility. Please desist from asking for it. Seek some other boon whatever you wish. A creature who is born has to die, they cannot be free from old age or death. Except for Siva and Visnu, no one else is immortal. If penance is performed for the harassment of the world, it shall be understood as gone.

It is only a well performed penance that can be fruitful. So I ask you again to choose another boon.

The Asuras said: —

Oh Lord, we have no mansion where we can stay happily. Please build us three beautiful cities endowed with wealth and all good things.

Sanatkumara exclaimed: —

Then the three brothers explained their desires.

Tarakaksa said: —

Let Visvakarma make a city which cannot be broken even by the gods. Let that golden city be mine.

Kamalaksa said: —

I wish to have a great silver city.

Kamalaksa said: —

Please give me a steel-set magnetic city.

The brothers said: —

We will join these cities together at the end of a thousand years during midday at the time of Abhijit when the moon shall be in the constellation Pusya. Oh Brahma, when these cities are joined together, may Siva discharge a wonderful single arrow and pierce our cities. Lord Siva is free from enmity with us. He is worthy of our worship and respect. How can he burn us? This is what we think in our minds. A person like him is difficult to get in the world.

Sanatkumara said: —

On hearing their words, Brahma agreed to it. He ordered Maya to build the three cities. Then Brahma returned to his abode. Then the intelligent Maya built the cities as asked. The golden one for Tarakaksa, the silver one for Kamalaksa and the steel one for Vidyunmall. The three fortlike excellent cities were in order in heaven, sky and on the earth.

After building the three cities for the Asuras, Maya established them there, desiring their welfare. Entering the three cities thus, the sons of Taraka, of great strength and valour experienced all enjoyments.

Thus, the Asuras, sons of Taraka, after acquiring the boons, lived there subservient to Maya, a great devotee of Siva. A long time elapsed as they were enjoying and living happily, ruling over their three kingdoms.

The Prayer of the Gods

Vyasa said: —

Oh son of Brahma, please narrate. What happened after that? What did the gods do when the three Asuras made the three worlds suffer due to their cities?

Brahma said: —

On hearing the words of Vyasa, Sanatkumara spoke after remembering the lotus-like feet of Siva.

Sanatkumara said: —

Indra and other gods scorched and distressed by the brilliance of the three cities sought refuge in Brahma. They narrated their grievances to him after awaiting the proper opportunity.

The gods said: —

Oh Brahma, the heaven-dwellers have been subjected to great distress by Maya the virtual ruler of the three cities, accompanied by the sons of Taraka. Hence, we are distressed and we seek refuge in you. Please plan out the way of their annihilation whereby we can be happy.

Brahma said: —

Oh gods, do not be afraid of those Asuras. Siva will hit upon a good way of killing them. The Asuras have flourished due to my favour. They do not deserve destruction at my hands. All of you gods including Indra pray to Siva. If the Lord of all is pleased, he will carry out your task.

Sanatkumara said: —

On hearing the words of Brahma, the distressed gods including Indra went to Siva and eulogised him. Eulogising the bull-bannered, the trident-bearing Lord Siva with various kinds of divine hymns, the gods then described their plight.

The gods said: —

Oh Lord Siva, the gods including Indra have been defeated by the Asura accompanied by his brothers. All the gods have been defeated by the sons of Taraka. The three worlds have been brought under their sway. The entire universe has been exterminated by them. The terrible Asuras take the entire share of the sacrificial benefits to themselves. They have initiated evil activities. They have prevented the sages from performing their virtuous rites. Oh Lord Siva, except you no one else can kill them. Please help us. Free us from them.

Sanatkumara said: —

On hearing these words of Indra and other heaven-dwellers who were expatiating on their distress, Siva spoke in return.

The Virtues of the Tripuras

Siva said: —

A meritorious person is the presiding ruler of the Tripuras now. He who practises meritorious deeds should not be killed by sensible persons. I know the misery of the gods completely. Those Asuras are very strong. They cannot be killed by the gods or demons. The sons of Taraka and Maya are equally meritorious. How can I knowingly commit malicious deeds to my friends though I am hardy and powerful in battles? Even Brahma has said that there is a great sin attending to even casual malicious actions. Those Asuras are my devotees. Oh Gods, how can they be slain by us? Let this aspect be thought over by you who know what virtue is. You must consider this virtuously. They should not be slain as long as they continue their devotion to me. Yet, this reason may very well be intimated to Visnu.

Sanatkumara said: —

Oh sage, thus when they heard these words, Indra and other gods immediately intimated this to Brahma in the first instance. Then, with Brahma at their head, the gods quickly went to Vaikuntha to see Visnu. They eulogised Visnu and told him everything.

Visnu said: —

This is true that where eternal virtue reigns supreme, no misery raises its head like darkness when the sun is seen.

The gods said: —

How are we going to go about our activities? How can our misery be dispelled? How can we be happy? As long as the Tripuras are alive, how can we observe virtuous activities? All the residents of the three cities give us trouble.

Sanatkumara said: —

On seeing them in that plight, distressed and humiliated, Visnu thought within himself, 'I am the benefactor of the gods. But what can I do in this affair? The sons of Taraka are the devotees of Siva.' After thinking like this, he thought upon the Supreme Visnu, the Lord of sacrifices.

Immediately on being thought upon by Visnu, all the sacrifices came where Visnu was stationed. The eternal Lord Visnu saw the eternal sacrifices and told them to look at the gods too, including Indra.

Visnu said: —

In order to destroy the three cities and to bring about prosperity in the three worlds, Oh gods perform the worship of Lord Siva along with the Lord of sacrifices.

Sanatkumara said: —

On hearing the words of Visnu, the gods eulogised the Lord of sacrifices. The gods worshipped the Sacrificial Being in accordance with the rules. Then from the sacrificial pit rose up thousands of Bhutas of huge size and armed with tridents, spears, iron clubs and other weapons.

Visnu said: —

Oh Bhutas, listen to my statement. You are all very powerful. All of you go immediately to the three cities. Strike at, break and burn the three cities of the Asuras.

Sanatkumara said: —

The hosts of Bhutas bowed to the Lord of the gods and went to the three cities of the Asuras. Immediately after their entry into the cities they were reduced to ashes like moths in the fire. Those who escaped fled out of the cities and came grief-stricken to Visnu. On seeing them and hearing the incidents in detail, Lord Visnu pondered over this.

He realised that these Asuras and the other residents of the three cities are virtuous. Hence they have become invincible. They are devotees of Siva and have perpetrated all sins. These Asuras devote themselves to the phallic worship of Siva. So if obstacles are put during their virtuous rites by means of magic, the three cities can be destroyed. After thinking thus, Lord Visnu set himself the task of interfering with the sacred rites of the Asuras.

Visnu said: —

Oh gods, you go to your own abodes. Undoubtedly I shall carry on the task of the gods to the extent of my intellect. Strenuously I shall make them averse to Siva. Coming to know that they are devoid of devotion to him he will reduce them to ashes.

The Tripuras are Initiated

Sanatkumara said: —

For causing obstacles in their virtuous activities, Visnu of great brilliance, created a Purusa born of himself. In a faltering voice he was muttering, 'Dharma, Dharma.' He bowed to Visnu and spoke to him.

Purusa said: —

Oh laudable, revered one, please tell me what my names are and what my place shall be.

Visnu said: —

Oh intelligent one, born of me, you are certainly identical with me in form. Let your name be Arihat. You will have other auspicious names too. Oh you who wield Maya, create a deceptive sacred text of sixteen hundred thousand verses, contrary to Srutis and Smrtis wherein Varnas and Asramas shall be eschewed. Let that holy text be in Apabhramsa language. You shall strain yourself to extend it further. I shall bestow on you the ability to create it. Different kinds of magic arts shall be subservient to you.

Arihat said: —

Oh Lord, command me quickly what I shall do. At your bidding, all activities shall be fruitful.

Visnu said: —

These Asuras, the residents of the three cities, shall be deluded. Oh intelligent one, they shall be initiated by you. They shall be taught strenuously. At my bidding you will incur no sin on that account. Go to the three cities and destroy them after revealing the Tamasika rites. Make four disciples and teach them the same. After this is done, you and your followers will attain great boons.

Sanatkumara said: —

At the bidding of the Lord Siva, Visnu, the powerful, commanded him thus and vanished.

Then Arihat created four disciples and taught them the deceptive cult. The four disciples had shaven heads and were of auspicious features. They habitually wore dirty clothes. They did not talk much. Delightfully they used to speak, 'Dharma is the great gain, the true essence,' and some similar words.

Then, bowing to Visnu who carried out the wishes of Siva, the deceptive sage went joyously to the three cities accompanied by his disciples. They then created an illusion.

Stationing himself in a garden at the outskirts of the city, accompanied by his disciples he set his magic in motion. That was powerful enough to fascinate even the expert magicians. This magic though was ineffective in the three cities. Arihat became distressed on realising this. He continued to meditate on Visnu and expressed his distress. Visnu, on realising this, immediately sent Narada to the three cities where Arihat was. Narada, an excellent in the magic art, entered the city and stationed himself. Then he approached the Lords of the three.

Narada said: —

A certain sage, very virtuous and excellent master of lores has arrived here. He possesses complete knowledge of the Vedic lore. Many cults have been observed by me but none of them is like his. Seeing the eternal virtue in this cult we have got ourselves initiated into it. Oh excellent Asuras, if you have any interest in that cult, you shall get yourself initiated into it.

Sanatkumara said: —

On hearing his words full of significance, the Lord of the Asuras was deluded and exclaimed with surprise in his heart. He thought that if Narada had initiated himself, so should he. Then Asura approached the sage. He was instantly deluded by his magic.

The Tripura ruler: —

Oh sage of pure mind, you shall perform my initiation. I shall become your disciple.

The sage said: —

Oh excellent Asura, if you are prepared to act according to my commands I shall initiate you, otherwise not.

The Asura said: —

I shall carry out whatever command you are pleased to give. I will not transgress your orders.

Sanatkumara said: —

On hearing the words of the Tripura-ruler, the excellent sage removed the cloth from his mouth and started initiating the ruler of Asuras, in accordance with his cult observing rules. Then all the three Asuras and the people of the three cities also initiated themselves in the cult.

Prayer to Siva

Vyasa said: —

When the ruler of the Asuras, his brothers and the citizens were deluded by repulsive Vedic teachings, what happened? Were they convinced that Siva was not the supreme? Please mention everything.

Sanatkumara said: —

The Asuras were convinced that Siva was not the supreme Lord. They had abandoned the worship of Siva. Without realising, an evil conduct came to stay. The Asuras were truly deluded.

When Visnu was told about this, he was happy. He praised Siva's intelligence and went to Kailsa. All the gods, Brahma and Indra also went along. They eulogised Siva.

Visnu said: —

Obeisance to you, great Lord, the great soul, Narayana, Rudra and Brahma, obeisance to you in the form of Brahman.

Sanatkumara said: —

Visnu repeated the mantra fifteen million times standing in water and concentrating his mind on him. In the meantime, the gods too eulogised him with devotion.

The gods said: —

Obeisance to you, the soul of all, obeisance to Siva the remover of distress, obeisance to the blue-necked Rudra, obeisance to the knowledge-formed Siva of great mind. Oh Lord Siva, they are now deluded by your magic. Oh Lord, they have gone astray from the virtuous path through the expedient taught by Visnu. They have resorted to Budhha's religion.

Siva said: —

Oh Lord of gods, all the intentions of the gods have been understood by me now. There is no doubt I am the one who kills them but as they are my devotees and have abandoned their beliefs under false pretext, how can I kill them? Let Visnu or anyone else slay them now.

Brahma said: —

Oh Siva, hear me. The Asuras cannot be killed by anyone else but you. This is a boon I have given them and hence no one else can kill them. You are the emperor of the gods, you are the only one who can restore the happiness of his subjects.

Siva said: —

Oh Brahma, if I am to be proclaimed the emperor of the gods, I do not have any characteristic of an emperor. I do not have a divine chariot and charioteer. I do not have bows and arrows needed to win a battle. If I had these, I could have killed the Asuras.

The gods said: —

Oh Lord of the gods, fret not, we shall make these available to you and head to the battlefield.

The Gods Pray

Sanatkumara said: —

On hearing the words of the gods and others, Siva accepted the proposal. In the meantime Parvati arrived there with her two sons. Everyone was surprised to see her there. They bowed to her but remained silent as they didn't know the cause of her arrival.

The goddess said: —

Oh Lord, see the sportive six-faced Karttikeya, refulgent like the sun, our excellent son embellished by excellent ornaments.

Sanatkumara said: —

Thus addressed by Parvati, Lord Siva was never satiated in drinking nectar of the beauty of Skanda's face. He recollected the Asuras who had come (to fight and) pounded by his splendorous valour. Embracing and kissing Skanda on the head Lord Siva rejoiced much.

Then the mother of the universe stayed there for a while and held conversation with the Lord. Afterwards the goddess stood up. Lord Siva went into his apartment with Parvati and Nandin. The gods and others stood on the other side of the door, worried and anxious. They began to mutter, 'What shall we do? Where shall we go? Who will make us happy? What will happen next? We are doomed.' Some gods said, 'We are sinners.' Others said, 'We are unfortunate.'

On hearing their multifarious voices, Kumbhodara beat the gods with a baton. The terrified gods fled from there. The terrified gods shouting 'Ha Ha' fled from there. The sages faltered and fell on the ground. There was excitement and great confusion.

Unnerved and languid, Indra crawled on his knees. The celestial sages dropped to the ground. Then the sages and gods approached Brahma and Visnu. They narrated their worries to them. On hearing this, Visnu consoled the sages and the gods and spoke thus.

Oh gods, Oh sages, why are you distressed? Eschew your sorrows. Siva will be propitiated but not so easily. Ponder over this greatly, how can Lord Siva ne made favourable immediately?

Visnu said: —

Oh scholars, I am giving you a mantra. You must repeat this. Utter the syllable 'Omkara' first, then repeat the word 'Namah' (obeisance). Then say 'Sivaya' (to Siva). Then repeat 'Subham' twice and 'Kuru' twice. Afterwards say 'Sivaya Namah Om.' If you repeat this mantra a crore times, Siva will be delighted and carry out your task.

Sanatkumara said: —

When this was mentioned by Visnu, the gods began to propitiate Siva. For the fulfilment of the task Visnu and Brahma also meditated on Siva. After the sages had repeated the mantra over a crore times, Siva appeared before them in his real form and spoke to them.

Lord Siva said: —

Oh Visnu, Oh Brahma, Oh gods and Oh sages of auspicious rites, I am delighted by your Japa. Speak out the desired boon.

The gods said: —

Oh Siva, Lord of the gods, if you are pleased, realising that the gods are unnerved, let the Tripuras be destroyed. Oh merciful one, save us. We, gods, have always been saved from adversities by you alone.

Oh Visnu, Oh Brahma, Oh gods, Oh sages, all of you listen to my words with attention considering that the three cities have been already destroyed. Hence make arrangements for the chariot, charioteer, divine bow and excellent arrows as agreed to by you all. Do not delay. Oh Brahma, Oh Visnu, provide me with the paraphernalia of an emperor, Lord Siva said.

Sanatkumara said: —

On hearing these words of Siva, the gods derived more pleasure than Visnu and Brahma. At his bidding, Visvakarman made a splendid chariot of good features, consisting of all the gods, for the welfare of the people.

Siva's Campaign

Sanatkumara said: —

Brahma handed over the divine chariot of various wonderful features to Siva after yoking the Vedas as the horses. He then requested Siva to mount the chariot. The great Lord Siva got into that chariot that had various scaffoldings attached to it. He was then eulogised by the gods, Gandharvas, serpents, sages, Visnu, and Brahma.

Glancing at the charioteer when he mounted the chariot, the horses constituted by the Vedas fell headlong to the ground. The earth quaked. The mountains became tremulous. Then Lord Visnu assumed the form of a Lordly bull and went under the chariot. He lifted it up and steadied it for a short while.

But in another instant, unable to bear the weighty splendour of Lord Siva seated in the chariot, the Lordly bull had to kneel down and crawl on the ground. But the Lord touched the bridle and steadied the horses. Then Brahma seated in the excellent chariot, drove it with the velocity of mind and wind. They headed to the three cities of the Asuras. The chariot was then in the sky. Lord Siva was seated inside.

Lord Siva said: —

Give me the Lordship of the animals. Then I shall kill the Asuras. The excellent Asuras can be killed only after assigning separate animalhood to the gods and others. Not otherwise.

Sanatkumara said: —

On hearing these words, the gods became distressed. Siva realised their worries and consoled them.

Siva said: —

Oh excellent gods, you will not fall even in your animal hood. Let it be heard, and let the process of release from animal hood be practised. Once you perform the divine rite of Pasupata you will be released from animal hood. He who renders service perpetually or for twelve years, becomes relieved of animal hood. Hence, oh excellent gods, perform this divine rite. You will be released from animal hood. There is no doubt about this.

Sanatkumara said: —

On hearing these words of Lord Siva, Visnu, Brahma and other gods became the animals of Lord Siva. Siva became the Lord of animals. Then the name Pasupati, that bestows welfare, spread in all the worlds and became renowned.

Then Siva went ahead to destroy the three cities. All the gods and others went on elephants, horses, lions, bulls and chariots to kill Tripuras, leaders of the Asuras. All of Siva's Ganas and Ganesvaras were capable of burning the entire world including the mobile and immobile beings, within a trice by their very thought. Surrounding Siva, the great Lord, they went ahead.

The Burning of the Tripuras

Sanatkumara said: —

Then Siva, the great Lord, seated in the chariot and equipped with everything, got ready to burn the three cities completely, the cities of the enemies of the gods. The bow was well strung and kept near the head. The arrow was fixed. The fingers clenched at the bow firmly. The eyes were fixed.

Ganesa was stationed on the thumb. During this time the three cities did not come within the target path of the trident-bearing Lord. Then from the firmament, the odd-eyed Siva who was standing there holding the bow and the arrow heard an auspicious voice. It said, 'Oh Lord, master of the universe, you will not kill the Tripuras as long as Lord Ganesa is not adored.'

On hearing these words, Siva called Bhadrakali and worshipped the elephant-faced god Ganesa. When Ganesa was worshipped, when he was standing ahead pleased, Lord Siva saw the three cities of the powerful Asuras, joined together.

When Bhadrakali stood up after worshipping Siva, the three cities joined together into one unit. Oh sage, when the three cities came to a unified whole, a tumultuous shout of joy rose up among the noble Gods and others.

Then Brahma and Visnu, the Lords of the worlds, said — 'The time for killing the Asuras has arrived. The three cities of the sons of Taraka have come into one unified whole. Oh Lord of the gods please discharge the arrow and reduce the three cities to ashes lest they should be separated again.' Holding the bow and arrow in his hands, Siva waited. For some reason, he looked at the three cities with contempt.

Seeing this, Visnu, Brahma and the other gods eulogised him. On being eulogised thus, Lord Siva desired to reduce the three cities to ashes with his arrow. In the auspicious moment called Abhilasa, he drew the bow and made a wonderful and unbearable twanging sound. He addressed the great Asuras and proclaimed his own name. Siva discharged an arrow that had the refulgence of countless suns.

The arrow, which was constituted by Visnu and whose steelhead was fire god, blazed forth and burnt the three Asuras who lived in the three cities. It thereby removed their sins.

The three cities reduced to ashes fell on the earth's ground by the four oceans. Since they had refrained from the worship of Siva, hundreds of Asuras were burnt by the fire generated by the arrow. Tarakaksa was burnt along with his two brothers. He remembered his Lord Siva and mentally appealed to him.

Tarakaksa said: —

Oh Siva, you are known to be pleased with us, if in the future we are to be burned again, let our kinsfolk burn with us. Let our intellect be purified by our thoughts on you in every birth.

Sanatkumara said: —

Oh sage, at the bidding of Siva, those Asuras were burnt and reduced to ashes by the fire. Other Asuras, children and old men were burned out too but quickly so the pain was lessened. Except Maya, everything else burned with the Tripuras.

The Gods' Prayer

Vyasa said: —

Oh son of Brahma, oh most excellent among the devotees of Siva, you are blessed. Tell me please where did Maya who was spared go? Where did the ascetics go? Please narrate all, if it relates to Siva's story.

Suta said: —

On hearing the words of Vyasa, Sanatkumara the holy son of the creator remembered the feet of Siva and spoke.

Sanatkumara said: —

Listen oh Vyasa, son of Parasara, listen. When the three cities of Asuras were utterly burnt, the Gods became surprised. The gods including Indra, Visnu and others became silent and bewildered on seeing the excessively brilliant Siva. He had a huge form, blazing with a thousand suns' fire and eyes that were red. Everyone was terrified.

Then Brahma too, who was excessively afraid after seeing Siva's terrible form, was delighted at heart and fervently prayed along with the gods. Visnu who was also afraid prayed to Siva, the slayer of the Tripuras. He was accompanied by his consort Parvati. Everyone eulogised the great Lord.

Brahma said: —

Oh Lord of the gods, bestower of blessings to the devotees, be pleased, Oh bestower of wholesome blessings to all the gods, be pleased, Oh Lord of the worlds, be pleased. Be pleased, Oh destroyer of the Tripuras. Oh great Lord, save, save us all the frightened gods. By burning the three cities, the gods have been satisfied and content. Oh slayer of the Tripuras, Oh Siva, let my devotion to you remain eternal.

Visnu said: —

Obeisance to you devoid of the attributes. Again obeisance to you possessed of attributes. Again obeisance to you of the form of Prakrti and Purusa. Obeisance to Siva, the Lord of the worlds. Let my devotion to you steadily increase.

The gods said: —

Oh Lord of gods, oh great Siva, you are the creator of everything. We bow to you joyously. Let our devotion to you be steady and endless.

Siva said: —

Oh Brahma, oh Visnu, oh gods, I am very much pleased with you all. All of you consider carefully and then let me know the boon you desire.

The gods said: —

Oh Lord, if you are pleased, if the boon is to be granted by you to us, be pleased to appear always whenever misery befalls us and destroy the misery.

Siva said: —

Let it be so.

The Gods Go Back to Their Abodes

Sanatkumara: —

In the meantime the Asura Maya who was not burnt due to the strength of grace, came there on seeing Siva delighted. With palms joined in reverence and with stooping shoulders he bowed to Siva again. Then he got up, with his mind full of devotion and voice choked with emotions of love, he eulogised facing Siva.

Maya said: —

Oh great Lord, oh Siva, obeisance to you. Oh sanctified soul, obeisance to you, Oh holy one. Oh great Lord, fond of eulogy, I know not how to eulogise you. Oh Lord of all, be pleased. Save me, I have sought refuge in you.

Siva said: —

Oh Maya, I am delighted. Oh excellent Asura speak out the boon you wish to have. I shall grant you what you desire.

Maya said: —

Oh great Lord, if you are delighted and if I deserve the grant of a boon, please grant me permanent devotion to you. Oh Lord Siva, let there be no demoniac instinct in me at any time. Oh Lord, let me be fearless forever engrossed in your auspicious worship.

Lord Siva said: —

Oh excellent Asuras, you are my devotees and are blessed. You are free from aberrations. All the boons desired by you are granted now. At my bidding you go to the region Vitala, more beautiful than heaven. Go in the company of your family and kinsmen. You stay there without fear. Be devout always. At my bidding you will never have a demoniac instinct.

Sanatkumara said: —

Then Maya went to Vitala as commanded by Siva. In the meantime those heretics of tonsured heads came there, knelt before Visnu, Brahma and others and spoke.

'Oh gods, where shall we go? What shall we do now? We are ready to carry out your behests. Please command us quickly. Wicked deeds have been performed by us. We have destroyed the devotion to Siva of all the Asuras who were great devotees of Siva. We will have to stay in hell for countless Kalpas. Certainly there is no redemption for us that have offended devotees of Siva. Please tell us the mode of atoning for the same. We have sought refuge in you,' the tonsured heads pleaded.

Visnu and others said: —

Oh tonsured ones, you need not be afraid at all. These excellent activities have taken place at the bidding of Siva. Since you are the servants of Siva and have carried out the activities conducive to the welfare of the gods and the sages, no mishap shall ever befall you bringing you to distress. He is pleased with those who work for the welfare of the gods and sages. No mishap befalls those who work for the welfare of the gods and sages.

Sanatkumara said: —

Thus bidden by the great gods, the tonsured heads bowed to them and went to their allotted abode. Then Lord Siva was duly worshipped by Brahma and others. He vanished after that with Parvati, his sons and his Ganas. Then Brahma, Visnu, the gids, sages and all other returned to their abodes with hearts full of happiness and peace.

The Resuscitation of Indra in the Context of the Destruction of Jalandhara

Vadsa said: —

Oh holy Lord, son of Brahma, I heard that Lord Siva killed the great Asura Jalandhara. Will you please narrate this tale?

Suta said: —

On being requested thus by Vyasa, the great sage spoke about it with excitement.

Oh sage, once Brhaspati and Indra went to Kailasa with great devotion, to see Lord Siva. Coming to know of the arrival of Brhaspati and Indra eager to see him, Lord Siva wished to test their knowledge. Accordingly, the Lord stood blocking their path in the naked form with matted hair and beaming face.

Brhaspati and Indra were walking on gleefully. On their way they saw this wonderful person of huge size. He was quiet and composed and very refulgent with matted hair on his head. He was fair-complexioned with long arms and wide chest. He was terrible to look at. Without realising that the person who stood there blocking their path was Siva himself, Indra who was proud of his authority said to him, Sanatkumara said.

Indra inquired: —

Oh, who are you? Where have you come from? What is your name? Tell me truly. Is Lord Siva in his apartment or has he gone anywhere?

Sanatkumara said: —

Oh sage, on being asked by Indra thus, he did not say anything. Indra asked him again. But the naked person did not say anything. The naked Lord, though asked repeatedly by Indra, did not say anything, for he wanted to test the knowledge of Indra. Then the Lord of Gods, proud of the wealth of the three worlds, became enraged. Rebuking the Lord with matted hair he spoke these words.

Indra said: —

Oh evil-minded one, though asked you did not reply to me. Hence I am going to kill you with my thunderbolt. Who can save you?

Sanatkumara said: —

After saying this and looking at him ferociously, Indra raised his thunderbolt in order to kill him. On seeing Indra lifting up his thunderbolt, Siva prevented the fall of the thunderbolt by making his hand numb. Then Siva became furious. His eyes became terrible. He blazed with his burning splendour. Indra too became agitated on having his arms numbed.

On seeing him resplendent, Brhaspati realised immediately that he was Lord Siva himself and bowed to him. He then eulogised Siva in an attempt to calm him down.

Brhaspati said: —

Obeisance to Siva, the chief Lord of the gods, the supreme soul, the three-eyed, possessed of matted hair. You are the fire, the wind, the ether, the waters, the earth, the sun, the moon, the stars, and the solar system. You alone are Visnu, Brahma, and you are eulogised by them; you are the great Lord. You are Narada, the great saint.

Oh Siva, with the strength of meditating on you, the clouds shower water. Indra protects the worlds like his sons. Be pleased oh Siva, be pleased.

Sanatkumara said: —

In the meantime, Indra, having realised his mistake, fell at Siva's feet.

Brhaspati said: —

Oh please quieten the anger rising from your eyes. Oh great Lord, be pleased. Protect Indra who has sought refuge in you. Let this fire rising from the eye in the forehead be rendered calm.

Lord Siva said: —

Oh Brhaspati, how can I take up the fury that has already come out of my eye? A serpent does not wear again the slough that has been cast off.

Brhaspati said: —

Oh holy Lord, indeed the devotees should be pitied always. Oh Siva, thus please make your name Bhaktavatsala (favourably disposed towards the devotees) true. You deserve to cast elsewhere the fierce brilliance. Oh uplifter of all devotees, raise up Indra.

Siva said: —

Oh dear one, I am delighted by your eulogy. I shall grant you the excellent boon. Henceforth you shall be famous as Enlivener because you have conferred life on Indra. I shall cast off this fire born of my eye in the forehead intended to kill Indra lest it should afflict him.

Sanatkumara said: —

On saying this he held that wonderful brilliance born of the eye in the forehead and cast it off in the briny ocean. Then the Lord Rudra vanished.

The Birth of Jalandhara and His Marriage

Vyasa asked: —

Oh omniscient Sanatkumara, what happened after Siva cast off his blazing eye in the ocean?

Sanatkumara said: —

Oh dear one, the brilliance of Siva born of the eye in the forehead and cast off into the briny sea immediately assumed the form of a boy. At the confluence of the river Ganga and the ocean, the boy of terrific features cried loudly.

At the sound of the crying boy, the earth quaked frequently. The heaven and the Satyaloka became deafened by the noise. All the worlds were frightened. The guardians of the quarters became agitated in the mind. Then the distressed gods and the sages immediately sought refuge in Brahma.

The gods said: —

This mysterious sound has arisen. Oh Lord of the world, we are frightened. Please quell it.

Sanatkumara said: —

On hearing their words, Brahma the grandfather of the worlds wished to go there. Then Brahma descended from Satyaloka to the Earth along with the gods. He went to the ocean desirous of knowing what it was.

When Brahma came there, he saw the boy in the lap of the ocean. On seeing Brahma coming, the ocean, assuming the form of a god, bowed to him and placed the boy in his lap. Then the surprised Brahma spoke these words to the ocean—'Oh ocean, tell me quickly about the parentage of this boy.'

The ocean said: —

Oh Brahma, this boy was suddenly seen in the confluence of the river Ganga. I do not know about the origin of this boy. Oh creator, let me know your predictions about his future according to his horoscope

Sanatkumara said: —

Even as the ocean said these words, the son of the ocean caught hold of the neck of Brahma and shook it several times. In due course tears came out of the eyes of Brahma, afflicted by the joggling and jolting. Brahma somehow extricated himself from the grip of the son of the ocean by means of his hands and spoke to the ocean.

Brahma said: —

Oh ocean, listen, I shall narrate the future as predicted from the horoscope, entirely. Since he was able to make my eyes water, let him be famous in the name of Jalandhara. He will become a youth now itself. He will become a master of all sacred lores, very valorous, courageous, heroic, invincible and majestic like you. Like Karttikeya, he will be the conqueror of all battles. This boy will become the emperor of Asuras. He will conquer even Visnu. He will face defeat from no quarter. He cannot be slain by any one except Siva. He will return to the place from where he sprang up. His wife will be a chaste lady who will increase good fortune. She will be exquisitely beautiful in every limb. She will be an ocean of good conduct and will speak pleasing words.

Sanatkumara said: —

After saying so he called Sukra and performed his coronation. Brahma then took leave of the ocean and disappeared. The ocean then took him to his abode. With a joyous heart he nurtured the boy with diverse great means. The boy grew into a beautiful youth of exquisite limbs and wonderful splendour. Then the ocean invited the great Asura Kalanemi and requested him to give his daughter named Vrnda in marriage to his son.

He gave his beloved daughter to Jalandhara, the brave son of the ocean, in marriage performing the nuptial rites according to the Brahma style. Oh sage, great festivities were held in the marriage. The rivers and Asuras were happy.

Those Asuras who had been formerly defeated by the gods and had sought shelter in Patala came fearlessly to the Earth and resorted to him. Then Jalandhara and his wife ruled over their kingdom.

The Fight Between the Gods and Jalandhara

Sanatkumara said: —

Once the son of the ocean was seated along with his wife and the Asuras. The brilliant Bhargava came there joyously illuminating the ten quarters as the embodied brilliance. On seeing him, Jalandhara received him with respect. Then he noticed the headless Rahu and enquired.

Jalandhara enquired: —

Oh Lord, by whom was this done to Rahu? By whom was his head cut? Please tell me, Oh preceptor, everything in detail as it had happened.

Bhargava said: —

Oh Jalandhara, listen to the account. Once there was a strong hero Bali, the son of Virocana and great-grandson of Hiranyakasipu. The gods including Indra being defeated by him sought refuge in Visnu. Eager to gain their ends they told him all the details.

Oh dear, at his bidding, the gods, very clever in deception, made an alliance with the Asuras, to further their own interest. All those gods, the assistants of Visnu churned the ocean eagerly for the gain of nectar, along with the Asuras. The enemies of the Asuras extracted jewels from the ocean. The gods seized the nectar and drank it deceitfully.

Then the gods including Indra increased in strength and prowess by the drinking of the nectar and harassed the Asuras with the assistance of Visnu. This Visnu who is always a partisan of Indra, cut off the head of Rahu as he was drinking the nectar along with the gods.

On hearing about the churning of his father, the heroic son of the ocean, the valorous Jalandhara became furious and his eyes turned red with anger. Then he called his excellent emissary Ghasmara and told him everything. He then lovingly honoured the clever emissary in various ways, assured him of protection and sent him to Indra as his messenger. After going there, the emissary entered the assembly of the gods and spoke to Indra, Sanatkumara said.

Ghasmara said: —

Jalandhara, the son of the ocean, is the Lord and emperor of all the Asuras. He is excessively heroic and valorous. He has the support and assistance of Bhargava. Please listen to what he says.

Oh base god, why was my father, the ocean, churned by you with the mountain? Why were all the jewels of my father taken away?

What you have done is not proper. Return all of them to me immediately. Pondering over this, come along with the gods and seek refuge in me. Otherwise you will have a great cause to fear. You will run the risk of the annihilation of your kingdom, Jalandhara said.

Sanatkumara said: —

On hearing the words of the messenger, Indra was bewildered. Remembering the previous incidents he was frightened as well as angry. He spoke to him thus.

Indra said: —

He gave shelter to the mountains who were terribly afraid of me. Others too, some of my enemies, the Asuras, were formerly saved by him. It was due to this that I took away his jewels. Those who oppose me can never remain happy. Formerly the Asura Sankha, the son of the ocean was stupid enough to be inimical to me. He was spared by me because he was associated with saintly men. But when he became violent towards the saintly men, he was killed in the interior of the ocean by Visnu, my younger brother.

Hence, oh messenger, go immediately and explain to the Asura, son of the ocean, our purpose for churning the ocean.

Sanatkumara said: —

Dismissed thus by Indra, the intelligent emissary Ghasmara hastened to the place where the heroic Jalandhara was present. All the words thus spoken by Indra were narrated to the king of Asuras by the intelligent emissary.

On hearing it, the lips of the Asura throbbed with anger. Desirous of conquering the gods he exerted himself immediately. In that enterprise of the Lord of the Asuras, countless Asuras from all the quarters and the nether region took part and helped him. Then the extremely heroic and valorous son of the ocean set forth with countless generals, Sumbha, Nisumbha and others.

Very soon, he reached heaven along with his force. He blew his conch. All the heroic soldiers roared. After going to heaven he stationed himself in Nandana. On seeing a vast army surrounding the city, the gods came out of Amaravati fully equipped with armour for the battle.

Then a battle between the armies of the gods and Asuras ensued. They rushed against one another with iron clubs, arrows, maces, axes and spears. They hit one another. Within a short time both the armies began to wade through streams of blood.

Bhargava resuscitated the Asuras killed in the battle with the Vidya of Amrtajivini and drops of water infused with mantras. The sage Angiras too resuscitated the gods in the battle with the divine herbs frequently brought from the mountain Drona. Jalandhara saw the gods restored to life again in the battle. He then spoke angrily to Bhargava.

Jalandhara said: —

The gods have been killed by me. How do they rise up again? The Vidya of Sanjivini has not been heard by me to exist elsewhere.

Bhargava said: —

Angiras is bringing divine herbs from the mountain Drona and enlivening the gods. If you wish for victory listen to my auspicious suggestion. Immediately you shall uproot the mountain Drona with your arms and hurl it into the ocean.

Sanatkumara said: —

Thus addressed by his preceptor Bhargava, the Lord of the Asuras, hastened to the lofty mountain. With his powerful arms, the Asura brought the mountain Drona and hurled it immediately into the ocean. Then the great hero, the son of the ocean, took a vast army with him, came to the battle ground and began to kill the gods with various weapons.

On seeing the gods being killed, Brhaspati went to the mountain Drona. On realising that the mountain Drona had been removed by the Asuras, Brhaspati was terrified. He returned and said dejectedly.

Brhaspati said: —

Oh gods, run away, all of you. There is no trace of the great mountain Drona. Certainly it has been destroyed by the Asura, the son of the ocean. Jalandhara is a great Asura. He cannot be conquered since he is born of a part of Siva. He will pound all the gods.

Sanatkumara said: —

Thus addressed by his preceptor Bhargava, the Lord of the Asuras, hastened to the lofty On hearing these words uttered by the preceptor of the gods, they abandoned all hopes of victory. They became excessively terrified. All the gods including Indra, struck by the king of the Asuras all round, lost courage and fled in all directions.

On seeing the gods routed, Jalandhara entered Amaravati with sounds of victory from the conches and drums. When the Asura entered the city, Indra and other gods entered the cavern of the golden mountain Meru and remained there. They had been extremely harrassed by the Asuras. At the same time the Asura appointed Sumbha and other Asuras severally in the places of authority of Indra and others. He then went into the cavern of the golden mountain.

The Battle of the Gods

Sanatkumara said: —

On seeing the Asura coming again, the gods including Indra trembled with fear. They fled together. With Brahma at the head they went to Vaikuntha. All of them including Prajapati eulogised Visnu after bowing down to him.

The gods said: —

Oh Visnu, obeisance to you who holds the earth, the support of people. Obeisance to Visnu. Obeisance to Visnu the younger brother of Indra, the Lord who deceived the king of Asuras in the guise of a Brahmin. Obeisance to a great yogin and saint who expounds great wisdom. Obeisance to the creator of the form of knowledge whereby the soul is delighted.

Oh thunderbolt for the destruction of gods' misery harassed by the Asuras. Obeisance to you lying on the Serpent-bed. Oh Lord of Laksmi, oh ocean of mercy, save us who have sought refuge in you. All the gods have been driven out of heaven by Jalandhara. While men freely move about, the gods do not shine. We have sought refuge in you. Let measures for his annihilation be thought of.

Visnu said: —

Oh gods, cast off your fear. I shall come to the battle-ground. I shall show my valour to Jalandhara.

Sanatkumara said: —

Having said this with a distressed mind, Visnu got up quickly and immediately mounted his vehicle Garuda. On seeing her Lord departing along with the gods, Laksmi, the daughter of the ocean, spoke with palms joined in reverence and tears welling up in the eyes.

Laksmi asked: —

Oh Lord, I am your beloved. If I am always devoted to you, Oh storehouse of mercy, how will my brother's death be at your hands?

Visnu said: —

Since I have been eulogised by the gods I shall go to the battle ground immediately. I can only show my valour to Asura Jalandhara. He cannot be slain by me because he is a part of Siva. Moreover Brahma has said so. Furthermore, you love him too.

Sanatkumara said: —

Having said this and seating himself on Garuda with the conch, discus, mace and the sword held in his hands, Visnu hastened to the fight along with Indra and other gods.

Roaring like a lion and accompanied by the gods, he reached the place where Jalandhara was waiting. Then the Daityas were blown here and there by a gush of wind. On seeing the Asuras afflicted by the gusts of wind, Jalandhara rushed against Visnu shouting out cries of bravery angrily.

In the meantime the delighted gods equipped with a vast army began to fight with their strength increased by the brilliance of Visnu. Seeing the army of the gods present there ready to fight, Jalandhara commanded the invincible Asuras thus.

Jalandhara said: —

Oh excellent Asuras, put up a stiff fight with Indra and other gods who are always cowardly though they have a huge army. At my bidding let all these come out with their entire army—the Mauryas numbering a hundred thousand, the Dhumras in hundreds, the Asuras and the Kalakeyas in crores and the Kalakas, the Daurhrdas and the Kaiikas in lakhs. All of you come out readily equipped with many divisions of the army and different kinds of weapons. Be fearless and free from hesitations.

Sanatkumara said: —

Thus the Asuras, clever and efficient in battle, commanded by Jalandhara on the one hand and gods equipped with the four sorts of fighting groups on the other, fought one another with maces, arrows, javelins, spears. They hit one another with axes and spears. Thus the fight between the gods and the Asuras was terrific. It was very fierce, frightening the sages and the Siddhas.

The Fight Between Visnu and Jalandhara

Sanatkumara said: —

Then the heroic Asuras hit and struck the gods with the spears, axes and clubs. With their bodies cut and pierced by the weapons of the Asuras, the gods including Indra became distressed in mind by fear and they fled from the battle.

On seeing the gods fleeing, Visnu hastened to the battle ground seated on his vehicle Garuda. By means of his discus Sudarsana he diffused his splendour all round. Holding the conch, sword, mace and the bow, the heroic deity was very furious. He was efficient in the battle using fierce weapons.

The Lord Visnu who was highly infuriated, cut off the heads of countless Asuras by means of the arrows discharged from his bow. Seeing Visnu suppressing and pounding the Asuras, the lips of the heroic Asura throbbed and he rushed at Visnu to fight with him. The king of Asuras shouted and roared, terrifying both the gods and the Asuras.

Striking with a single arrow, Visnu smote the heart of the Asura. With innumerable arrows he cut off the umbrella, banner, bow and arrows of the demon. Seizing the mace with his hand, the Asura jumped up quickly, hit Garuda on his head and felled him to the ground. The infuriated Asura with throbbing lips hit Visnu in his heart with his sharp spear diffusing its splendour.

Visnu laughingly split the mace with his sword. The destroyer of Asuras twanged his bow and split him with sharp arrows.

The infuriated Jalandhara, invincible in war, hurled a trident, resembling fire, at Visnu. Immediately Visnu remembered the lotus-like feet of Siva and cut the trident with his sword Nandaka. When the trident was split, the Lord of the Asuras leapt and rushed against Visnu and hit him in the chest with his fist. Without minding the pain in the least, the heroic Visnu hit Jalandhara in the chest with his firm fist.

Then both of them equally powerful had a hand to hand fight hitting each other with arms, fists and knees. Fighting with the Asura thus, for a long time, Visnu was surprised. Then he assumed a delightful aspect. He addressed the king of Asuras in a thundering voice.

Visnu said: —

Oh excellent Asura, you are blessed. You are invincible in war. Since you are a great Lord you are not at all afraid of even great weapons. Many Asuras have been killed by these very same weapons in great battles. The wicked and haughty people have been pierced through their bodies and killed.

Oh great Asura, I am delighted by this fight with you. You are really great. A hero like you has not been seen in the three worlds. Oh Lord of Asuras, choose a boon. I am pleased at your valour. I shall give you anything, even that which cannot be given, whatever is in your mind.

Sanatkumara said: —

On hearing these words of Visnu, skilled in magic, the intelligent king of the Asuras replied thus.

Jalandhara said: —

Oh brother-in-law, if you are pleased give me this boon. You stay in my house with all your followers, my sister and myself.

Sanatkumara said: —

On hearing these words of the great Asura, Lord Visnu said distressingly — 'So be it.'

Then Visnu came to the city called Jalandhara along with his followers, the gods and Laksmi. Asura Jalandhara returned to his abode and stayed very delightedly in the company of his sister and Visnu. Thereafter Jalandhara appointed Asuras in the authoritative posts of the gods. Joyously he returned to the Earth. The son of the ocean confiscated whatever gem or jewel the gods, Gandharvas or Siddhas had hoarded.

Making gods, Gandharvas, Siddhas, Serpents, Raksasas and human beings, the denizens of his capital, he ruled over the three worlds. After making the gods thus subservient to himself, Jalandhara protected them all virtuously, like his own sons. When he was ruling the kingdom virtuously, none in his realm was sick or miserable or lean and emaciated or indigent.

The Conversation Between Narada and Jalandhara

Sanatkumara said: —

When the great Asura was ruling over the Earth virtuously, the gods were reduced to be mere slaves. The distressed gods mentally sought refuge in Siva the benefactor. They eulogised the great Lord by means of pleasant words.

Siva then called Narada and commissioned him with a desire to carry out the task of the gods. Then Narada went to the gods in the city of the Asuras at the bidding of Siva.

On seeing the sage Narada coming, the distressed gods, Indra and others, stood up. After bowing to Narada, the great sage who sat comfortably, the distressed gods, Indra and others spoke to him again.

The gods said: —

Oh excellent sage, listen to our misery. You are powerful and the favourite of Siva. The gods have been routed by the Asura Jalandhara from their abodes and positions of controlling authority. Hence we are miserable and distressed.

The gods have been harassed by that powerful Asura. We who have been subjected to great grief now seek refuge in you. The great Asura Jalandhara who has suppressed the gods and who is very powerful has made Visnu subservient to him in the battle.

Becoming subservient and granting Jalandhara a boon, Visnu has now begun to stay in his palace along with Laksmi. Please Narada, help us now.

Narada said: —

Oh gods, I know that you have been defeated by the king of Asuras, that you are miserable and harassed and have been deposed. There is no doubt in this that I shall carry out your task according to my ability. Oh gods, since you are in misery I shall be favourable to you.

Sanatkumara said: —

After saying so and consoling the gods, the excellent sage went to the assembly chamber of Jalandhara to see the favourite Asura. On seeing the excellent sage, the king Jalandhara stood up and offered him a splendid seat with great devotion. After worshipping him duly, Jalandhara laughed loudly and spoke to the excellent sage.

Jalandhara asked: —

Oh brahmin, where do you come from? What did you see here? Oh sage, what is the aim of your present visit here?

Narada said: —

Oh Jalandhara of great intellect, listen to the purpose for which I have come here. I shall explain it to you.

I had been to the summit of Kailasa casually. It is ten thousand Yojanas wide. It has a grove of Kalpa trees. Hundreds of Kamadhenus are found there. It is illuminated by Cintamani gems. It abounds in gold. It is divine and wonderfully brilliant.

There I saw Siva seated along with Parvati. He is fair-complexioned and exquisitely handsome. He has three eyes and the moon for his crest. On seeing this wonderfully great thing, a doubt arose in my mind. Can there be any other splendour as this in all the three worlds? Oh Lord of Daityas, then the idea of your prosperity struck into my mind. That is why now I have come to see you personally.

Sanatkumara said: —

On hearing these words of Narada the Lord of Daityas Jalandhara showed all his glory to Narada. On seeing it, the wise Narada, eager to realise the interests of the gods, spoke to the king of Daityas, Jalandhara, induced by the Lord.

Narada said: —

Oh foremost among heroes, you have everything conducive to prosperity. You are the Lord of the three worlds. No wonder that you possess this wealth. Whatever valuable thing there is in the world finds a place here.

Oh great hero, I am highly delighted to see your great affluence consisting of diverse objects. But Oh Jalandhara, your mansion is deficient in the most excellent of all ladies. You deserve to bring that. Oh Jalandhara, one who possesses all excellent things but does not possess the most excellent of women does not shine. His life is rendered waste.

Sanatkumara said: —

On hearing these words of Narada the noble soul, the king of Daityas, with his mind excited by passion, spoke.

Jalandhara said: —

Oh celestial sage, Oh Narada, obeisance be to you. Where is this most excellent of all ladies? Please tell me now. Wherever it may be in the whole of this universe, if such a lady exists anywhere, I will bring her here. Truth, it is certainly the truth.

Narada said: —

Kailasa is very beautiful and it possesses all sorts of things conducive to prosperity. Siva lives there assuming the form of a naked Yogin. His wife Parvati is exquisitely beautiful in every limb. She is charming and has all the characteristics of a beautiful lady. Such an exquisite beautiful form has never been seen anywhere. It incites the enthusiasm of everybody. It fascinates even the Yogins. It is worthy of being seen. It is conducive to great prosperity.

This occurs to my mind, there is none more prosperous in the three worlds than Siva who possesses the most excellent of all ladies. Even the four-faced Lord Brahma, immersed in her ocean of beauty, lost his mental steadiness formerly. Who can be compared to such a beautiful lady?

Even Siva reputed to be free from infatuation has been won over by her womanly sports. He enjoys prosperity from indulging in dalliance with her. This prosperity has not come to you. You have all the other prosperities except this.

Sanatkumara said: —

After saying this, the world-renowned celestial sage, Narada, pursuing his attempt to help the gods departed from there by the aerial path.

Jalandhara's Emissary to Siva

Vyasa said: —

Oh omniscient Sanatkumara, what did the king of Daityas do after the departure of Narada to heaven? Please tell me in detail.

Sanatkumara said: —

When Narada departed to heaven, the king of Daityas who had heard of the exquisite beauty of Parvati became harassed with pangs of love. The deluded Daitya, Jalandhara, who had lost clear thinking, being swayed by Time (the annihilator) called his messenger Rahu.

The infatuated son of the ocean, Jalandhara, addressed him politely with these words.

Jalandhara said: —

Oh Rahu of great intellect, most excellent of my emissaries, go to the mountain Kailasa. A sage and a Yogin named Siva lives there. He has matted locks of hair. His body is smeared with ashes. Go there and tell the detached Yogin Siva with matted locks of hair, fearlessly this: —

'Oh Yogin, of what avail is an exquisitely beautiful wife to you who stays in the jungle and is attended by ghosts, goblins, spirits and other beings? Oh Yogin, this state of affairs is no good in a world with me as the ruler. Hence you give up your wife, the most excellent lady, to me, the enjoyer of all excellent things. I have forcibly seized the most excellent elephant of Indra, the most excellent horse, and the celestial tree. I have seized everything excellent to all the powerful people and gods. Everyone has bowed to me, hence you do too. Everyone has surrendered, hence Oh ascetic you too surrender your wife, the most excellent of all ladies to me.'

Sanatkumara said: —

On hearing his words Rahu went to Kailasa and was allowed to enter by Nandin. With surprise and mystery manifest in his eyes, he went to the assembly chamber of Siva. Rahu was desirous of speaking to him. He sat in front of Siva. Urged by his gesture Rahu spoke to the three-eyed god Siva.

Rahu said: —

I am the messenger of the Lord of the three worlds, worthy of being served forever by Daityas and serpents. I have come here to you on being sent by him. The son of the ocean Jalandhara became the Lord of all Daityas and now he is the Lord of the three worlds. He is the emperor of all.

Oh Siva, listen to what he has to say to you. He asks how can the auspicious daughter of Himavat be a wife unto you who habitually stays in the cremation ground wearing garlands of bones and assuming the form of a naked ascetic. He is the possessor of all excellent things. She is the most excellent of all ladies. She deserves Jalandhar who is better than you in every sense. Hence, you must surrender Parvati to him. He shall possess her.

Sanatkumara said: —

When Rahu spoke thus, a terrific being, resonant like the thunder, came out from the space between the eyebrows of Siva. He had a leonine mouth with a moving tongue; his eyes shed fiery flames ; his hair stood at its end; his body was dry and rough. He appeared to be the man-lion incarnation of Visnu.

He was very terrible. He immediately rushed to Rahu. On seeing him rushing to devour, Rahu was terrified. He ran out when he was caught by the terrible being.

Rahu said: —

Oh great Lord, Oh Lord of the gods, save me who have sought refuge in you. You are always worthy of being worshipped by the gods and Asuras. Your terrible servant has come here to swallow me, a brahmin. Oh Lord of gods save me lest he should devour me. Obeisance be to you again and again.

Siva said: —

Leave off this brahmin Rahu, the emissary who has sought refuge. Oh excellent Gana, those who seek shelter shall be protected, not punished.

Sanatkumara said: —

Commanded thus by the Lord of Parvati, the Gana set Rahu free. After leaving Rahu, the Gana came near Siva and pleaded to the great Lord in piteous words.

Oh great Lord, my prey has been taken away. Oh Lord, I am tormented by hunger. So I am utterly emaciated. Tell me Lord, what should I eat now? Please command me, the Gana said.

The Lord said: —

If you are badly in need of food, if hunger torments you, eat up immediately the flesh of your own hands and feet.

Sanatkumara said: —

On being commanded thus by Siva, the being ate up the flesh from his limbs. He was then left only with his head. On seeing the Gana left only with his head, the delighted Sadasiva spoke smilingly.

Siva said: —

Oh great Gana, you are blessed since you carried out my request to the very letter. Oh excellent one, I am pleased with this action of yours. You shall hereafter be known by the title Kirtimukha. You shall be my door-keeper. You shall be one of my great Ganas, very heroic and terrible to all wicked persons.

The Fight Between the Rank and File of the Ganas and the Asuras

Vyasa said: —

Oh omniscient Sanatkumara, tell me what happened after that. When released by that being, where did Rahu go?

Suta said: —

On hearing the words of Vyasa, the great sage, the delighted son of Brahma, replied.

Rahu had been let off in the land of the outcastes. He too became an outcast and came to be known in the world as such. Considering that as his second birth he became humble. He became free from haughtiness. He slowly wended his way to the city of Jalandhara.

Sanatkumara said: —

After approaching Jalandhara, he explained everything concerning Siva in detail. On hearing it, the powerful son of the ocean Jalandhara became furious from head to foot. Then the infuriated Asura commanded the entire army of the Daityas to enter into the fray.

Jalandhara said: —

Let all the Asuras with their entire divisions start the fight.

Sanatkumara said: —

After ordering thus, the Lord of the Asuras, set out quickly accompanied by crores of Daityas. Then Sukra and Rahu with his severed head went ahead of him. In his quick jerky movement, his crown became dislodged and fell on the ground.

On seeing his enterprise, the gods including Indra went to Kailasa, the abode of Siva without being observed. After going there and seeing Siva, Indra and the gods joined their palms in reverence and eulogised.

The gods said: —

Oh Siva the merciful, obeisance be to you. Save us who have sought refuge in you. We are very much distressed by this harassment. All including Indra are deposed and compelled to stay on the earth. Hence in order to protect us please kill him.

Oh Siva, we have approached you unobserved by him. That powerful son of the ocean is coming hither to fight with you. You shall kill Jalandhara in the battle without delay. Save us who have sought refuge in you.

Sanatkumara said: —

On hearing the words of the gods, the bull bannered deity laughed. He called Visnu immediately and spoke these words.

Lord Siva said: —

Oh great Visnu, the distressed gods harassed by Jalandhara have sought refuge in me. How is it that Jalandhara was not killed in battle by you? Leaving off your own

Vaikuntha you have gone to his mansion, why? As I wanted to be free and sportful, I had appointed you for the protection of the good and the curbing of the wicked.

Visnu said: —

He was not killed in war by me because he was born from a part of yours. Moreover he is Laksmi's brother. Hence I couldn't kill him. He is very powerful, heroic and indefatigable. In fact a war was fought with him by me in the company of the gods. But my strategy was ineffective in regard to this great Danava. Seeing his great valour, I gave him a boon. For the boon, he asked me and Laxmi to stay in his mansion. Oh Lord, I could not deny him this boon.

Lord Siva said: —

Oh Visnu, foremost among the gods, please listen to my words attentively. I will kill the great Daitya Jalandhara. There is no doubt about this. Go back to your abode fearlessly. Let the gods too go back without fear and hesitation, considering the ruler of the Asuras already killed.

Sanatkumara said: —

On hearing the words of Lord Siva, the Lord of Laksmi immediately went to his abode without doubts along with the gods. In the meantime, Jalandhara reached Kailasa. Accompanied by a vast army he laid siege to Kailasa. He stood there like the god of death roaring like a lion.

On hearing the tumultuous roar of the Daityas, Lord Siva became very furious. He commanded Nandin, Vighnesvara, Kumara and all the other Ganas to get ready for the battle. Then at the ridges, valleys and sides of Kailasa, a terrible battle was fought between the leaders of the Pramathas and the Daityas. Weapons clashed with weapons.

The whole earth shook resonant with the sounds of great war drums. The whole atmosphere was filled with javeline, iron clubs, arrows, great pestles, iron rods, pikes and other weapons. With so many of the warriors killed, Bhargava only resuscitated the forces of Jalandhara using the Sanjivani. When Siva found out about it, he was terribly furious.

A terrible Krtya came out of Rudra's mouth. Her calves were as stout as Palmyra trees. Her mouth was huge and deep like mountain caverns. With her breasts she crushed huge trees.

She rushed immediately to the battle ground. The terrible Krtya roamed the battleground devouring the great Asuras. Fearlessly she rushed amid the battle-field where Bhargava was stationed.

Oh sage, she enveloped the whole sky with her terrible brilliance. She split the ground she trod; she stuffed Bhargava into her vaginal passage and vanished in the sky.

On seeing Bhargava seized, the invincible armies of the Daityas became dejected and fled from the battle ground. On seeing their army running away, the three most powerful Asuras started to kill all the Ganas. On seeing their army thus shattered, the infuriated leaders Nandin, Ganesa and Karttikeya hurriedly checked the rushing Daityas.

Description of the Special War

Sanatkumara said: —

On seeing the leaders of the Ganas, Nandin, Ganesa and Karttikeya, the Danavas rushed at them for a duel. Kalanemi clashed with Nandin; Sumbha fought Ganesa and Nisumbha hesitatingly rushed at Karttikeya.

With five arrows Nisumbha hit the peacock of Karttikeya in the chest and it fell unconscious. Then the infuriated Karttikeya discharged five arrows at his chariot and pierced the horses and the charioteer. The invincible hero hit Nisumbha with another sharp arrow quickly and roared. The Asura Nisumbha hit Karttikeya in the battle with his arrow as he roared. By the time the furious Karttikeya seized his spear, Nisumbha struck him with it.

Thus, a great fight between Karttikeya and Nisumbha ensued as they shouted heroically.

On the other side Nandin hit Kalanemi with seven arrows and pierced his horses, banner, chariot and charioteer. With very sharp shafts discharged from his bow, the infuriated Kalanemi cut the bow of Nandin. Defying the great demon Kalanemi the heroic Nandisvara hit him in the chest with his spear. With his horses and charioteer killed and himself wounded in the chest, he broke the top of a mountain and hit Nandin.

Then Sumbha and Ganesa seated respectively in a chariot and on a mouse fought each other with volleys of arrows. Ganesa hit Sumbha in his chest with an arrow and felled his charioteer with three arrows on the ground. Then the infuriated Sumbha covered Ganesa with a shower of arrows. Hitting the mouse with three arrows he roared like thunder. The mouse, pierced by the arrows, shook with acute pain. Ganesa was thrown off his vehicle and he became a foot soldier. Then Ganesa hit Sumbha in his chest with his axe and felled him to the ground. Thereafter he mounted his mouse again.

Then the Bhutas ran here and there devouring the Danavas. They jumped up and danced in the battle field and threw the Asura on the ground.

Then the army of the Daityas became agitated and dejected with many Daityas wounded, killed, felled to the ground and devoured. Thus Nandin, Karttikeya the formidable and valorous, Virabhadra and the other Ganas roared much in the battle.

On seeing the army destroyed, the powerful son of the ocean rushed at the Ganas in his chariot of waving and wafting colours. Hitting Nandin and Ganesa with five arrows each and Virabhadra with twenty he roared like thunder. Then Karttikeya the heroic son of Siva then swiftly hit the Daitya Jalandhara with his spear and roared. After falling down, Jalandhara got up again and attacked Kumara and Virabhadra both.

Virabhadra, the leader of the Ganas, fell on the ground with his head shattered by the iron club and shed much blood. On seeing Virabhadra fallen, the terrified Ganas abandoned the battle ground and fled to Lord Siva.

On hearing the tumultuous uproar of the Ganas, Siva asked them.

Siva said: —

Peace shall be established by me, of course. Then Lord Siva assured them of freedom from fear, increasing their enthusiasm.

Outraging the Modesty of Vrnda

Sanatkumara said: —

Then the great Lord Siva, assuming a terrible form, went laughingly to the battle-field and sat on his bull, accompanied by his heroic Ganas. On seeing Siva coming, the Ganas who were formerly defeated returned to fight roaring like lions.

On seeing Siva the terrible, all the Daityas fled for fear. On seeing the Daityas returning from the battle field, Jalandhara rushed at Siva discharging thousands of arrows. Thousands of leading Daityas, Nisumbha, Sumbha and others rushed at Siva, biting their lips. Similarly Kalanemi the hero, Khadgaroma, Balahaka, Ghasmara, Pracanda and others rushed at Siva.

Oh sage, the heroes Sumbha and others, covered the Ganas of Rudra with arrows and cut their limbs. On seeing his army of Ganas enveloped in darkness, Siva split the net of their arrows and encompassed the sky with his own.

He afflicted the Daityas with the gusts of wind raised by the arrows. He felled them to the ground with fierce volleys of arrows. He severed the head of Khadgaroma from his body with his axe. He shattered the head of Balahaka with his club into two pieces. He tied the Daitya Ghasmara with his noose and dashed him on the ground. With his trident, he chopped off the great hero Pracanda.

Some of the Asuras were killed by the bull. Some were struck by the arrows. Like elephants harassed by lions, the Asuras were unable to stay there. Then the great Asura Jalandhara became infuriated and rebuked the Daityas in the battle. The courageous Daitya mocked Sumbha and others and spoke thus.

Jalandhara said: —

Of what avail is your boasting about the pedigree of your mother if you flee back on being attacked? To die cowardly while you profess to be heroes is not commendable, nor does it yield heaven. Death in battle is preferable. It yields all cherished desires. It is especially conducive to fame. No sensible man should ever be afraid of death. Hence, cast off all fear for death. Come and fight in war joyously.

Sanatkumara said: —

Saying this, he tried to encourage his heroes in several ways. But the frightened demons did not regain courage. They fled from the battle in a trice.

On seeing his army run away Jalandhara became very furious. Then the infuriated Jalandhara challenged for a battle in a stentorian voice like the sound of fierce thunderbolt.

Jalandhara said: —

Oh ascetic, fight with me now. What is the use of slaying these? Show me what little strength you have.

Sanatkumara said: —

After saying this, Jalandhara hit the bull-bannered Siva with an incessant volley of arrows. Laughingly, Lord Siva split all the arrows of Jalandhara by discharging his own sharp arrows even before his arrows reached him.

Then with seven arrows, he split the horses, banner, umbrella and the bow of Daitya Jalandhara. The infuriated Asura, devoid of a chariot and with bow split up, rushed at Siva lifting his mace vigorously. Siva immediately split the mace hurled at him. Yet Jlandhara rushed at Siva with the mailed fist lifted up. By a volley of arrows Jalandhara was hurled back a Krosa by Siva of indefatigable enterprise.

Then, considering Siva more powerful, Jalandharaa, created the illusion of Gandharvas that mysteriously fascinated even Siva. By the power of his Maya, hosts of Gandharvas and celestial damsels came into view for fascinating Siva. They were dancing and singing songs in their beauty. On seeing that wonderful feat, Siva was fascinated. He was not conscious of even the garments let down from the hands.

On seeing Siva concentrated on the dance, Jalandhara, urged by lust, immediately went to the place where Gauri stood. With his demoniac Maya he assumed the form of Siva. He was seated on the great bull. In every respect, Oh Vyasa, Jalandhara appeared like Siva. On seeing Siva coming, the beloved of Siva came out from the midst of her female friends within the range of his vision. When the Lord of Asuras saw the bountiful Parvati, he let drops of semen fall and his limbs became numb.

On realising that he was the demon, the terrified Gauri vanished immediately to the northern shore of the Manasa lake. Unable to see her and touch her, the Daitya immediately went to the place where Lord Siva stood to fight him. Then Parvati remembered Lord Visnu mentally. Immediately she saw the Lord seated near her. On seeing Visnu bowing to her with palms joined in reverence, Parvati the beloved of Siva, the mother of the universe, spoke.

Parvati said: —

Oh Visnu, is it not known to you that the wicked Daitya Jalandhara perpetrated a wonderfully base deed?

Visnu said: —

Oh mother, by your favour that incident is known to me. Whatever command you give me I shall obey.

Parvati said: —

He himself has shown the path. The same shall be done to him. At my bidding, violate the chastity of his wife.

Outraging the modesty of Vrnda

Vyasa said: —

Oh omniscient Sanatkumara, please narrate, what did Visnu do?

Sanatkumara said: —

After going to the city of Jalandhara, Visnu thought of violating the chastity of Vrnda. He assumed a wonderful body and stationed himself in a park in the city. He made Vrnda see a dream.

The gentle lady Vrnda, though pure, had a very bad dream at night on account of Visnu's power of illusion. In the dream she saw the naked form of her husband anointed with oil and seated on a buffalo. He was proceeding in the southern direction. His head had been completely shaved. He was wearing black flowers to decorate himself. He was being served by a number of Asuras. He was completely encompassed by darkness. Later, towards the end of the night she had various bad dreams.

Then the lady woke up still thinking of the dream she had. She saw the rising sun with a hole in the middle and fading repeatedly. On realising that it was a bad portent, the terrified lady began to cry.

With two of her friends she then went to the park in the city. Even there she did not find herself at ease. Then she wandered from forest to forest. She was not even conscious of herself. The wandering lady saw two demons with terrible faces with shining curved fang like teeth. Terrified on seeing them, the lady fled from there and saw an ascetic of calm countenance observing silence and accompanied by his disciple.

Putting her tender creeper-like hands around his neck due to fright she gasped out— 'Oh sage, save me. I have sought refuge in you.' Seeing the agitated lady followed by the demons, the sage drove them back with a loud bellowing sound of 'Hum'. On seeing them go away, freed from the fear, she bowed down to the great sage and spoke.

Vrnda said: —

Oh leader of the sages, you have saved me from those wicked demons. You are competent in every respect. You are omniscient. I wish to submit a query. Be pleased to hear it.

Oh Lord, Jalandhara my husband has gone to fight Siva. How does he fare in the war? Please tell me.

Sanatkumara said: —

On hearing her words, the sage feigned a deceptive silence and looked at her sympathetically. Right then, two monkeys came and bowed to him. At a significant gesture from his eyebrows, the monkeys rose into the sky. Within a trice, they came back with Jalandhara's head, body and limbs. On seeing the head, body and limbs of her husband, Vrnda fell unconscious, extremely pained at the misery of her Lord.

Vrnda said: —

Oh Lord, please get up. Talk to me again and humour me. How can you be defeated? You defeated the greatest of gods including Visnu then how can you be killed now? Oh great Daitya, you did not know the reality of Siva nor did you pay heed to my words when I told you not to go against Siva, the supreme Brahman.

Oh excellent sage, take pity on me and resuscitate my Lord. Oh great sage, I know that you are competent to enliven him again. Hence please resuscitate my beloved husband.

The sage said: —

This Daitya cannot be enlivened because he has been killed by Siva in the battle. Those killed in battle by Siva never return to life. Still, knowing the eternal Dharma that those who seek refuge should be protected, I shall resuscitate him urged by pity.

After saying this and restoring him to life, that sage who was Visnu, vanished from the scene. Jalandhara thus revived to life. Delighted in mind, he embraced Vrnda and kissed her face. On seeing her husband, Vrnda too was delighted. She forgot her sorrow. She considered everything a dream.

Delighted in the heart and with all the dormant passions kindled up, she sported with him for many days in the middle of that forest. Then, after many days, at the end of the sexual intercourse, she realised that it was Visnu. Vrnda rebuked him angrily and spoke thus, Sanatkumara said.

Vrnda said: —

Fie on this misdeed of Visnu in outraging the modesty of another man's wife. I have now realised you as the wielder of illusion, appearing in the guise of an ascetic.

Sanatkumara said: —

Oh Vyasa, saying thus, in great anger she showed her brilliant powers as a staunch chaste lady by cursing Visnu.

Vrnda said: —

Oh foe of the Daityas, defiler of other people's virtue, take this curse from me. The two persons whom you made to appear in front of me shall become Raksasas and abduct your wife. You will be distressed on account of separation from your wife. You will seek the help of monkeys in the forest.

Sanatkumara said: —

After saying this, Vrnda entered into fire though prevented by Visnu. Then the great wife of Jalandhara immediately went to Sivaloka. The refulgence of Vrnda became merged in Parvati. Thus Vrnda attained salvation. Visnu stood there, looking at the pyre. He was not at peace.

Jalandhara is Slain

Oh great son of Brahma, what happened thereafter in the battle? How was Asura killed? Please narrate.

Sanatkumara said: —

Unable to see Parvati, the king of Daityas returned to the battle ground. The groups of deceptive Gandharvas vanished. It was only then that the bull-bannered deity regained awareness of the surroundings.

On seeing the illusion vanish, Siva woke up. The annihilator became very furious. He approached Jalandhara angrily in order to fight with him. On seeing Siva approaching again, the Asura showered him with arrows. Lord Siva immediately split the cluster of arrows by means of his own excellent arrows.

Seeing Siva exhibiting wonderful feats of valour, Jalandhara created Parvati by means of his illusion in order to delude Siva. Siva saw Parvati tied to the chariot and crying. She was being harassed by Nisumbha, Sumbha and other Daityas.

On seeing that, Siva became dispirited and dejected in the mind. He remained silent with face drooping down, utterly dejected, exhausted and forgetful of his own prowess.

Then Jalandhara hurriedly hit Siva in his chest, belly and the head with three arrows that went deep down as far as their feathered tail. Then witin a trice, Lord Siva assumed a terrific form, dreadfully blazing.

On seeing his excessively terrible form, the Daityas fled to the ten different quarters. They were unable to stay facing him. The illusion created by Jalandhara had vanished in an instant. On seeing Sumbha and Nisumbha fleeing, the infuriated Siva rebuked them and cursed as follows.

Siva said: —

You are wicked and excessively roguish. You have offended me by harassing Parvati. Now both of you have deserted the battle ground. A person fleeing the battle ground shall not be killed. So I will not kill you. Since you have escaped from a fight with me you would be killed by Parvati.

Sanatkumara said: —

Even as Siva was saying, Jalandhara became very furious with Siva. One after the other, he showered many sharp arrows on Siva in the battle. The whole of the Earth became enveloped in darkness by his arrows. Siva split the arrows swiftly.

Becoming excessively angry, Siva made a mysteriously terrible wheel in the great waters by means of his big toe. Creating a sharp wheel in the waters of the ocean and remembering that the three worlds had been harassed by Jalandhara, Lord Siva laughingly said.

Siva said: —

Oh Jalandhara, if you are powerful enough to lift the wheel created by me with the leg, you will be competent to stand and fight with me, not otherwise.

Jalandhara asked: —

After uplifting the wheel, I shall be killing you with your Ganas. Oh Lord Siva, who is there in the three worlds that can escape being pierced by my arrows? Even in my childhood, Lord Brahma had been defeated by my vigour. Indra, Agni, Yama, Kubera and others were unable to endure my valour. I have destroyed and conquered everything that I desired. How can you think that I will not be worthy to fight with you?

Sanatkumara said: —

After saying this to Lord Siva, the son of the ocean did not move. On hearing the inauspicious words of the Daitya, Lord Siva laughed mockingly and became furious.

Siva held in his hand the wheel Sudarsana which he had made with his toe and got ready to kill him. Lord Siva hurled the discus Sudarsana which resembled a crore suns and the fire of dissolution.

Blazing the heaven and the earth, the discus hit Jalandhara and severed his head with wide gaping eyes. The body of the son of the ocean fell on the ground from the chariot making the earth resonant. The head too fell. There was a great hue and cry.

His body fell in two halves. The whole universe was filled with his terrible blood. His entire blood and flesh, at the bidding of Siva was taken to the hell Maharaurava and became a big pit of blood there.

His splendour that came out of his body merged into Siva just like the splendour that came out of the body of Vrnda merged into Parvati.

On seeing Jalandhara killed, the gods, the Gandharvas and the serpents became highly delighted. The gods, Siddhas and great sages were delighted. Making showers of flowers they sang his glory loudly.

Oh sage, the quarters became clear when Vrnda's husband was killed. The three winds, gentle to the touch and sanctifying, blew. Thus the entire universe of the three worlds regained their earlier health and normalcy.

The Vanishing of Visnu's Delusion

Vyasa said: —

Oh son of Brahma, after enchanting Vrnda what did he do? Where did he go?

Sanatkumara said: —

Oh Vyasa, listen. When Brahma and other gods became silent after eulogising Lord Siva, he spoke delightedly.

Siva said: —

Oh Brahma, Oh you excellent gods, it is for you that Jalandhara has been killed by me although he was a part of myself. Have or have not you attained happiness now? It is for you that I indulge in sports though I am always free from all aberrations.

Oh great Lord, all the gods have been saved by you from the danger of the enemy but another event has happened. What shall we do in that respect?

The gods said: —

Oh Lord, Vrnda was fascinated by Visnu. She burnt herself on the pyre and attained the great goal. But Visnu, deluded by your illusion, is excessively agitated by the beauty of Vrnda. He has smeared himself with the ashes from her pyre. We have tried a lot but Visnu, deluded by your illusion, does not come to his former self. Oh Lord Siva, be pleased. Restore Visnu to his former self.

Lord Siva said: —

Oh Brahma, Oh gods, you listen to my words attentively. My illusion deludes all the worlds. It cannot be transgressed. That illusion is given various names : Uma, Mahadevi, the mother of the three deities, the greatest, primordial Mulaprakrti and the lovely woman Parvato. Seek refuge in that fascinating goddess named illusion, for the removal of Visnu's delusion. Sing the eulogy that satisfies my Sakti. If she is delighted, she will carry out your tasks.

The gods said: —

We bow to the primordial Prakrti from which emanate the three attributes, Sattva, Rajas and Tamas. These that cause creation, sustenance and annihilation, and by whose desire the universe is evolved and dissolved. May the great illusion save us.

Oh great goddess, please carry out our tasks. O Parvati, please remove the delusion of Visnu. Oh goddess Durga, obeisance be to you.

Oh Siva, when the fight between Jalandhara and Siva started, for killing Jalandhara, Vrnda was deluded by Visnu at the bidding of Gauri. She was made to forsake her virtue and reduced to ashes in the fire. She attained salvation. Then Jalandhara was slain in the battle by Siva who took pity on us and who always blesses his devotees. We have been relieved from his fear.

It is at his bidding that we all have sought refuge in you. Infatuated by the beauty of Vrnda, Visnu is staying there itself. He has lost his balance. He is deluded. He has smeared himself with the ashes from her pyre.

Oh great goddess, be merciful. Enlighten Visnu so that he shall return to his region and carry out the task of the gods with a settled mind.

Sanatkumara said: —

Eulogising thus, the gods saw a sphere of refulgence in the sky pervading all the quarters with its flames. They heard a celestial voice from the sky bestowing their desire.

The celestial voice said: —

Oh gods, it is I who stand in three forms by the variety of the three attributes. Rajas, Sattva and Tamas. The three forms are Gauri, Laksmi, and Sarasvati. Hence, you go to them respectfully at my bidding. If they are pleased they will fulfil your desire.

Sanatkumara said: —

On hearing the speech, the gods, urged by it bowed respectfully to Gauri, Laksmi and Sarasvati. Brahma and other gods eulogised the goddesses with various speeches and bowed their heads.

Then the goddesses appeared in front of them. On seeing them, the gods eulogised them with great devotion and delighted minds. They submitted what they wanted to be carried out. Being pleased, the goddesses addressed them after giving them seeds.

The goddesses said: —

Sow these seeds in the place where Visnu is standing. Then your task will be fulfilled.

Sanatkumara said: —

Oh sage, after saying this, the goddesses vanished. Then Brahma, Indra and the other gods went to the place where Visnu was. The gods sowed those seeds in the ground where the pyre of Vrnda had been lit. Oh sage, they stayed there thinking these as parts of Siva's Sakti.

Out of the seeds sown, three plants shot up—the Myrobalan, the Jasmine and the holy basil.

The Myrobalan is born of the creator's Sakti, the jasmine of Laksmi and holy basil of Gauri. On seeing the plants in the forms of ladies Visnu stood up with excitement of infatuation over them. On seeing them he was deluded and his mind became overwhelmed by lust. The two plants—the holy basil and Myrobalan looked at him lovingly. The womanlike plant born out of the seed by the Sakti of Laksmi became jealous of him.

Then Visnu forgot his sorrow. Accompanied by them he went to Vaikuntha fully satisfied. He was bowed to by all the gods. On seeing Visnu settled again in Vaikuntha, Brahma, Indra and other gods bowed to and eulogised him and then left for their respective abodes.

The Birth of Sankhacuda

Sanatkumara said: —

Oh sage, now listen to another story of Siva lovingly. The story narrates how the heroic Danava Sankhacuda who harassed the gods was killed by Siva.

The sage Kasyapa son of Marici and grandson of Brahma was a virtuous Prajapati engaged in creation. He possessed great learning. Daksa gave him his thirteen daughters in marriage.

Among the wives of Kasyapa the excellent lady Danu was one. She was very beautiful, chaste and tenderly nurtured by her husband. Many powerful sons were born to that lady Danu. One of them is Vipracitti who was very powerful and valorous. His virtuous son Dambha of self-control was a great devotee of Visnu.

No son was born to him. Hence the hero became worried. He made the preceptor Sukra his initiator and learnt the mantra of Krsna. He performed a great penance in the holy centre Puskara for a hundred thousand years. Seating himself in a stable pose he performed the Japa of Krsna mantra for a long time.

While he was performing the penance, an unbearable refulgence sprang up blazing from his head and spread everywhere. All the gods, sages and Manus were scorched by that. With Indra ahead they sought refuge in Brahma. Bowing to Brahma, the bestower of riches, they eulogised him and narrated this event to him.

On hearing that, Brahma accompanied them to Vaikuntha in order to tell the same to Visnu in its entirety. After going there they eulogised Visnu the Lord of the three worlds. Then they told him everything.

The gods said: —

Oh Lord of gods we do not know how this happened to cause this. Please tell us. By what refulgence have all of us been scorched? You are the protector of the distressed and dispirited servants. Save us oh Visnu.

Visnu said: —

Oh gods, be calm and unperturbed, do not be afraid. The Asura Dambha, a devotee of mine, is performing a penance seeking for a son. I shall bestow a boon and quieten him.

Sanatkumara said: —

Oh sage, on being consoled thus, Brahma and other gods became encouraged and they returned to their respective abodes. In order to grant the boon, Visnu went to Puskara where Dambha was performing penance. On reaching there Visnu consoled Dambha who was repeating his name and spoke to him.

Visnu said: —

Mention the boon you wish to be granted.

Dambha said: —

Oh Lord of gods. Obeisance be to you, oh Lord of Laksmi, oh Lord of the three worlds, please take pity on me. Please give me a powerful and valorous son who will be your devotee, who will be invincible to the gods and who will conquer the three worlds,

Sanatkumara said: —

On being thus requested by the Lord of Danavas, Visnu granted him the boon. Oh sage, making him desist from the penance he vanished from the place.

Within a short time, his fortunate wife became pregnant. Oh sage, it was Sudama, a cowherd, one of the leading comrades of Krsna who had been cursed by Radha, that entered her womb.

At the proper time the chaste lady gave birth to a brilliant son. The father invited sages and performed the post-natal rites. The boy was named Sankhacuda. In the abode of his father he grew up like the moon in the bright half. Learning all the lessons in childhood he became resplendent.

The Penance and Marriage of Sankhacuda

Sanatkumara said: —

As instructed, Sankhacuda performed a penance in Puskara for a long time in order to propitiate Brahma with devotion. He concentrated his mind, controlled the senses and organs of activities, and muttered the mantra of Brahma imparted by his preceptor.

Lord Brahma went to Sankhacuda who was practising penance in order to grant him the boon soon.

Brahma said to him, 'Tell me the boon you wish to choose.'

On seeing Brahma, the king of Danavas bowed to him humbly and eulogised him with words of devotion. He requested Brahma to grant him the power of being invincible to the gods. With a delighted mind, Brahma said, 'Be it so'.

He gave him the divine amulet of Srikrsna the most auspicious of all auspicious things in the universe, that yielded victory everywhere.

Brahma said: —

You now go to Badari. There you marry Tulasi who is performing penance just at her own will. She is the daughter of Dharmadhvaja.

Sanatkumara said: —

Brahma instructed him thus and vanished. Then Sankhacuda, whose penance had been fruitful, tied the most auspicious amulet round his neck. At the behest of Brahma, the Danava went to Badarikasram with delight beaming in his face.

The Danava Sankhacuda casually visited the place where the daughter of Dharmadhvaja, Tulasi was performing the penance. The smiling beautiful gentle woman fully bedecked in ornaments cast loving glances at the great man. On seeing that charming, tender, beautiful and chaste lady, he stopped near her and spoke to her sweetly.

Sankhacuda said: —

Who are you, please? Whose daughter? What are you doing? Why do you stay here and observe silence? Consider me as your devoted slave.

Tulasi said: —

I am the daughter of Dharmadhvaja. I am performing penance. I stay in this hermitage. Who are you? You can go as you please.

Sankhacuda said: —

Oh gentle lady, what you said now is not entirely false. It is partially true also. You are the foremost among chaste ladies. I am not a lusty person of sinful nature. I think you too are not like that. I come to you now at the behest of Brahma. Oh gentle lady, I shall take your hand by the Gandharva rites of marriage. I am Sankhacuda, the router of the gods. Oh gentle lady, don't you know me? Have you never heard of me? I am a scion of the Danu family. I am Danava, the son of Dambha. In the previous birth I was the cowherd Sudama, a comrade of Krsna. Due to the curse of Radha I have become a Danava now. By the favour of Krsna I remember events of my previous birth. I know everything.

Sanatkumara said: —

After saying this to her, Sankhacuda stopped. Tulasi, who was thus addressed truthfully and respectfully by the king of Danavas, was delighted and she spoke smilingly.

Tulasi said: —

I have now been overpowered by you who have Sattvika thoughts. That man is blessed in the world who is not overwhelmed by a woman. You have been tested by me in order to know your knowledge and power. A woman must test her bridegroom before wooing him.

Sanatkumara said: —

Even as Tulasi was saying so, Brahma, the creator, came there and spoke these words.

Brahma said: —

Oh Sankhacuda, why do you hold discussion with her? Marry her according to the Gandharva form of marriage. You are a jewel among men. And she, the chaste lady, is a jewel among women. The union of an intelligent lady with an intelligent man must necessarily be virtuous.

Oh chaste lady, why shall you test such a good and noble husband? He can suppress the gods, Asuras and Danavas too. You may sport with him for as long, as you please, in different centres all over the world. In the end, he will attain Srikrsna again in the Goloka. After he is dead, you will attain the four-armed Lord in Vaikuntha.

Sanatkumara said: —

After conferring blessings, Brahma returned to his abode. The Danava accepted her by means of the Gandharva rite. After marrying her he went to his father's place. In the beautiful apartment he sported with her.

The Previous Birth of Sankhacuda

Sanatkumara said: —

When Sankhacuda returned home duly married, after performing the penance and receiving the boons, Danavas and others rejoiced. Leaving their world and accompanied by their preceptor, the Asuras assembled and approached the Danava. They stayed with him alone.

On seeing the family preceptor, Sankhacuda bowed to him with devotion and prostrated before him with respect. After conferring his excellent benediction, Sukra, the family preceptor, narrated the tales of the gods and Danavas.

He expatiate on the natural enmity of the two, the invariable defeat of the Asuras, the victory of the gods and the help rendered by Brhaspati. With the consent of the Asuras, the preceptor Sukra made him the emperor of Danavas, Asuras and others with jubilant festivities.

The delighted Asuras were highly joyous. They offered him presents lovingly. The son of Dambha, Sankhacuda shone as the emperor of Asuras. Taking a vast army of Daityas, Danavas and Raksasas and seated in his chariot, he marched quickly to the city of Indra with the intention to conquer it.

On hearing that Sankhacuda was coming, Indra, accompanied by the gods, made preparations for a fight. Then a tremendous fight ensued between the Asuras and the gods delighting the heroic and terrifying the cowardly.

When the warriors roared in the battle, there was a tumultuous noise. The powerful gods fought with the Asuras ferociously and defeated them. They were afraid and fled.

On seeing them fleeing, their leader Sankhacuda roared like a lion and fought with the gods. With his power and force he distressed the gods. The gods could not endure his dazzling brilliance. They fled. The gods took shelter in the caves of the mountains. They lost their independence. They were subjugated.

Thus the son of Dambha, conquered all the worlds and took up the powers of the gods. He kept the three worlds under his control. He partook of all the shares in sacrifices. He became Indra and ruled the universe. Thus Sankhacuda enjoyed the kingdom of the worlds for many years. He became a great emperor. There was no famine, plague or pestilence in his realm. The planets were not inauspicious. There was no worry or sickness among the people. The subjects were happy forever. Except for the gods all living beings were happy and free from distress.

Sankhacuda was a close friend of Krsna, the resident of Goloka. He was powerful, and always engaged in devotion to Krsna. Although he was a Danava, his nature was different. He was born as a Danava due to a previous curse.

Oh dear, thereafter, the defeated gods, deprived of their kingdom, consulted among themselves and went to Brahma's assembly chamber along with the sages. They saw the creator and bowed to and eulogised him. With distress they explained to him everything in detail.

After consoling the gods and the sages, Brahma accompanied by them went to Vaikuntha.

Accompanied by the gods, Brahma saw the Lord of Laksmi decorated with a crown, earrings and a garland of wild flowers.

On seeing Visnu, they bowed to the Lord. They eulogised him with palms joined in reverence.

The gods said: —

Oh Lord of the universe, save us who have sought refuge in you. Oh Lord Visnu, you alone are the protector of the worlds. Obeisance be to you.

Visnu said: —

Why have you come to Vaikuntha inaccessible even to Yogins? What distress has befallen you? Tell me just here.

Sanatkumara said: —

On hearing the words of Visnu and bowing to him, they narrated to him the activities of Sankhacuda and the distress suffered by the gods. On hearing that Visnu who knew everything laughed. The Lord then told Brahma the secret of Sankhacuda, Sanatkumara said.

Lord Visnu said: —

Oh lotus-born Brahma, I know everything about Sankhacuda, a great devotee of mine, of great splendour and who had been formerly a cowherd. Hear all the details about him, the old narrative. There is nothing to be suspected. Siva will necessarily perform what is good.

The Goloka is near Kailasa. Siva's cowshed is situated there. Krsna having my form stays there at Siva's behest. It is to tend his cows and bulls that he has been ordered by him. Deriving happiness from him he took up sports there. His wife Radha is the mother of the universe. Her form is greater than Prakrti. Many cowherds and cowherdesses born of her live there. They are sportively inclined and follow Radha and Krsna.

That very same Sudama, now born as Sankhacuda, has been fascinated by Siva's illusion. Cursed by Radha he is born as a Danava to his distress. Krsna has already ordained that the death of Sankhacuda will be by Rudra's trident. Casting off his body he will become his comrade again. Oh Lord of gods, knowing this you need not have any fear. Let us seek refuge in Siva. He will do everything conducive to our good.

Sanatkumara said: —

After saying this and mentally thinking upon Siva, Visnu went to Sivaloka accompanied by Brahma. Radha was a cowherdess and a favourite mistress of Krsna. She is worshipped among the Vaisnavas as an incarnation of Laksmi as Krsna is of Visnu.

Upon reaching, they eulogised Siva with devotion and love. Then they narrated the plight of the gods. They told Siva about Sankhacuda who was born as a Danava after Radha cursed him. They told the mighty Lord about the harassment faced by the gods at his hands. They eulogised and requested Siva to kill him as he cannot be killed by anyone else.

Siva's Advice

Sanatkumara said: —

On hearing these words of the distressed Visnu and Brahma, Siva laughingly spoke in the rumbling tone of the cloud.

Siva said: —

Oh dear Visnu, O Brahma, cast off your fear from all sides. Certainly something good will result from the activities of Sankhacuda. I know all the details of his activities factually as well as those of Sudama the cowherd devotee of Krsna. At my bidding Visnu has assumed the form of Krsna and is stationed in the cowshed in the beautiful Goloka presided over by me. Considering himself independent under a delusion, he indulged in many kinds of sportive dalliance like a deluded licentious person.

On seeing his excessive delusion as a result of my deceptive art, I suppressed their virtuous intellect and made them suffer curse. Having thus performed my sport, I suppressed the illusion. Regaining knowledge, they got rid of delusion and became well-intentioned. They came to me in a piteous plight. Overwhelmed by shame, they told me all the details. Dejected, they asked me to save them.

Then I, becoming delighted, told them these words, 'Krsna, you forget your fear at my behest. I am the protector, always infused with love. Good will befall you. All this has happened at my will. Go to your abode along with Radha and your comrade. He will become a Danava here in Bharata, certainly. At the proper time I shall redeem you from the curse'.

Then Srikrsna and Radha accepted readily. Srikrsna the intelligent rejoiced and returned to his abode. There they engaged themselves in propitiating me and biding their time. Realising that everything is subject to my control and his will is not independent, Sudama became the Lord of Danavas as a result of the curse of Radha. The virtuous demon Sankhacuda distresses and harasses the gods with his might. He is evil minded to this extent. He has been deluded by my deception and hence he seeks the help of evil ministers. But myself being the chastiser of the wicked you can get rid of his fear quickly.

Sanatkumara said: —

Oh sage, by the time Siva completed this expatiation, another event happened there. Listen to it.

In the meantime, Krsna came there along with Radha and his attendant cowherds in order to propitiate Lord Siva. Devoutly bowing to the Lord, meeting Visnu with respect and honoured by Brahma with love he stood there awaiting Siva's behest. Realising the principle of Siva and getting rid of his delusion Krsna eulogised Siva.

Lord Krsna said: —

Oh supreme God, be pleased. Oh Siva, everything originates from you. Oh supreme Lord, everything merges in you. Be pleased.

Considering myself above all, I sported about, under the delusion. I reaped the fruit thereof. He who went astray was cursed. Oh Lord, my leading comrade Sudama the cowherd is born as a Danava. Uplift us. Please redeem us from the curse. Save us who have sought refuge in you.

Lord Siva said: —

Oh Krsna, O Lord of cowherdesses, leave off your fear. Be happy. Oh dear, all this has been brought about by me with blessing in disguise. Good will befall you. Go back to your excellent abode. You shall be cautious and guarded in your position of authority. Sport about as you please. Accompanied by Radha and your comrades, carry out your task duly. Oh Krsna, your comrade, the most beloved Sudama is born of a Danava now and he harasses the universe. He has become a Danava, an enemy of the gods, named Sankhacuda as a result of the power of Radha's curse. He hates and belongs to the party of Daityas. It is for their sake that Brahma and Visnu have come here and sought refuge in me. There is no doubt in this that I will relieve them of their distress.

Oh Visnu, Oh Brahma, lovingly listen to my words. Be fearless. Go to Rudra, a resident of Kailasa, who has my excellent and perfect form. He has manifested himself for the task of the gods with a separate form and features. It is for this purpose that the Lord assumes my form fully and perfectly stays on the mountain Kailasa. There is no difference in him from us both. He shall be served by you two and all living beings.

Sanatkumara said: —

Oh Vyasa, Visnu and Brahma became delighted and relieved of fear. After bowing again and again to Siva they hastened to Vaikuntha. Having come there and mentioning everything to the gods, Brahma and Visnu went to Kailasa taking the gods with them.

On seeing Lord Siva there, who had taken a body for protecting the distressed, they eulogised him as before with devotion and choking words. They joined their palms in reverence humbly and with drooping shoulders.

The gods said: —

Oh great god, Oh Siva, we seek refuge in you. Please save the terrified gods. Please slay Sankhacuda, the king of Asura and the destroyer of the gods. The gods have been defeated and harassed by him. Like men they are roaming on the earth divested of their powers. Their region the Devaloka has become very dreary to look at due to fear. Oh great Lord, save Indra from fright by killing that ruler of Danavas.

Lord Siva said: —

Oh Visnu, Oh Brahma, Oh Gods, return to your own abodes by all means. I shall kill Sankhacuda along with his followers and attendants. There is no doubt about it.

Sanatkumara said: —

On hearing the words of Lord Siva they were excessively delighted considering the Danava already killed. After bowing to Lord Siva, Visnu went to Vaikuntha and Brahma to Satyaloka. The god and others went to their own abodes.

The Emissary Is Sent

Sanatkumara said: —

Then Lord Siva decided in his mind to slay Sankhacuda in accordance with the wishes of the gods. He made his friend Puspadanta his messenger and sent him in a wonderful chariot hurriedly to Sankhacuda.

Reaching there, he saw the excellent abode of Sankhacuda in the middle. Passing beyond that door he joyously went in. Going in he saw Sankhacuda, the ruler of Danavas, seated on a gem-set throne in the midst of heroic warriors. Seeing him, Puspadanta was struck with wonder. He gave the message of war as conveyed by Siva.

Puspadanta said: —

Oh great king, I am the Emissary of Siva named Puspadanta. Please listen to what is mentioned by Siva himself. I am telling you the same.

Siva said: —

Now, give back their kingdom to the gods and their authority. If not, fight with me, the greatest of the good warriors. The gods have sought refuge in me. If you do not do so, I will certainly slay you.

I am Siva, the destroyer. I have granted protection to all the gods. Oh Lord of Danavas, consider and let me know one of the two alternatives specifically, whether you will return the kingdom or fight.

Puspadanta said: —

Oh Lord of Danavas, what has been stated by Siva has been conveyed to you. Siva's words have never gone in vain. I wish to return to my Lord Siva immediately. After going back, what shall I tell Siva?

Sankhacuda said: —

I will never return the kingdom to the god. The earth shall be enjoyed by heroic warriors. Oh Siva, I shall fight with you. The hero who allows another to supersede him is the basest in the world. Hence Oh Siva I shall certainly march towards you just now. I will reach there in the morning. Oh messenger, go and tell all this to Siva.

Sanatkumara said: —

On hearing these words of Sankhacuda, the emissary of Siva laughed aloud and then spoke haughtily to the Lord of the Asuras.

Puspadanta said: —

Oh Great king, you will not be able to face even the Ganas of Siva then how do you think you can face Siva himself? So return the positions of authority to the gods entirely. Move immediately to Patala if you wish to live.

Oh excellent Danava, do not regard Siva an ordinary deity. He is indeed the great soul, the Lord of the Lord of all. Indra and other gods abide by his commands. The Siddhas, the patriarchs, the sages and the serpent Lords all follow suit.

Siva is the perfect form of gods, the cause of the annihilation of the worlds, the goal of the good, the destroyer of the wicked. He is the overLord of Brahma. He is Lord Siva even into Visnu. Oh excellent Danava, his behest should never be slighted.

Return their kingdoms to the gods as well as their positions of authority. Oh dear, thus you will fare well. Otherwise, terror will strike you.

Sankhacuda said: —

I shall neither give up the kingdom nor the positions of authority, without a fight with him. This is certain. I tell you the truth. Go and tell Siva exactly what I have said to you. Let him do what is proper. Do not talk much.

Sanatkumara said: —

Oh good sage, Puspadanta thus addressed by the Asura, returned to Lord Siva and told him everything duly.

March of the Victorious Lord Siva

Sanatkumara said: —

On hearing those words of the emissary, the infuriated emperor of the gods, Siva spoke to Virabhadra and other Ganas.

Siva said: —

Oh Virabhadra, Oh Nandin, Oh eight Bhairavas, the frontier guards, let the Ganas start along with my sons, at my bidding. Let those strong ones be ready and fully equipped with weapons. Let Bhadrakali start with her army for the war. I shall start just now for slaying Sankhacuda.

Sanatkumara said: —

Having ordered thus, Lord Siva started along with his army. His delighted heroic Ganas followed him. In the meantime Karttikeya and Ganesa, the overall generals of the army, came near Siva joyously, fully equipped with weapons and ready for war.

Each of the chiefs had an army of a few hundred crores. With thousands, hundreds and twenties of crores, many heroes came there to take part in that festival of War. Virabhadra came there with a thousand crores of Bhutas, three crores of Pramathas and sixty four crores of Lomajas.

These and other leading Ganas, powerful and innumerable, started to fight fearlessly with Sankhacuda. They resembled Brahma, Indra and Visnu. They were as refulgent as a crore suns.

Oh sage, some of them were the residents of the earth; some of the Patala, some of the sky and some of the seven heavens. All the Sivaganas, residents of different regions went to fight with the Danavas.

The great goddess Bhadrakali herself with hundred arms was seated in an aerial chariot studded with gems. Her tongue was as long as a yojana and terrible. She bore many divine weapons that she held in her hands.

She came and stood there with three crores of Yoginis and three crores of terrible Dakinis. Bhutas, Pretas, Pisacas, Kusmandas, Brahmaraksasas, Vetalas, Yaksas, Kinnaras and Raksasas too came there. Skanda was surrounded by them all. He bowed to Siva and at his bidding stayed near his father to assist him.

The fearless, fierce Siva gathered his armies and went to fight Sankhacuda. The great god stationed himself at the foot of a beautiful Banyan tree on the banks of the river Candrabhaga for the emancipation of the gods.

The March of Sankhacuda

Vyasa said: —

Oh dear son of Brahma, live long for many years. When Siva's emissary had departed, what did the valorous Danava, Sankhacuda do? Please mention that in detail.

Sanatkumara said: —

When the messenger returned, the valorous Sankhacuda went in and told his wife Tulasi all the details.

Sankhacuda said: —

Oh dear lady, infuriated by the words of Siva's messenger, I have prepared for a war. Hence I am going to fight. You carry out my directions.

Sanatkumara said: —

After saying this and slighting Siva, that demon professing to be wise advised his wife in various ways and sported with her with delight. Throughout that night, the couple indulged in sexual dalliance. Uttering coaxing and cajoling words, practising various erotic arts, they immersed themselves in the ocean of happiness.

He got up in the Brahma Muhurta, and finished his daily routine in the morning. He then performed the offering of charitable gifts. He crowned his son as the Lord of Danavas. He entrusted his wife, his kingdom and his riches to the care of his son. Then he called his general and ordered him to be ready for the war.

Sankhacuda said: —

Oh general, let the heroic warriors start the war. Let them be ready for action; they have been trained well for the war. At my bidding, let the hundred armed families of Dhaumras speedily set out to fight with Siva. At my behest, let the Kalakeyas Mauryas, Dauhrdas and the Kalakas set out ready for the fight with Siva.

Sanatkumara said: —

After ordering thus, the powerful Lord of Asuras and the Emperor of the Danavas set out, surrounded by thousands of warriors and great armies. His general was an expert in the science and technique of warfare. He was the best of charioteers, a great hero and skilled in warfare.

Mounting on an aerial chariot of exquisite build and inlaid with gems, and making obeisance to the elders and preceptors he set out for the battle.

In the holy land of Bharata, to the east of the western ocean and to the west of Malaya mountain, on the banks of river Puspabhadra, there is a hermitage of Kapila with an auspicious holy Banyan tree. It is called Siddhasrama. It is the place where holy men achieve the result of their action.

The Conversation Between Siva and the Emissary of Sankhacuda

Sankhacuda said: —

Stationing himself there, the Lord of Danavas sent a leading Danava of great knowledge as his emissary to Siva. The emissary went there and saw the moon-crested Lord Siva, seated at the root of the Banyan tree. He saw him sitting in a yogic pose, showing the mystic gesture with his eyes, with a smiling face and body as pure as crystal. On seeing him, the messenger descended from his chariot and bowed to him as well as to Kumara.

He saw Bhadrakali to his left and Karttikeya standing before him. Kali, Karttikeya and Siva offered him the conventional benediction.

This emissary of Sankhacuda had full knowledge of the sacred texts. He joined his palms in reverence and bowing to him spoke the auspicious words.

The Emissary said: —

Oh Lord, I am the emissary of Sankhacuda and have come to you. What is it that you desire? Please tell me.

Sanatkumara said: —

On hearing these words of Sankhacuda, Lord Siva became delighted and spoke.

Lord Siva said: —

Oh messenger of great intellect, listen to my words conducive to happiness. After pondering over this, without disputation, this shall be mentioned to him.

Brahma is the creator of the worlds and father of Dharma. He knows virtue. Marici is his son. Kasyapa is Marici's son. Daksa gave him his thirteen daughters, with pleasure. Among them the chaste lady Danu increased his fortune to a great extent. Danu gave birth to four sons called Danavas. They were vigorous and powerful. Vipracitti of great strength and valour was one of them. His son, the virtuous Dambha of great intellect was the ruler of Danavas. You are his excellent son, a pious soul, and the Lord of Danavas. In your previous birth you were a cowherd and an attendant of Krsna. Among the cowherds you were virtuous. As a result of Radha's curse, you are born as Danava and have become the king of Danavas. You are casually born as a Danava. You are really no Danava. Realising your previous birth you leave off your inimical attitude to the gods. Don't be malicious towards them. You can enjoy your kingdom zealously. Do not try to expand your kingdom nor spoil it. Oh Danava, return their kingdom to the gods. Maintain my affection. Stay in your kingdom happily. Let the gods stay in their region.

Sanatkumara said: —

These and many such words of advice, auspiciously based on injunctions of Sruti and Smrti, Siva said to him enlightening him in an excellent manner. The emissary who had been well instructed by Sankhacuda, who knew his duties well but who had been deluded by destiny, spoke these words humbly.

The messenger said: —

Oh Lord, what has been narrated by you is true. It cannot be otherwise. But let my submission based on certain factual elements be heard.

Oh Lord Siva, verily a great sin has been cited as the result of offence to kinsmen by you now. But does it concern only Asuras and not the gods? Please tell me. If it applies to all alike, I shall consider it and let you know. Please tell me your decision at the outset and clear my doubts. Oh Lord Siva, why did the discus-bearing Lord Visnu sever the heads of Madhu and Kaitabha, the excellent Daityas in the ocean of dissolution?

Your Majesty too is famous as a partisan of the gods. Why did you fight with the Tripuras and reduce them to ashes? After divesting him of everything, why was Bali packed off to Sutala and other regions? Did Visnu go to his threshold as his uplifter? Why was Hiranyaksa harassed by the gods along with his brother? Why were Sumbha and other Asuras subjected to fall by the gods?

The enmity of the gods and the Danavas is perpetual and sparked off due to some reason or other. By turns, subject to the whims of Kala they enjoy victory or defeat. Interference on your part in the dispute between the two is futile. This does not behove you, the Lord who are equally in touch with both. Your rivalry to us is excessively shameful since you are Lord unto the gods as well as to the Asuras. You are the supreme soul.

In the event of your victory your fame is not enhanced. In the event of your defeat you suffer a great loss. Let this disadvantage be pondered over.

Lord Siva said: —

We are subservient to our devotees. We are never independent. We carry out their tasks at their wish. We are not the partisans of any one in particular.

Formerly the fight of Visnu with the excellent Daityas Madhu and Kaitabha in the ocean of dissolution was due to the prior request of Brahma. For the sake of Prahlada, at the request of gods, Hiranyakasipu was slain by him acting in the interest of his devotees. I fought with the Tripuras and reduced them to ashes, only at the request of the gods.

Parvati, the mother of all, fought with Sumbha and others, and killed them only at the request of the gods. Even today, the gods have sought refuge in Brahma. And he along with the gods and the Lord Visnu has sought refuge in me.

Oh emissary, paying heed to the request of Visnu, Brahma and others, I, though Lord of all, have come here in the battle of the gods. Really you are the foremost of the comrades of Krsna, the great soul. Those Daityas who had been formerly killed are not on a par with you.

What is excessively shameful in my fight with you, Oh king? I have been urged humbly to carry out the task of the gods. Go to Sankhacuda and tell him what I have said. Let him do what is proper. I shall carry out the task of the gods.

Sanatkumara said: —

On saying this, Siva the great god, stopped. The emissary stood up and returned to Sankhacuda.

Mutual Fight

Sanatkumara said: —

The emissary returned and mentioned the words of Siva. He conveyed his decision as it was. On hearing that, the valorous Danava Sankhacuda accepted lovingly the alternative of a fight. Hurriedly he got into his vehicle along with his ministers. He commanded his army against Siva.

Siva too hastened to urge his army and the gods. The Lord of all was ready himself with his sport. Oh sage, the mutual fight between the gods and the Danavas ensued. Both the hosts of the gods and the Danavas fought righteously.

Visnu fought a great battle with Dambha, Kala with the Asura Kala and the fire god fought with Gokarna. Kubera fought with Kalakeya and Visvakarman with Maya. Nandisvara and the rest fought with leading Danavas in the great battle.

Oh sage, then Siva stayed at the foot of the Banyan tree along with Kali and his son. The hosts of the two armies fought continuously against each other.

Then ensued a great war in which both gods and Asuras were crushed. Using the divine weapons, the heroes severed the heads of each other. It was a jubilant occasion for the roaring heroes of the armies. The soldiers running in the battlefield saw several headless bodies that jumped with many weapons in their hands.

Fighters of duel rushed against one another, challenging, thrusting and diving in at the vulnerable points. Everywhere groups of heroes were seen in that terrible war roaring like lions with various weapons displayed in their hands. The heroes in their joy shouted and leapt blowing on their conches of loud sound severally.

Thus for a long time the great combat between the gods and Danavas continued, terrible and tumultuous but delightful to the heroes.

Sankhacuda Fights with the
Full Contingent of his Army

Sanatkumara said: —

Then the gods were defeated by the Danavas. Their bodies were wounded by weapons and missiles. Terrified, they took to flight. Returning to Siva, the Lord of the universe, they sought refuge in him. In agitated words they cried, 'Oh Lord of all, save, save us.'

He glanced at the gods sympathetically and assured them of his protection. With his brilliance he enhanced the strength of his Ganas. Commanded by Siva, the great hero Karttikeya, fought fearlessly with the hosts of Danavas in the battle. Shouting angrily and roaring like a hero, the slayer of Taraka killed a hundred Aksauhinisin the battle.

Clipping off their heads, Kali with eyes like a red lotus, drank off the blood and devoured the flesh rapidly. She drank the blood of the Danavas all round.

Again Karttikeya became furiously angry and showered volleys of arrows. He struck crores of leaders of the Asuras within a trice. The Danavas wounded in their bodies fled in fright. Those who remained were killed. Mahamari also fought. All of them afflicted by Karttikeya's spear were wounded.

On seeing the wonderfully terrible fight of Karttikeya and Mahamari, Sankhacuda became furious and himself got ready for the battle. He got into his excellent aerial chariot that contained different weapons and missiles. Sankhacuda drew the string of the bow to his ear and discharged volleys of arrows from his seat in the middle of the chariot. He was accompanied by many heroes. His volley of arrows was terrifying. It could not be withstood. A terrible darkness spread on the battlefield.

The gods Nandisvara and others fled. Only Karttikeya stayed behind in the battle field. The king of Danavas showered mountains, serpents, pythons and trees so terrifyingly that it could not be withstood.

Oppressed by that shower Karttikeya, the son of Siva, looked like the sun enveloped by thick sheets of frost. He exhibited many types of illusions in the manner indicated by Maya. None of the gods or Ganas understood it.

At the same time, the powerful Sankhacuda of great illusion split his bow with a divine arrow. He split his divine chariot and the horses pulling it. With a divine missile he shattered the peacock too. The Danava hurled his spear fatally on his chest where he fell unconscious by the force of the blow.

Regaining consciousness, Karttikeya mounted his vehicle of sturdy build. With his divine missiles, the son of Siva split the serpents, mountains, trees and rocks, everything furiously. Then he hurled his spear refulgent like the sun at the chest of the Lord of Danavas. At the blow he fell unconscious.

That powerful Asura got rid of the affliction in a Muhurta and regained consciousness. With a leonine vigour he got up and roared. He hit Karttikeya with his spear and he fell on the ground.

Taking him on her lap, Kali brought him near Siva. By his divine sport and perfect wisdom Siva enlivened him. Siva gave him infinite strength. As a result of that, the valorous Karttikeya stood up and felt inclined to go to the battlefield.

In the meantime the heroic Virabhadra of great strength fought with the powerful Sankhacuda in the battle. Whatever arrows were discharged by the Danava in the battle were split playfully by Virabhadra by means of his own arrows. Then the valorous Sankhacuda became infuriated and hit him after which he fell on the ground. Regaining consciousness in a trice the leader of the Ganas, Virabhadra caught hold of his bow again. In the meantime Kali went to the battle ground again at the request of Karttikeya to devour the Danavas and to protect her own people. Nandisvara and other heroes, the gods, Gandharvas, Yaksas, Raksasas and serpents followed her.

Kali Fights

Sanatkumara continued: —

Going to the battle ground, the goddess Kali roared like a lion. On hearing that the Danavas fainted. She laughed boisterously again and again, boding ill to the Asuras. She drank the distilled grapevine and danced on the battle ground.

On seeing Kali, Sankhacuda hastened to the battle ground. The Danavas were frightened but the king Sankhacuda assured them of protection. Kali hurled fire as fierce as the flame of dissolution which the king put out sportively by means of Vaisnava missiles. Immediately the goddess hurled the Narayana missile at him. The missile developed its power on seeing the Danava Sankhacuda. On realising it as fierce as the flame of fire of dissolution, the Danava Sankhacuda fell flat on the ground and bowed again and again.

On seeing the Danava humbled the missile turned away. Then the goddess hurled the Brahma missile with due invocation through the mantra. On seeing the missile blazing he bowed and fell on the ground. The leader of the Danavas thus prevented the Brahma missile from attacking him.

Then the infuriated leader of the Danavas drew the bow violently and discharged divine missiles at the goddess with due invocation through the mantras. Opening the mouth very wide, she swallowed the missiles and roared with a boisterous laugh. The Danavas were terrified.

He then hurled a Sakti, a hundred Yojanas long at Kali. By means of divine missiles she broke it into a hundred pieces. He hurled the Vaisnava missile on Kali. She blocked it with the Mahesvara missile. Thus the mutual combat went on for a long time. All the gods and Danavas stood as mere onlookers.

Then the infuriated goddess Kali, as fierce as the god of death on the battleground, angrily took up the Pasupata arrow sanctified by mantras. In order to prevent it from being hurled, an unembodied celestial voice said—'Oh goddess, do not hurl this missile angrily at Sankhacuda. Oh goddess, the death of this Danava will not take place even through the never failing Pasupata missile. Think of some other means for slaying this warrior Sankhacuda.'

On hearing this, Bhadrakali did not hurl the missile. Sportively she devoured ten million Danavas as if in hunger. The terrible goddess rushed at Sankhacuda to devour him. The Danava prevented her by means of the divine missile of Rudra. Then the infuriated leader of the Danavas hurled a sword with a sharp and terrific edge. On seeing the blazing sword approaching, Kali furiously opened her mouth and swallowed it even as Sankhacuda stood watching.

The goddess then hit him with her fist forcefully and angrily. The king of Danavas whirled round and fainted for a short while. Immediately the Danava regained consciousness and got up. He did not fight her with his arms by the thought that she was a woman like his mother. The goddess seized the Danava, whirled him again and again and tossed him up with great anger and velocity. The valorous Sankhacuda fell down after being tossed up very high. He got up and bowed down to Bhadrakali. Highly delighted thereafter, he got into a beautiful aerial chariot of exquisite workmanship set with gems and did not lose the balance of his mind in the battlefield.

Hungrily Kali drank the blood of the Danavas. In the meantime an unembodied celestial voice said, 'Oh goddess, a hundred thousand haughty leading Danavas have been left out in the battle still roaring. Devour them quickly. Do not think of slaying the king of Danavas. Oh goddess, Sankhacuda cannot be killed by you. It is certain.'

On hearing these words from the firmament, Bhadrakali drank the blood and devoured the flesh of many Danavas and went near Siva. She then narrated to him the events of the war in the proper order.

The Annihilation of the Army of Sankhacuda

Vyasa said: —

Oh intelligent one, on hearing the narrative of Kali, what did Siva say? What did he do? Please tell me. I am eager to know.

Sanatkumara said: —

On hearing the words of Kali, Lord Siva laughed. Siva consoled her. On hearing the celestial voice, Siva went himself to the battle along with his Ganas. He was seated on his great bull and surrounded by Virabhadra and others, the Bhairavas and the Ksetrapalas all equal in valour to him.

Assuming a heroic form, Lord Siva entered the battlefield. On seeing Siva, Sankhacuda got down from the aerial chariot, bowed with great devotion and fell flat on the ground. After bowing to him he immediately got into his chariot. He speedily prepared for the fight and seized the bow and the arrows.

The fight between Siva and the Danava went on for a hundred years and they showered arrows fiercely like clouds pouring down incessantly. The heroic Sankhacuda discharged terrible arrows playfully. Siva split all of them by means of his arrows.

There was a terrific tumult in the midst of that battle. All round amongst the Ganas, the shouts of heroes rose up. The Danavas were frightened by those harsh and terrible sounds. On hearing them the powerful king of Danavas became very furious.

When Siva shouted, 'Oh wicked one, stay by. Stay by', the gods and the Ganas rapidly shouted 'victory, victory.' Then coming again, Sankhacuda hurled his spear with shooting flames at Rudra. While it came on, blazing brilliantly, it was immediately suppressed by Ksetrapala by means of the meteor springing from his mouth. Again the great battle between Siva and the Danava was resumed. Siva split up the arrows discharged by the son of Dambha by means of hundreds and thousands of his fierce arrows. Similarly the arrows of Siva were split up by the Danava.

Then the Danava seized his mace and accompanied by a huge army rushed at Siva with the intention to kill him. The infuriated Siva split the mace of the Danava rushing headlong by means of a sharp-edged sword. When the mace was split, the Danava became very furious. The brilliant Danava took up a spear that blazed unbearable to the enemies. By means of his trident, Siva hit the comely king of Danavas rapidly in the chest even as he approached with the spear in his hand.

From the chest of Sankhacuda pierced by the trident, a valorous huge being came out and said, 'Stand by. Stand by.' Laughing noisily, Siva severed the terrible head of the being that was coming out, by means of a sword. He fell on the ground. Then spreading her mouth wide open, Kali furiously devoured innumerable Asuras whose heads were crushed by her fierce fangs.

Virabhadra furiously destroyed many other heroes. Nandisvara killed many other demons. Thus the other Ganas, readily prepared and furiously heroic, destroyed many Daityas, Asuras and suppressors of the gods. Thus a major portion of his army was destroyed there.

Sankhacuda is Slain

Sanatkumara said: —

On seeing the important and major portion of his army killed, including heroes as dear to him as his life, the Danava became very furious. He spoke to Siva.

Sankhacuda said: —

I am here standing ready. Be steady in the battle. What is it to me, if these are killed? Fight me standing face to face.

Sanatkumara replied: —

Oh sage, after saying this and resolving resolutely the king of Danavas stood ready facing Siva. The Danava hurled divine missiles at him and showered arrows like the cloud pouring rain. He exhibited various kinds of deceptive measures invisible and inscrutable to all the excellent gods and Ganas and terrifying as well.

On seeing that, Siva sportively discharged the excessively divine Mahesvara missiles that destroyed all illusions. All the illusions were quelled rapidly by its brilliance.

Then in the battle, the powerful Lord Siva suddenly seized his trident which could not be withstood even by brilliant persons, in order to slay him. In order to prevent him then, an unembodied celestial voice said to Siva.

The celestial voice said: —

Oh Siva, do not hurl the trident now. Please listen to this request. Oh Siva, by all means, you are competent to destroy the entire universe in a trice. Why do you doubt this in regard to a single Danava Sankhacuda?

Oh Lord Siva, it has been mentioned by Brahma, that, as long as he wears the armour of Visnu and as long as his wife maintains the marital fidelity, Sankhacuda has neither death nor old age. Please make those words truthful.

Sanatkumara said: —

On hearing this celestial voice, Siva said, 'So be it'. Visnu came there at the wish of Siva. Siva, who is the goal of the good, commanded him. Then, in the guise of an old brahmin, Visnu, the foremost of those who wield magic, approached Sankhacuda and told him.

The aged brahmin said: —

Oh Lord of Danavas, give me the alms for which I have come to you. I shall not say openly what I wish to have from you. I shall tell you when you have promised me first.

Sanatkumara said: —

On hearing the brahmin, Sankhacuda agreed and promised to give him what he desired.

The old brahmin said: —

I am the supplier for your armour.

Sanatkumara said: —

On hearing that, the Lord of Danavas, a well wisher of the brahmins and of truthful word, handed over the divine armour, his vital breath, to the brahmin. This is how Visnu snatched off his armour by means of deception. Then, in the guise of Sankhacuda, Visnu approached Tulasi.

Lord Visnu, an expert in wielding magic, went there and deposited his semen in her vaginal passage for the protection of gods. In the meantime the Lord of Danavas approached Siva without the armour. He took up his trident that blazed to slay Samkhacuda.

That trident, named Vijaya, shone, illuminating heaven and earth. It could neither be prevented nor withstood. It was never ineffective in destroying enemies. It had a fierce halo all round. It was the best of all weapons and missiles. It was unbearable to gods and Asuras. It was terrible for everyone.

That trident whirling around over the head of Sankhacuda for a while, fell on the head of the Danava at the behest of Siva and reduced him to ashes.

Oh brahmin, then it rapidly returned to Siva and having finished its work went away by the aerial path with the speed of the mind.

A continuous shower of flowers fell over Siva. Visnu, Brahma, Indra, other gods and sages praised him. Sankhacuda the king of Danavas was released from his curse by the favour of Siva. He regained his original form.

After slaying him thus, Siva went to Sivaloka seated on his bull, joyously, accompanied by Parvati, Karttikeya and the Ganas. Visnu went to Vaikuntha. Krsna became complacent. The gods went to their abodes with great delight. The universe regained normalcy.

The Curse of Tulasi

Vyasa said: —

How did Visnu manage to deposit his semen in the vaginal passage of Tulasi? Please narrate the same.

Sanatkumara said: —

It was in the guise of Sankhacuda that he indulged in sexual dalliance with his wife. Visnu went to Tulasi's place. Very near the entrance to Tulasi's palace he caused the drum Dundubhi to be beaten and cries of victory to be raised. He thus made the beautiful woman wake up. On hearing it that chaste lady was highly delighted. Eagerly she peeped through the window into the highway. Knowing that her husband had returned she observed all auspicious rites and offered monetary gifts to the brahmins. She then beautified herself. After descending from the chariot, Visnu who had assumed the guise of Sankhacuda by deceptive art went to the apartment of the queen. On seeing her husband come before her she became delighted. She washed his feet, bowed to him and cried.

Tulasi said: —

Oh Lord, how did you fare in the battle with Siva who renders help to the gods? You had gone to fight Siva who is the foremost of the gods, who is the annihilator of innumerable universes, whose behests are strictly adhered to and carried out by Visnu, Brahma and other gods always. You have happily returned after defeating him, the great Lord. How did you win? Please mention that to me.

Lord Visnu replied: —

When I, fond of war, reached the battle ground there was a great tumult. A great battle ensued. There ensued the battle between the gods and the Danavas both desiring victory. The daityas were defeated by the gods who were proud of their strength. Then I fought with the powerful gods. The gods defeated by me sought refuge in Siva. In order to help them Siva came to fight. Proud of strength, I fought with him for a long time. My dear wife, we fought continuously for a year. Oh lovely woman, all the Asuras were destroyed. Brahma made us come to a peace. At the bidding of Brahma the powers of authority were reassigned to the gods. I have returned home. Siva has returned to Sivaloka. Everyone has resumed health and normalcy. The torment has receded.

Sanatkumara said: —

After saying this the Lord of the worlds lay down on his bed. Then out of joy, Visnu indulged in sexual intercourse. That lady began to suspect on observing a change in her happiness, endearment and attraction and asked him, 'who are you?'

Tulasi said: —

Who are you? Tell me quickly. I have been enjoyed by you deceptively. My modesty has been outraged. Hence I am going to curse you.

Sanatkumara said: —

On hearing the words of Tulasi, Visnu became afraid of the curse. Oh Brahmin, sportively he re-assumed his own real beautiful form. On seeing the characteristic signs she guessed that it was Visnu. Infuriated by the violation of her chastity she said to him.

Tulasi said: —

Oh Visnu, you are ruthless. Your mind is like a rock. Since my chastity has been outraged, my husband is doomed. Hence due to my curse you will become a rock. Those who call you ocean of mercy are erring. There is no doubt. How was a devotee killed for another man's sake, even without any offence?

Sanatkumara said: —

After saying this Tulasi lamented again and again in the excess of her grief. On seeing her crying, Visnu remembered Lord Sankara, Paramesvara, by whom the universe is deluded. Then Sankara appeared in front of them. He was bowed to and eulogised humbly by Visnu. On seeing Visnu distressed and the beloved lady lamenting, Siva tactfully enlightened both of them.

Siva said: —

Oh Tulasi, do not cry. Every one reaps the fruit of his actions. In the world that is an ocean of actions and rites there is no external entity that bestows happiness and sorrow. Both of you listen. I shall mention what is beneficent to both and conducive to happiness.

Oh gentle lady, penance has been performed by you. The fruit thereof has been attained now. How can it be otherwise? Cast off this body. Take up a divine body and indulgence in dalliance with Visnu forever. Be equal unto Lakshmi.

The body that you caste off shall become a river in Bharata. That will be a sacred river famous as Gandaki. Oh great lady, as a boon granted by me, Tulasi (holy basil) will be the most important constituent of the materials of worship of the gods some time. In heaven, earth and the nether worlds you will become the Tulasi plant more excellent than flowers. As a result of your curse, Hari shall assume the form of a rock on the banks of the river Gandaki and shall preside on the same in Bharata. Crores of terrible sharp-toothed germs shall penetrate and erode the rock and carve rings on it. Those pieces shall be known as Salagrama rocks and will be meritorious. Oh gentle lady, if anyone plucks the leaves of Tulasi lying on Salagrama he will be separated from his wife in the next birth. He who keeps Salagrama, Tulasi and Sankha in one place shall become wise and a favourite of Visnu.

After saying so, Siva narrated the greatness of Salagrama stone and Tulasi, that is highly meritorious. After delighting Visnu and Tulasi, Siva the benefactor of the good, vanished from there and went to his abode.

Sanatkumara said: —

On hearing the words of Siva, Tulasi was delighted. She cast off that body and assumed a divine form. The Lord of Laksmi went to Vaikuntha with her. Immediately the river

Gandaki took its origin from her cast off body. On its banks, Visnu became a mountain conferring merit on men. Oh sage, germs made different kinds of holes therein. The pieces that fell into the water were highly meritorious.

Hiranyaksa is Slain

Narada said: —

Please narrate another story of that great Lord Siva who indulges in divine sports delightful to the devotees, by resorting to magic practices.

Brahma said: —

Then Sanatkumara narrated to Vyasa—the son of Satyavati—the auspicious and admirable story of Lord Siva.

Sanatkumara said: —

Oh Vyasa, listen to the auspicious story of Lord Siva in relation to Andhaka how the latter obtained the leadership of Ganas from Siva.

Oh great sage, it was after a great fight with the gods and by propitiating Lord Siva again and again with Sattvika devotion that he attained the leadership.

Vyasa said: —

Oh holy one, who is this Andhaka? In which warrior family on the earth was this powerful great Andhaka born? What was his parentage? What is his importance? How did he obtain the leadership of the Ganas from Siva of great splendour? Really that Andhaka was blessed since he became the Lord of the Ganas.

Sanatkumara said: —

Formerly Siva, the emperor of the gods, came to Kasi from Kailasa accompanied by Parvati, his Ganas because he was desirous of sporting there. He built his capital there. He appointed the hero Bhairava as its protector. Then he performed many sports, pleasing the people, in the company of Parvati.

Once he went to the mountain Mandara to see its excellent grandeur. He sported much in the company of Siva and the various principal heroic Ganas. While sporting on the eastern ridges of the Mandara mountain, Parvati sportively and playfully closed the eyes of Siva. When Siva's eyes were closed, a great darkness spread immediately. By this contact with Lord Siva, a rapturous rutting juice exuded from her hands and became hot by the fire of the eye on his forehead and flowed out. Conception took place and a terrible inhuman being manifested itself. It was furious, ungrateful, blind deformed, and black in colour. It had matted locks of hair and fine hair all over the body. It sang, cried, laughed, danced, put out its tongue like a serpent and thundered fiercely. When this curious creature arose, Siva smilingly spoke to Parvati.

Lord Siva said: —

You did it yourself by closing my eyes. Oh my beloved, why are you afraid of it now?

Parvati said: —

Oh Lord, what is this ugly hideous being that is born in front of us? Please tell me the truth. Why was it created? By whom? Whose child is it?

Sanatkumara said: —

On hearing these words of his beloved, Lord Siva smilingly said to Parvati.

Lord Siva said: —

Oh Parvati of mysterious activities, listen. When my eyes were closed by you, this being of wonderfully fierce might was born of my sweat. He shall be named Andhaka. You are the cause of his creation though not in the natural way. He shall be guarded by the Ganas lovingly as well as by you along with your friends. His well being rests with you. Oh noble lady, pondering over this intelligently, you shall do everything.

Sanatkumara said: —

On hearing the words of her Lord, Parvati was very compassionate. Accompanied by her friends, she made arrangements for his safety in diverse ways and means as if he were her own son.

At that time, the Asura Hiranyaksa desired to obtain a son at the pressure of his wife who was envious at the sight of many sons of her husband's elder brother. Accordingly he set out in the season of late winter.

He resorted to the forest and performed penance for obtaining a son. In order to see Lord Siva, he performed a rigorous penance conquering the passions of anger and remaining insensible to external sensation as does a log of wood.

The trident-bearing Lord was pleased at his penance. Oh great brahmin, he went there in order to grant him the boon. After reaching that spot, Lord Siva spoke to the leading Daitya.

Lord Siva: —

Oh Lord of Daityas, do not curb your senses so much. Why have you taken up this sacred rite? Speak out what you desire. I am Siva, the granter of desires. I shall grant whatever you desire.

Sanatkumara said: —

On hearing the pleasing words of Lord Siva, the Daitya Hiranyaksa was delighted. He joined his palms in reverence and humbly bowed his head. Eulogising and bowing in various ways he spoke to Lord Siva.

Hiranyaksa said: —

Oh moon-crested Lord, I have no powerful son befitting the race of Daityas. It is for this purpose that I have resorted to penance. Oh Lord of gods, give me a powerful son. My brother has five sons of infinite valour, Prahlada being the eldest. I don't have any son. My family is likely to be extinct. Who will inherit my kingdom after me? An abode in heaven is enjoined only for those who have sons as mentioned by the learned and the virtuous. All living beings are active in that respect. A person whose family is extinct cannot have higher regions. It is for obtaining the son that people worship the deities.

Sanatkumara said: —

On hearing these words of the king, the kindhearted Siva was satisfied and spoke thus.

Siva said: —

Oh ruler of Daityas, there may not be a son born of your semen. But I shall grant you a son. My son Andhaka has a prowess equal to yours. He cannot be defeated by any. You choose him as your son. Cast off your distress and accept him as your son.

Sanatkumara said: —

After saying this, the delighted Lord gave the son to Hiranyaksa. Then Siva vanished. After getting a son from Siva, the Daitya circumambulated Siva and worshipped him with many hymns. Joyously the noble Asura returned to the kingdom. Having obtained a son from Siva, the demon of great and fierce valour conquered all the gods and took the earth to Patala.

Then the gods, sages and the Siddhas propitiated Visnu. He appeared in the form of a celestial boar that was terrific in form. He split the earth by beating and striking with his snout and entered Patala. He powdered hundreds of Daityas with his nose and the formidable curved fangs. He smashed the armies of the Asuras by kicking with his legs dazzling like lightning. With his Sudarsana dazzling like a crore of suns he chopped off the burning head of Hiranyaksa and reduced the wicked Daityas to ashes. He was then delighted to crown his son Andhaka as the king of Daityas.

Then Visnu, the great boar, returned to his abode. He lifted up the earth from the Patala by means of his fangs. He sustained the Earth as before. Eulogised by the gods, the delighted sages, and Brahma, Lord Visnu who had assumed the form of a boar finished the task and returned to his abode.

Hiranyakasipu is Slain

Vyasa said: —

Oh Sanatkumara of great intellect, when Asura was killed what did his elder brother, the great Asura, do? Oh great sage, I am eager to hear this. Oh son of Brahma, please narrate the same.

Brahma said: —

On hearing these words of Vyasa, that great sage, Sanatkumara spoke after remembering the lotus-like feet of Siva.

Sanatkumara said: —

When his brother was thus killed by Visnu in the form of a boar, Oh Vyasa, Hiranyakasipu was distressed with grief and excited by anger. Always fond of enmity with Visnu that he was, he instigated heroic Asuras to wreak havoc among the people.

Receiving the command of their Lord with bowed heads, they did as instructed. Thus when the universe was utterly disturbed by the evil-minded Asuras, the gods abandoned heaven and roamed on the Earth unobserved.

After performing the last rites of his younger brother, the distressed Hiranyakasipu consoled his wife and others. Then the emperor of the Daityas desired to make himself invincible, undying, unageing, unrivalled and sole ruler.

He performed a severe penance in the ravine of the Mandara mountain. Keeping his arms lifted up he fixed his eyes on the sky. He stood on the Earth on his big toes alone. When he was performing penance, the gods accompanied by their forces defeated the Daityas and regained their lost seats. The smoking fire of penance springing from his head, spreading everywhere scorched the worlds all round, above and below.

The gods scorched by that, abandoned heaven and went to Brahma's region. With their faces turned pale and deformed by his penance they informed the creator of everything.

Oh Vyasa, thus informed by the gods, the self-born Brahma went to the hermitage of the Daitya accompanied by Bhrgu, Daksa and others.

The Asura who had already scorched the worlds saw that the lotus-born deity had arrived. In order to grant him the boon, Brahma said— 'Choose a boon'. On hearing the sweet words of the creator, the Asura of undismayed intellect spoke thus.

Hiranyakasipu said: —

Oh creator, Oh Lord of subjects, never may I have the fear of death from weapons, missiles, thunderbolts, dry trees, mountains, water, fire. May I never be killed by the onslaught of enemies— gods, Daityas, sages, Siddhas or in fact from any living being created by you. Why should I expatiate on it? Let there be no death for me in heaven, on earth, in the day time, at night, from above or below!

Sanatkumara said: —

On hearing these words of the Asura, the merciful lotus-born deity bowed to Visnu mentally and spoke.

Brahma said: —

Oh Lord of Daityas, I am delighted. Attain everything. Stop your penance which has already run onto ninety six thousand years. You have realised your desires entirely. Stand up. Rule over the kingdom of the Danavas.

Sanatkumara said: —

After being granted his boon, he became inclined to destroy the three worlds. The highly elated Asuras disturbed all righteous activities and defeated all the gods in battle. Then the terrified Indra and other gods harassed by him got the permission of Brahma and went to the milk ocean where Visnu was lying.

On learning their misery in entirety, Visnu granted them boons. Getting up from his couch, Visnu consoled the gods and the sages by means of different words befitting himself.

The Lord said: —

Oh leading gods, I shall kill the Daitya with force. Return to your own abodes fully assured, all of you.

Sanatkumara said: —

Oh great sage, on hearing the words of Visnu, Indra and other leading gods, fully assured and satisfied, went to their abodes thinking that the younger brother Hiranyaksa was already killed.

The noble soul Visnu assumed the form partly of lion and partly of man. His head was matted and full of manes. Sharp fangs were his weapons. The claws were keen and pointed. The snout was finely shaped. The mouth was wide open. The body was terrible and refulgent like a crore of suns, blazing and powerful like the fire at the time of dissolution. He was identical with the universe.

When the sun was about to set, the Lord went to the city of the Asuras. The Man-lion fought with the powerful Daityas. He killed many of them. He held them up and whirled. Exhibiting wonderful prowess, he smashed and crushed the various Asuras. On seeing that omniformed lion, the son of the Lord of Daityas, Prahlada said to the king, his father.

Prahlada said: —

Is it the universe-formed Lord who has come as the majestic lion? The infinite Lord in the form of Man-lion has come within your city. Desist from fighting and seek refuge in him. I see the terrible form of the lion. Since there is none to fight him in all the three worlds, it is better that you submit to him and continue to be the ruler.

Sanatkumara said: —

On hearing the words of his son, the wicked Asura said to his son.

Hiranyakasipu said: —

Oh son, why are you so afraid?

Sanatkumara said: —

Thus addressing his son, the king of the Daityas ordered the heroes among the Daityas to catch the lion-man deity. At his behest, the leading Daityas who desired to catch the lion approached him but they were burnt in a trice. When the Daityas were burnt the king himself fought with the lion with all kinds of weapons, missiles, spears, swords, nooses, goads, fire and the like.

Oh Vyasa, a day, according to the calculation of Brahma, passed by even as they fought with weapons in their hands, roaring heroically and furiously at each other. Then suddenly the Daitya assumed many arms holding weapons. He looked angrily at the fighting man-lion and pounced upon him in a rush.

Then after a terrific battle fought by all sorts of weapons and missiles they were exhausted. Then the great Daitya himself seized up a spear and rushed to the man-lion. He was seized by the Lord of beasts with hands as powerful as mountains. He was placed on the knee, torn and scratched in the chest by the claws piercing every vulnerable joint in the body. His heart lacerated by his claws was filled with blood. He lay dead like a log of wood, his limbs being reduced to powder.

When he was killed, the heroic Visnu was pleased. He beckoned to Prahlada who bowed to him. He crowned him king and then left for his abode. Then the gods were delighted. They bowed to Lord Visnu who had finished their task and who deserved worship, Oh Brahmin. Thereafter Brahma and others returned to their abodes.

Andhaka's Attainment of the Leadership of Ganas

Sanatkumara said: —

Once Andhaka, the son of Hiranyaksa, was addressed jokingly by his haughty cousins in the course of their sports and games—'Oh blind fellow, what will you do with the kingdom? Hiranyaksa was a fool who adopted you as a son who is bereft of eyesight, fond of quarrel, ugly and hideous. You cannot lay claim to the kingdom. Can a person other than the son of a king ever aspire for the kingdom? You yourself can ponder over it. At the most we can give you some share.'

On hearing their words Andhaka was distressed. He thought over the matter intelligently. He then appeased his cousins with various words. In the night he went to a desolate forest.

For ten thousand years he performed a severe penance, repeating mantras. He stood on one leg, observed fast and lifted up his arms continuously. In short, he performed a penance that no god or Asura could do.

Every day he cut a piece of his flesh and consigned it to the sacred blazing fire along with his blood repeating the mantras all along. This he continued for a year. In the end only the bones and the nerves were left. The entire blood was exhausted. When there remained no flesh to offer, he desired to offer his whole body into the fire.

Then he was seen by the heaven-dwellers, all of whom became frightened and bewildered. Then Brahma the creator was immediately propitiated and eulogised by the gods. He stopped him and said thus, 'Oh Danava, choose a boon. Whatever is inaccessible in the universe, if you desire it, you can have it.'

On hearing the words of Brahma, the Daitya piteously bowed to him and asked for his boon.

Andhaka said: —

May Prahlada and others who have cruelly usurped my share in the kingdom be my slaves. I am now blind but let me be endowed with divine vision. Let Indra and others pay me tax and tribute. Let no death come to me from gods, Daityas, Gandharvas, Yaksas, serpents or human beings. Nor shall I meet with death from Narayana, the enemy of leading Daityas, or from the omniscient and omniformed Siva.

Brahma said: —

Oh leader of Daityas, whatever you ask shall take place. But accept some cause of death because none who is born or who will be born can escape the jaws of death. Good men like you should rather avoid a long life.

Andhaka said: —

The most excellent of the ladies in the world for all time whether of mature, middle or young age shall be like a mother unto me. She may be the rarest in the world, unapproachable to all men, bodily, mentally or verbally. Oh self-born Lord, should I covet her, let destruction befall me instantaneously depriving me of the position of the ruler.

Brahma said: —

Oh leader of Daityas, whatever you desire shall necessarily be realised. Oh king of Daityas, stand up. Realise your ambition. But always fight with heroic people.

Sanatkumara said: —

Oh great sage, after listening to these words of the creator, and immediately bowing to him with devotion, the son of Hiranyaksa spoke to the Lord.

Andhaka said: —

Oh Lord, how can I enter the hosts of the enemy with this body and fight? Make me whole again. Heal all my wounds.

Sanatkumara said: —

On hearing his words, Brahma touched his body with his hand and returned to his abode accompanied by the great gods and worshipped by the sages and Siddhas.

The moment he was touched, he became full bodied and strong. With eyes regaining sight he became beautiful and stout. Thus he entered his city. Considering him blessed with the boon, on his arrival Prahlada and other leading Danavas surrendered the entire kingdom to him and became his slaves.

Then Andhaka went to heaven to conquer it, accompanied by his army and attendants. After defeating the gods in battle he made Indra pay him tribute. He conquered all the three worlds. He acquired thousands of women beautiful in appearance, amiable and faithful. He indulged with them in sexual dalliance on the beautiful banks of the rivers, mountains and other places.

Thus, indulging in sports he spent ten thousand years beautified and rendered pleasant and mysteriously wonderful stuff. The haughty fellow attacked leading scholars by using fallacious arguments. Posing as a great soul he roamed about with his Daitya friends destroying Vedic rites.

Proud of his affluence he slighted the Vedas, gods and preceptors. Then many crores of years passed by. Once, roaming about on the Earth with his army, he joyously went to the Mandara mountain. The haughty demon roamed there along with his armies admiring its golden splendour. Having gone there ostensibly for some sport and pastime he finally resolved to stay there as destiny would have it.

He built a wonderful stable and auspicious city on the ridges of the Mandara and forced people to settle there gradually. His three ministers Duryodhana, Vaidhasa and Hasti once saw a beautiful woman in an excellent spot on the mountain. They hastened to their Lord joyously and lovingly told him what they had seen there.

The ministers said: —

Oh Lord of Daityas, in a mountain cavern we have seen a certain sage. His eyes are closed in meditation. He is handsome. He is wearing an elephant hide round his hips. He holds a trident and a staff. This fair-complexioned four-armed sage of matted hair has smeared ashes over his body. Not far from him, another person was seen. He has simian features, very terrible in face and demeanour. Equipped with weapons his hands are rough and brawny. He is the guard on duty. There is a white bull, too old but firm and steady. A woman of very auspicious features, young and beautiful was seen at the side of that sage. She is a gem under the sun. Her necklaces are fine and auspicious. He who has seen her can alone be called a man of sight. Oh Lord of Daityas, that divine lady, wife and the beloved of that meritorious sage, is worthy of being seen and fetched here.

Sanatkumara said: —

On hearing their words, the Daitya became lustful. He shook with excitement. Immediately he sent Duryodhana and others to the sage. Oh great sage, they approached the inscrutable sage of exalted rites. After bowing they conveyed to him the behest of the Daitya.

The ministers said: —

Andhaka the noble soul, son of Hiranyaksa, the king of Daityas, the emperor of the three worlds, is camping here now at the instance of Brahma and is sportively inclined. Oh great sage, we are his ministers possessed of great prowess. We have come to you at his behest. Listen with attention to what he says.

Andhaka told Siva: —

Whose son are you? Why are you stationed here in a carefree manner? Whose wife is this young beautiful lady? Oh great sage, this auspicious lady is to be given to the Lord of Daityas. Surrender your wife unto me peacefully. Oh foolish fellow, why do you perform your penance in the company of a lady? Leave off your weapons, at my behest and carry on your penance. If my order is transgressed you will have to pay dearly with this very body.

Siva proclaimed: —

l am Siva. Why do you utter false things? Oh Lord of Daityas, listen to my prowess. It is improper on your part to speak like this. I do not remember any father of mine. Ignorant and hideous that I am, I do not know my mother. In a cavern I am performing this severe Pasupata rite, the like of which none has yet performed. This is well known that I have no roots. I cannot get rid of all these things. This young and beautiful wife is mine. She bears everything patiently. She is the achievement of one that has gone everywhere. Oh Raksasa, whatever appeals to you at present you can take.

Sanatkumara said: —

On hearing his profound words, the Danavas bowed to him and returned to their leader Andhaka who had taken a vow to destroy the three worlds. The ministers narrated everything that Siva had smilingly told them. Then they commented as follows.

The Ministers said: —

Oh king, you are the emperor of all the Daityas. You have been mockingly disparaged by the sage, a pitiable penance-monger. Indeed he considers the three worlds insignificant by his poor understanding. He has Viraka as his bodyguard whom he thinks to be very strong. He has mockingly challenged you to fight against him.

Oh gentle Lord of Danavas, these and similar words were uttered by that sage. Oh king, he says all this because he is proud and conceited. Is it not proper then to fight him?

Sanatkumara said: —

On hearing these words, Andhaka became furious. Proud of the boons granted to him he seized a sword. He emulated the fierce gust of wind. He got ready to go there.

The Beginning of the War and the
Conversation with the Messengers

Sanatkumara said: —

Andhaka, the great Daitya king, deluded and smitten by Kama's arrows, drank wine and started from his palace. He was accompanied by many of his soldiers. He was fierce and walked majestically like heroes. He saw the cavern guarded by Viraka, standing at the entrance. He was attacked with stones, trees, thunderbolts, water, fire and serpents. He was threatened with weapons and missiles. He was afflicted by Viraka repeatedly but ineffectively.

Andhaka began to fight Viraka when surprisingly and unbelievably he was defeated by Viraka in the battle. When his sword was shattered to pieces he fled from the battlefield divested of his conceited pride. His throat was parched with hunger and thirst. He was aggrieved.

Prahlada and other important Daityas then fought with Viraka. Though they were terrible themselves they were defeated by hundreds of weapons. While Siva's Ganas and Bhutas and everyone else celebrated, Siva consoled Parvati.

Siva said: —

Oh beloved, formerly I had performed the great Vrata called Mahapasupata. The strength that I derived therefrom is exhausted whence this fall of the immortals at the hands of the mortals. O goddess, merit has declined due to the physical contact with you. I will create a wonderfully divine and terrible forest and going there I shall perform a more severe vrata whereby, Oh beautiful lady, you shall be free from fear and sorrow.

Sanatkumara said: —

After saying this, the noble soul went to a holy and terrible forest. He proclaimed loudly his intention and performed penance highly illuminated. Parvati stayed behind in Mandara mountain awaiting for the return of the Lord. The chaste lady, endowed with good conduct, remained alone in that cavern. She was terrified and distressed. Of course she was guarded by her son Viraka.

Then the Daitya whose mental steadiness had been shattered by the arrows of Kama, became bold and haughty due to the boons that had been granted to him. He came to the cavern accompanied by his soldiers.

Forsaking food, drink and sleep, the infuriated Daitya accompanied by his army fought with Viraka a very wonderful battle for five hundred, five days and nights. Viraka was attacked with many weapons and he fainted at the entrance to the cavern. His body was pierced by the sharp weapons hurled by the Daityas. Viraka was covered by the weapons and could not be extricated. The goddess Parvatl was afraid at the sight. From within the cave she remembered Brahma and Visnu.

Thus remembered by the goddess, Brahma, Visnu, Indra and others assumed female forms and came there. Sages of great dignity, Siddhas, Nagas and Guhyakas became women and entered the cavern where Parvati was staying.

Since it was not customary to enter the harem of kings they assumed a female form of wonderful features and entered the cavern of Parvati for heroic activities.

Meanwhile Viraka of wonderfully fierce valour regained his consciousness and stood up. He seized the weapons of the warriors and hit the Daityas with them. All the goddesses also began fighting. The goddess of thousand eyes, fought steadily in war, undaunted and invincible with hundreds of Daityas. The goddess of fire was of none too gentle face and Yamya was fierce with staff in her lifted hands. The female form of fierce storm took up hunger for her physical body and held goad in her hand. The female form of Kubera held a mace in her hand, blazing like the fire at the end of a Kalpa.

On seeing this limitless vast army, the Daityas were bewildered and dejected in the heart. All these celestial damsels, the chief of whom was Brahmasakti and the general was Viraka, pacified the mind of Parvati and assured her.

The important ones among the Daityas and others who possessed strength derived from the boons granted to them, thought, in their minds, of their death or retreat and fought an unprecedented great battle with the ladies.

Making Viraka her general, Parvati fought a wonderful battle in the company of her friends and allies. Thinking upon Visnu and looking towards the southern direction the Daitya king, the heroic son of Hiranyaksa, quickly made a fierce array of soldiers with Gila at the head.

By the time this was done, the infuriated Lord came there. Clad in hides he had the lustre of a thousand fiery suns at the end of a Kalpa.

On seeing Lord Siva arrive after the lapse of a thousand years, the delighted women in the company of Viraka fought a very great battle. Parvati bowed her head to Siva. She exhibited great valour to her Lord. The delighted Parvati fought a terrific battle. Siva embraced her and then entered the cavern. The numerous women that had gathered were dismissed. Parvati honoured Viraka by hundreds of gifts and appointed him as the keeper of the gate.

Then the Asura chief, very clever in statesmanship, unable to see either Parvati or Siva sent his emissary Vighasa immediately to Siva. He entered the cavern, bowed to Siva and spoke these words haughtily.

The messenger said: —

I have been sent by him and so I have entered this cavern. You have nothing to do with a woman. Surrender this young and beautiful lady. You are extremely inimical to the Daityas. Show your might in fighting with me. Oh wicked ascetic, I shall send you to Yama's abode befitting the nether worlds.

Siva said: —

Manifestly your words are fierce. Hence hasten. Fight with me if you have the might. Let the haughty Daityas proud of their strength come. I have already thought of this and acted accordingly.

Andhaka Fights

Sanatkumara said: —

The king of Daityas, skilled in interpreting what he hinted at, seized his mace and hastened along with his army to the entrance of the cavern. The terrible demon Gila who could not be overwhelmed even by the foremost among the gods, was placed ahead. After reaching the cavern of the Lord Siva, the Daitya attacked with his weapons. The others showered weapons on Viraka and others on Parvati.

Then Siva collected his army. The infuriated trident-bearing deity called them together, the terrible living beings, the gods with their armies including Visnu and others. Immediately after being called, the gods came to Siva with chariots, elephants, horses, bulls, cows, and their weapons. When the gods had taken adequate rest along with their vehicles, the trident-bearing Lord Siva sent them to the battle ground with the steady and chief resolve of victory.

In a trice all of them including Brahma, Indra, Visnu, the sun and the moon were swallowed by Vighasa. When the armies were devoured, only Viraka was left behind.

Leaving off the battlefront Viraka entered the cavern and bowed to Siva. The eloquent but distressed Viraka then acquainted the destroyer of Kama with all the details. He told Siva how his army was devoured by Vighasa, including Visnu, Brahma and Indra.

Viraka said: —

Visnu the Lord who became invincible after tearing off Hiranyakasipu. He opened his mouth wide and began to blow off the three worlds although the Lord was subservient to the good. When the matter stood thus, he was cursed by the seven sages, 'You will be crushed by the Daityas for a long time.'

Then they were requested by Visnu—'Oh great sages, when will I get rid of this terrible curse?' Thereupon the infuriated sages said—'At the time of war you will be hit with fists and struck with terrible arrows. When swallowed by Vighasa with a mouth wide open, you shall stabilise yourself in the Badari forest in the holy residence of Siva, the cavern and shall then be freed from sins.' Thereafter in accordance with the curse of the sages he roams everyday in the battle ground, very hungry and swallows the Daityas and becomes delighted.

By using the science of reviving the dead to life and chanting verses of hymns, Sukra revives the Daityas killed by the gods and cures them of their hundreds of wounds. It would rather be better to give up our lives at the battle than yield. You, the witness of everything, have been chosen by us as the guide in the accomplishment of our task.

Sanatkumara said: —

On hearing this from his beloved son, the Lord of the three worlds meditated for a long time. He performed an incomparable miracle by chanting Saman songs. He laughed assuming a body as resplendent as the sun and thereby dispelled the darkness.

When the light spread, the sage Viraka fought again with the Daityas of deformed features. This time, Viraka was also devoured. Then Lord Siva got on to his bull and faced the Daitya Vighasa. Repeating the divine Mantra that compels the disgorging of what is swallowed, he stood there keeping the bow in readiness and the arrows as powerful as thunderbolts.

Then the sage Viraka came out of the mouth of Vighasa, accompanied by Visnu and his army. The lotus born Brahma, Indra—the enemy of Bala, the moon and the sun were also disgorged. Thus disgorged, the delighted army fought a great battle again. They defeated the Danavas.

But Sukra revived the Daityas slain in the battle by the virtue of his science. Then Sukra was bound like an animal and brought before Lord Siva, who swallowed him. When Sukra was no more, the entire residence of the Danavas was shattered and destroyed.

When the exhausted army entered the nether worlds, Andhaka the foremost of the Daityas, was divested of his haughtiness by Visnu by terrible blows from his mace.

Since he had secured boons, he did not leave the battle ground although his body had been afflicted much by the Lord of the gods by terrible blows and hits. Then by means of weapons and missiles, trees, mountains and waters he defeated the gods. Then he challenged the Lord of Pramathas, roaring loudly.

Fighting steadily by means of various weapons that fell on the battle ground, they were exhausted. Then the Asura inflicted pain on Parvati and Siva by means of uprooted trees, serpents, thunderbolts and other weapons and by indulging in deceptive practices. In order to conquer Siva, the Daitya created another juggler, a cheat.

Many Andhakas originating from the exudations of his body, with hideous faces, pervaded the surface of the earth. He was terribly pierced with the Trident by Siva. When fresh army cropped up from the army slain by Siva, from the hot drops of blood and cut pieces of flesh, from the wounds of those killed, Visnu called away the Lord of Pramathas and intelligently assumed a fierce form of a hideous woman employing his Yogic knowledge.

The goddess stood high in the battle field covering up the entire ground by her pair of feet. She was eulogised by the gods. Induced by the Lord, the hungry female form devoured the army, drank the hot blood of the Daityas and made the battle ground marshy. Then, only the chief of the Daityas was left. Still he fought on with Siva, beating terribly with his palms, knees, legs, and head. Although his blood had been sucked dry he remembered the traditional heroism of his race. Afterwards, he was quieted by the Lord of Pramathas. His heart was pierced. He was staked to the trident.

The Lords of the worlds worshipped the Lord of Pramathas, at the end of war, with different hymns pleasing and significant. Siva then spent the time rejoicing in the mountain cavern in their company.

Description of Swallowing Sukra

Vyasa said: —

What happened after Sukra was swallowed by Siva? Please narrate in detail what that great Yogin, stationed in the stomach of the trident-bearing Lord Siva did. How did the intelligent Sukra of bright refulgence, come out of the stomach of Siva? How long and in what manner did Sukra propitiate him? Oh sage, how did Andhaka get the position of the chieftain of Ganas after being released from the trident of Siva?

Sanatkumara said: —

Oh Vyasa of great intellect, listen then. In the battle, the Daityas emerged victorious first but then Siva came and fought to win the battle from them. On hearing that the Asura Andhaka was dejected. He began to think, 'How can I be victorious?' Going away from the battle ground the heroic and intelligent Andhaka went immediately to Sukra, unattended by anyone else.

Andhaka said: —

Oh holy Lord, we are never vanquished. We are always victorious. Due to our power we consider all the gods and their followers including Siva and Visnu as insignificant. But now the Asuras are harassed by the heroic enemy. They are killed. Save, save us Oh Brahmin.

Formerly you did a great penance drinking the smoke of husks or eating bits of grain for a thousand years and secured a great lore where you can resuscitate Asuras and Danavas. Now the opportunity has arrived to put it to a practical use. Oh Bhargava, resuscitate all the Asuras with that lore,.

Bhargava thought to himself: —

What shall I do? What will benefit me? Any living being has various activities to be performed. It may seem improper to me. This Vidya has been derived from Siva and I am going to use it on the heroes suppressed by the heroic Pramathas, the followers of Siva. But it is also my duty to protect those who seek refuge in me.

Sukra said: —

Oh dear, what has been mentioned by you is entirely true. I have acquired this lore just for the welfare of the Danavas. With this lore, I shall revive the Daityas destroyed in the battle by the Pramathas.

Within a Muhurta you will see these Daityas as if waking from sleep, healed from wounds, devoid of pain and very healthy.

Sanatkumara said: —

After saying this to Andhaka, Sukra repeated the mantra once for each of the Daityas after thinking upon Lord Siva. As soon as the mantra was repeated, the Daityas and Danavas rose up simultaneously as if from sleep, with the weapons lifted in their hands. Roaring with awful sounds, the fearless Asuras got ready to fight with Pramathas.

On seeing the Daityas and Danavas resuscitated to life by Sukra, Nandin and other Pramathas were surprised. Then Nandin approached Siva and told him about it.

Siva said: —

Oh Nandin, go very quickly and seize that great brahmin from the midst of the Daityas and bring him here like a vulture bringing the bird quail.

Sanatkumara said: —

Thus commanded by the bull-bannered deity Nandin bellowed like a bull and roared like a lion. Moving fast through the army, he reached the place where Bhargava was sitting. Nandin snatched away Sukra who was well guarded by all the Daityas. When the combat between the Asuras and gods deepened, the chief of Ganas burnt hundreds of the weapons of the enemy by the fire originating from his mouth and reached Siva taking Bhargava with him.

He said, 'Oh Lord, here is Bhargava', saying that he handed him over to Siva immediately. The Lord of gods caught hold of Bhargava like a present offered by a devotee. Without saying anything, the protector of the Bhutas, thrust Bhargava into his mouth like a fruit.

Swallowing of Sukra

Sanatkumara said: —

When Bhargava was swallowed by the Lord of Parvati, the Daityas gave up hopes of victory. When Bhargava was taken away by Nandin and swallowed by Siva, the Daityas became grief-stricken and their pride and jubilation for battle became curbed. On seeing Thunda, Hunda and other Daityas, devoid of enthusiasm, the courageous and valorous Andhaka replied.

Andhaka said: —

By seizing Bhargava forcibly from our midst we have been duped by Nandin. Our bodies have been rendered lifeless. With the taking away of Bhargava from us, our courage, valour, achievement, fame, strength, splendour and exploit have been simultaneously taken away. Hence do not waste time. Fight with the enemy. After killing these along with the gods including Indra, I shall obtain the release of Bhargava. Bhargava too is a Lordly Yogin. If he himself comes out of Siva's body, the rest of us are saved.

The Danavas said: —

If we are destined to live, the Pramathas cannot overwhelm us. If it is otherwise what avails running from the battle ground leaving our master behind. Those who leave their masters and run away professing to be honoured and desiring to be rich will surely fall into hell.

Sanatkumara said: —

After saying these words and deciding in accordance with them, those Daityas and Danavas pounded the Pramathas in the battle. They sounded the war-drums. There was a great noise everywhere.

There was great tumult caused by the war drums, trumpets, the trumpeting sounds of elephants and the neighing sounds of the horses. The vast space between heaven and earth was filled with loud reports causing horripilations to the courageous as well as the cowardly.

Oh sage, the heroic Nandin and other Pramathas slew all Asuras and won the victory. On seeing his army being shattered here and there Andhaka rushed at the Ganas driving in his chariot. Glancing at the in-coming or out-going Pramathas, far off or at close quarters, Andhaka hit them severally with as many arrows as the hair on their bodies.

On seeing the army shattered and smashed by the powerful Andhaka, Skanda, Vinayaka, Nandin, Somanandin and other heroic and powerful Pramathas, Siva's personal Ganas became furious and fought in diverse ways.

By Vinayaka, Skanda, Nandin, Somanandin, Viraka, Naigameya, the powerful Vaisakha and other terrible Ganas, Andhaka was rendered blind as they showered tridents, spears and arrows incessantly.

Then a great tumult arose in the midst of the armies of Pramathas and Asuras. At that great noise, Bhargava who was within the belly of Siva began to wander seeking an outlet. In Siva's body he observed seven worlds including Patala. He saw the diverse worlds of Brahma, Visnu, Indra, Aditya and celestial damsels as well as the battle between the Pramathas and Asuras.

Wandering round and round in the belly of Siva for a hundred years, he failed to see any outlet as a wicked person fails to see a vulnerable point in a good person.

Taking recourse to the Yoga of Siva he repeated the following mantra and assumed the form of Siva's semen. He thus emerged out of the belly of Siva through his penis. Thereafter he bowed to Siva and was accepted as a son by Parvati. He was made a Lord of the Ganas. On seeing Bhargava come out of the path of the semen, Lord Siva, the storehouse of mercy, laughed and said.

Lord Siva said: —

Oh son of Bhrgu, since you came out of my penis in the form of the semen you will be called Sukra henceforth. I accept you as my son. You may go if you please.

Sanatkumara said: —

Sukra then bowed to Siva and eulogised him. After eulogising Siva, Sukra took leave of Siva and entered the army of the Danavas as the moon does the cluster of clouds.

Suukra Learns Mritasanjivani Lore

Sanatkumara said: —

Oh Vyasa, listen how the lore of warding off death was gained by the sage Bhargava from Siva.

At first, Bhargava went to the city of Varanasi and performed penance for a long time meditating on Lord Visvesvara. There itself he fixed a phallic emblem of Siva, the great Atman. Assiduously he performed the ablutions of the Lord of the gods for a hundred thousand times. He eulogised Siva with various hymns and repeated a thousand names. He sang songs of Siva's glory. He danced and made offerings. Sukra worshipped Lord Siva in various ways for five thousand years.

When he did not see the Lord, he took up more unbearable and terrible observances and restraints. He drank the smoke of powdered husks or bits of grains or balls of iron-ash for a thousand years.

On seeing him performing the terrible penance thus by keeping the mind steady, Lord Siva was delighted. Coming out of the phallic image, Lord Siva appeared before him with a brighter refulgence than that of a thousand suns.

Lord Siva said: —

Oh great sage, Oh son of Bhrigu, Oh fortunate saint, by your perpetual penance I have been delighted. Choose anything that you wish as your boon. I shall lovingly bestow on you all your desires. There is nothing that cannot be granted to you.

Sanatkumara said: —

On hearing this, Bhargava was delighted and emotional. He offered his obeisance and eulogised Siva in his eight-forms. Eulogising the eight formed Siva by reciting the eight verses, Bhargava touched the ground with his head and bowed again and again. When he was eulogised by Bhargava, the great god stood up and lifted the brahmin from the ground where he was bowing to him. Holding him up, the Lord spoke in a rumbling voice like that of the cloud but gentle in effect.

The great Lord said: —

Oh excellent brahmin, Oh Bhargava, you are my faithful devotee. By your severe penance in this life, by the merit of installing my phallic image, and the adoration of it, I see you as my other two sons. There is nothing which cannot be given to you. With this body you shall enter the cavity of my belly and you will be born as my son through my excellent organ—the penis.

I am giving you now the boon inaccessible to even my attendants and which I have kept away even from Visnu and Brahma.

Oh pure one, I am giving unto you the lore in the form of Mantra, which is called Mrtasanjivani. It is pure and it has been formulated by me alone through the power of the penance. You have the capacity to receive that lore.

Whoever he may be, if you were to repeat this mantra in respect of anyone, he will truly return to life. This lore is the most excellent one. If any man or woman were to proceed on a journey in your direction, their work will perish by your glance. Your devotees will be prolific in progeny and profuse in the production of semen. The phallic image installed by you is called Sukresa.

Sanatkumara said: —

After granting him boons, the Lord vanished in the phallic image. The delighted Bhargava too returned to his abode.

The Story of Usa

Vyasa said: —

Oh omniscient one, I wish to know more of the story of the moon-crested Lord wherein he gave the Asura Bana the position of the chieftain of his Ganas.

Sanatkumara narrated: —

Oh Vyasa, here is the good story of Siva, the great Lord. Here too is the story of Siva's fight with Krisna when the former blessed Bana.

Marici, the sage of great intellect, was the mentally created eldest son of Brahma. He was a Prajapati too. His son Kasyapa was a noble soul. He was the most excellent of all sages. He made the creation flourish well. He was devoted to his father and to Brahma.

Oh Vyasa, thirteen daughters of Daksa were his wives. They were of good conduct and very faithful to their husband, the sage Kasyapa. The eldest of the wives was Diti. The Daityas were her sons. The eldest Diti had the heroic sons Hiranyakasipu the elder and Hiranyaksa the younger.

Hiranyakasipu had four sons. They were in order of Hrada, Anuhrada, Samhrada and Prahlada. Prahlada was a great devotee of Visnu. He had full control of his sense-organs. The Daityas were unable to destroy him. His son Virocana was the most excellent of donors. He even gave his head to Indra who requested for the same in the guise of a brahmin. His son was Bali who was a favourite of Siva and a liberal donor. The earth was given by him to Visnu who assumed the form of a dwarf. His son Bana became a devotee of Siva. He was highly respected and intelligent. He was truthful and a liberal donor making thousands of charitable gifts.

Staying in the Sonita town, he ruled over the three worlds after defeating several rulers forcefully. As a result of the grace of Siva, the gods became the virtual servants of Bana, the devotee of Siva.

They were distressed by his enmity although he practised high virtues. In accompaniment of the instrumental music played by his thousand arms, by means of the Tandava dance he propitiated Siva.

Siva was highly delighted and satisfied by his dance and he glanced at him with sympathetic eyes. The Lord of the worlds asked the great demon, the son of Bali, to choose a boon he liked.

The Asura Bana said: —

Oh great god, Lord of the gods, if you are pleased with me, be my guardian forever. Be present with me as the Lord of my city along with your sons and Ganas. Oh Lord, be delightful to me in every respect.

Sanatkumara said: —

Bana son of Bali, deluded by Siva's deception, did not request anything else from Lord Siva. He granted boons to him and stayed there lovingly along with his sons and his Ganas.

Once Siva performed divine sports in Sonita, the beautiful city of Bana, in the company of the gods and Asuras, on the banks of a river. The Gandharvas and the celestial damsels danced and laughed. The sages performed Japas, bowed to, worshipped and eulogised him. Then being glanced at by Kama who was not vanquished, the crescent-crested Lord Siva spoke to Nandin.

Siva said: —

Go quickly from this forest and tell Parvati everything and bring her here from Kailasa after she has bedecked herself.

Sanatkumara said: —

He quickly rushed to Kailasa to bring Parvati.

Nandisvara said: —

Oh goddess, the great Lord of the gods wishes to see you, his beloved, well-dressed. It is at his bidding that I say this.

Sanatkumara said: —

Oh excellent sage, then Parvati began to bedeck herself ardently.

Parvati said: —

I am coming. You return and so inform the Lord at my bidding.

Sanatkumara said: —

Then Nandin approached Siva with the velocity of mind. Siva, who was extremely agitated, told Nandin again, 'Dear, go again and fetch Parvati from there.'

He went to Parvati of sweet appearance and said, 'Your Lord wishes to see you beautifully and gorgeously dressed. Oh goddess Siva is eagerly waiting for various sports. Please go since the Lord is distressed with passion.'

In the meantime all the celestial damsels started to hold a challenge. They said that since Parvati isn't here, we shall assume the form of Parvati and try to woo Siva. Let us see if Siva can tell us apart. If any lady is able to touch Siva, let her go there unhesitatingly and fascinate him.

The daughter of Kumbhanda Citralekha said— 'I desire to attract Siva in the form of Parvati, just as Visnu assumed the form of Mohini.'

On seeing the change of form of Urvasi, Ghrtaci adopted the form of Kali and Visvaci that of Candika. Rambha assumed the form of Savitri, Menaka that of Gayatri; Sahajanya that of Jaya and Punjikasthali that of Vijaya.

On seeing their forms, the daughter of Kumbhanda, taking recourse to the Vaisnava and her own Yoga, knew everything and emulated the same. Usa, daughter of the Asura Bana efficient in divine Yoga, assumed the wonderfully auspicious and divine form of Parvati. Her feet were of excellent lustre. They shone like the great red lotus. They had all the divine characteristics bestowing every desired object. Knowing that she wanted to indulge in love-sport with Siva, the omniscient and omnipresent Parvati spoke.

Parvati said: —

Oh friend Usa, chaste and honourable lady since you have adopted my form out of passion, so you will have the monthly course in the appropriate time in the Karttika month. On the twelfth day in the bright half of Vaisakha, you will undertake a fast. During the night, while you are asleep in the harem, a man will come there and enjoy you. He has been made your husband by the gods. You will sport with him. This is because you have been devoted to Visnu ever since childhood without sinking into lethargy. She then mumbled to herself.

Then the goddess Parvati bedecked herself zealously and went to Siva. She then sported with him. Oh sage, at the end of the dalliance Lord Siva vanished from the place accompanied by his wife, the Ganas and the gods.

The Story of Usa Continues...

Sanatkumara recalled: —

Formerly the Asura Bana had pleased Siva by performing the Tandava dance. By adverse fate he became haughty. On realising that Siva was delighted in mind, the Asura Bana spoke.

Bana said: —

Oh great god, I am very strong, thanks to your favour. A thousand hands have been given to me by you. They are only a burden to me, since except you I do not find any match to oppose me having an equal strength. What can I do with these thousand mountain-like hands without a fight? Please suggest a fight unto me wherein my hands may fall shattered by the weapons hurled by the enemy or cause him to fall in thousand pieces. Oh Lord Siva, please fulfil this desire of mine.

Sanatkumara said: —

Becoming furious on hearing that, Siva laughed boisterously and in a wonderful manner he became very angry.

Siva said: —

Fie upon you, Oh haughty base Daitya, such a talk as this does not behove the son of Bali and a devotee. Very soon, you will meet a terrible challenge to your bluff by fighting a great battle against a person equal to me in strength. The battle will be sudden. Therein your mountain-like hands will be cut off by weapons and missiles. They will fall off like reeds or stumps of plantain trees. Oh wicked soul, when this flagstaff of yours falls without being blown off by a gust of wind, you can decide within your mind that a terrible battle is at hand. Go to that terrible war accompanied by all your generals. Now return to your abode where Siva is present.

Sanatkumara said: —

After hearing that, Bana worshipped Siva with palms joined in reverence in the form of buds and bowed to Lord Siva. He then went to his abode. On being asked, the delighted Asura mentioned everything to Kumbhanda in the manner it had happened. The Asura Bana eagerly awaited the particular conjunction of circumstances.

Once, by chance he saw the flagstaff broken and fallen. On seeing it, he was delighted and he set out for war. He called together his entire army. He was accompanied by his eight lieutenants.

In the meantime, in the month of Vaisakha after her monthly course, the daughter of Bana had her auspicious bath and auspicious rites after worshipping Lord Siva. At night she lay asleep in the well-guarded harem. It was then that Kama entered the place with Lord Siva.

She was seized by Krsna's grandson sent by Parvati. She began to cry helplessly. He enjoyed her forcibly. Within a moment he was carried to Dvaraka by Parvati's attendants. Rubbed and squeezed thus, she got up crying. She mumbled various words to her female attendants. She even decided to give up her life.

Oh Vyasa, she was then reminded by her friend of the fault she had committed previously. She then came to realise the entire incident that had occurred formerly. Oh sage, Usa, daughter of Bana, spoke sweetly to Citralekha, daughter of Kumbhanda.

Usa asked: —

Dear friend, if he is the person ordained as my husband by Parvati, how can I obtain him duly? In what family is he born who has fascinated my mind thus?

Citralekha said: —

Oh gentle lady, how shall I bring that man who was seen by you in the dream and whom I do not know?

Sanatkumara said: —

Thus said by her, the daughter of the Daitya, blinded by passion, was ready to end her life. She was saved by her friend on the first day.

Oh excellent sage, Citralekha, of great intellect spoke to Usa the daughter of Bana.

Citralekha said: —

I can dispel your grief if such a man could be anywhere in the three worlds. I shall bring him who has captivated your mind. Please mention the details of his features

Sanatkumara said: —

After saying this, she painted all the gods on a canvas together with the Daityas, Danavas, Gandharvas, Siddhas, Nagas, Yaksas and others. Similarly she painted all the excellent men. On seeing Aniruddha, the son of Pradyumna painted, she became bashful. Usa's heart was filled with delight. She stood with a downcast face.

Usa said: —

Oh this is the thief who has stolen my heart. This is the man whom I secured in the night. By his very contact I became fascinated. I wish to know more about him.

Sanatkumara said: —

On being thus asked by her, the lady, expert in yogic practice, mentioned the name of the family. Oh excellent sage, on hearing about his family, the eager and passionate daughter of Bana said.

Usa said: —

Oh my friend, ascertain some means lovingly so that I shall regain my beloved husband in a trice. Without him, my friend, I am not at all eager to live even for a moment. Please bring him here strenuously.

Sanatkumara said: —

On being thus requested by the daughter of Bana, Citralekha took her friend's leave and went to Dvaraka. After searching a little, she finally saw him. In the park of the harem the son of Pradyumna was seen by her playing with women and drinking wine. He was dark complexioned but beautiful in every limb, smiling and in the prime of youth. When he lay on the cot, she encompassed him with the shroud of darkness by employing her Tamasa Yoga. Thereafter she carried the cot on her head and within a moment reached the city of Sonita where the daughter of Bana eagerly awaited her.

Passionate that she was, she made various mad pranks displaying her emotions. On seeing that he was actually brought, she became frightened too. When they began their sexual dalliance in that fresh contact in the well-guarded harem, it became known to all in a moment.

The man with a divine body who carried on illegitimate affairs with a virgin was found out by the persons appointed at the doorway to the harem with cane sticks in their old hands. They understood that he was a young man, very comely in features, daring and fond of battle. On seeing him, the heroic men who guarded the harem went and told Bana, son of Bali, everything.

The gatekeepers said: —

Oh Lord, no one knows how this was done. Indra has entered your harem in secret and forcibly. He has outraged the modesty of your daughter by seizing her himself. Oh Lord, do whatever is proper. We are not at fault.

Sanatkumara said: —

Oh excellent sage, on hearing of the defilement of his daughter, the Lord of Danavas of great strength, became surprised.

The Dalliance of Usa and Aniruddha

Sanatkumara said: —

The infuriated Asura Bana went there and saw Aniruddha. The infuriated Bana, very efficient in war, was a bit surprised on seeing him and wondered why he had done like that and therefore said mockingly.

Bana said: —

Oh this man is really handsome, bold and daring. Who can this unfortunate deluded person be? His death is imminent. Oh angry ones, with terrible weapons, immediately kill the fellow who has outraged the traditional purity of my family and defiled my dear daughter. Oh heroic ones, bind the terrible fellow of evil conduct. Put him in a frightful prison for a long time.

Sanatkumara said: —

Commanded by him those heroic terrible fellows encircled the harem and tried to carry out the wishes of their Lord.

On seeing the army of the enemy, Aniruddha roared. He seized the big iron club from the harem-gate and came out of the apartment like the god of death armed with thunderbolt. With that iron club he killed the servants and returned to the harem. He killed ten thousand men.

When another hundred thousand soldiers had been killed, the Asura Bana furiously entered the fray taking with him Kumbhanda, expert in war. He then challenged Aniruddha for a duel in the course of that war.

Aniruddha then seized a spear blazing like the fire of death. Bana was hit with the spear even as he was seated in a chariot. In a trice the heroic demon vanished along with his horse. When he vanished, Aniruddha stood steady like a mountain observing all the quarters.

Remaining invisible, Danava Bana, practising deceptive fighting, hit him again and again with thousands of weapons. Then he bound him with serpent nooses. After binding him and putting him in a cage he stopped the battle. The infuriated Bana then spoke to the very powerful son of the charioteer.

The Asura Bana said: —

Oh son of the charioteer, cut off the head of this wicked fellow who has defiled my family. After chopping off the limbs, give them to the Raksasas. Or let the beasts of prey swallow his flesh and blood. Or kill this sinner and put him in a grassy well.

Sanatkumara said: —

On hearing his words, the Asura Kumbhanda, the most excellent of the ministers and righteous in thought, spoke to Bana.

Kumbhanda said: —

Oh Lord, this is not a proper thing to do. Please consider. I think by killing him we will be killing ourselves. Oh Lord, he seems to be equal to Visnu in exploits. His strength has been increased by the brilliance of the moon-crested Lord, your favourite.

Sanatkumara said: —

Then Kumbhanda spoke to Aniruddha.

Oh hero, who are you? Whose son are you? Tell us the truth. Oh meanest of men, of evil conduct, by whom have you been brought here? If you plead guilty and ask for forgiveness your life may be spared, Kumbadnda said.

Oh friend of the basest of Daityas, Oh demon of evil conduct, you do not know the laws of adversaries. I will not run away or plead for my life. A person who does so on a battlefield deserves worse than death. For a Ksatriya, death while fighting face to face with the enemy is commendable rather than joining the palms in reverence to have his life saved, Aniruddha said.

Sanatkumara said: —

These and many other heroic words he uttered. Hearing this, Bana was angry. Then a celestial voice was heard for the pacification of Bana which all the heroes, Aniruddha and the minister, stood listening to.

The celestial voice said: —

Oh Bana, you shall not be angry. Oh devotee of Siva, you are the son of Bali. Ponder over this. Siva, the Lord of all, the supreme Lord, is the witness of all activities. The Lord is omnipresent. Even a weak person becomes strong, thanks to his will. Oh intelligent one, realise this in your mind, be normal and complacent. If you do not do so, he will destroy your arrogance.

Sanatkumara said: —

Oh great sage, having spoken thus, the celestial voice stopped. On hearing these words the Asura Bana did not kill Aniruddha. Then he went to his harem and drank excellent beverages. His intellect was adversely affected, he forgot those words and began to sport. Aniruddha was bound by serpentine bodies emitting poison powerfully. His passion for his beloved had not been satiated fully. He remembered Durga then.

Aniruddha said: —

Oh goddess, you are worthy of being resorted to. I have been bound by serpents. Oh goddess, come and save me. Oh Siva, save me.

Sanatkumara said: —

Propitiated by him, Kali arrived there in the dark night of the fourteenth day in the dark half of the month Jyestha. With the heavy blows of her fists she broke the cage. She reduced the serpentine arrows to ashes. She released Aniruddha and let him enter the harem and then vanished from the scene. Oh great sage, thus, thanks to the grace of the goddess, Aniruddha got rid of the difficulty. Securing success by means of Siva's energy, Aniruddha gained access to his beloved, the daughter of Bana and rejoiced. In the company of his beloved, he carried on dalliance and was happy drinking the beverages till his eyes became red.

The Fight Among Bana, Siva, Krsna and Others

Vyasa said: —

Oh excellent sage, when Aniruddha the grandson of Krsna was abducted by the daughter of Kumbhanda what did Krsna do? Please narrate it to me.

Sanatkumara said: —

Oh excellent sage, on hearing the woeful cries of his women when Aniruddha had gone off suddenly, Krsna too became vexed. On hearing from Narada about the imprisonment and activities of Aniruddha the followers of Krsna, became dejected. On hearing everything, Krsna immediately called Garuda and went to the city of Sonita eagerly for fighting. They destroyed everything they saw.

On seeing the parks, fortresses, ceilings and minarets of the city thus broken, Bana became infuriated and set forth with an equal number of armies. In order to help Bana, Lord Rudra accompanied by his son and the Pramathas rode on the bull Nandin and arrived there to fight.

The fight was between Krsna and Siva; Pradyumna and Karttikeya; Kumbhandaka and Kupakarna, Bala and Sarhyuga.

Krsna, his brother Rama and the intelligent Pradyumna, fought an unequalled fight with the Pramathas. Krsna routed the Bhutas, Pramathas and Guhyakas, the followers of Siva with sharp-pointed arrows discharged from his bow. The heroes Pradyumna and others jubilant over the war destroyed the armies of the enemies and fought terribly.

On seeing his army being scattered, Siva became highly infuriated and roared terribly. On hearing that, Siva's Ganas too shouted and fought. They suppressed the opponents with their strength increased by Siva's brilliance.

Defeated by the opponents, the army of Krsna fled. It could not face the full refulgence of Siva. Oh sage, when his army was routed, Lord Krsna discharged a terrible fever missile named 'cold'. Oh sage, when the army of Krsna was routed, the cold fever missile of Krsna rushed at Rudra blazing the ten quarters. On seeing that coming, Lord Siva discharged his own fever missile. The two fever missiles fought each other. Oppressed by the fever missile of Lord Siva, the fever missile of Siva cried aloud. Then delighted Lord Siva, eulogised by Visnu's fever missile, spoke to the cold fever missile of Visnu.

Lord Siva said: —

Oh cold fever, I am delighted. Leave off your fear from my fever. There is no fear from fever to him who remembers this anecdote.

Sanatkumara said: —

Thus advised, the fever missile of Visnu went away after bowing to Siva. On seeing that activity, Krsna was surprised and dismayed.

Garuda, took up a thousand bodies and drank up the water from the great sea. He then began to wreak havoc by showering the sea-waters through Avarta clouds. Then the infuriated bull, the powerful vehicle of Lord Siva, hit him with great force by means of his horns. When his limbs were shattered by the blows of his horns, Garuda was dismayed. He forsook Visnu and fled from the battle ground immediately.

When the situation was like this, Lord Krsna, dismayed by Siva's refulgence, spoke to the charioteer suddenly.

Lord Krsna said: —

Oh charioteer, listen to my words. Drive the chariot immediately to Lord Siva so that I shall speak to him.

Sanatkumara said: —

Thus commanded by Visnu, the charioteer Daruka, drove the chariot immediately to Lord Siva.

Lord Krsna said: —

Oh Lord Siva, it is at your bidding that I have come here to cut off the hands of Bana. This haughty Bana was cursed by you who are the destroyer of haughtiness. Oh Lord, please return from the battle-ground. Let not your curse go in vain. Oh Lord, command me to cut off the hands of Bana.

Lord Siva said: —

Oh dear, what you say is true; the Lord of the Daityas has been cursed by me. It is at my bidding that you have come here to cut off the hands of Bana. But how can there be the chopping of Bana's arms while I am watching? Hence my bidding, make me numb by means of your missile. Thereafter you can do as you please and be happy.

Sanatkumara said: —

Oh great sage, thus urged by Siva, Lord Krsna fixed the missile to the bow and discharged it at Siva. After enchanting Siva, and making him numb, Visnu slew the army of Bana by means of swords, daggers and clubs.

The Chopping of Bana's Arms and His Humiliation

Vyasa said: —

Oh dear sage, now tell me what happened then?

Sanatkumara said: —

Oh Vyasa of great intellect, listen. When Siva became numb, Bana came to fight Krna. On seeing his army destroyed, the Lord of the Daityas became infuriated. The powerful son of Bali fought an incomparable battle. Drawing the string of his bow to the ear, the infuriated Visnu discharged sharp arrows on Bana. On seeing the arrows coming, Bana split them even before they reached him, by means of arrows discharged from his bow.

Thus the tumultuous fight between the two strong armies went on for a long time aggravating the wonder of the spectators.

Bana then discharged an unlimited number of arrows on Garuda, Krsna and Yadus separately. He hit Garuda with an arrow, Krsna with another, Bala with a third. The powerful hero hit others too. Then Krsna became angry and roared in the course of the battle. Thinking upon Siva he hit Bana and his terrible army simultaneously with the good arrows discharged with force from his bow.

A great battle went on for a long time between Krsna and that strong Asura who was the most excellent devotee of Siva. Oh great sage, the powerful Krsna fought for a long time with Bana. Deriving strength at the instance of Siva he became furious.

At the bidding of Siva, Lord Krsna, the destroyer of heroic enemies, chopped off several arms of Bana by means of Sudarsana. Only his four beautiful arms were left. Thanks to the grace of Siva, the demon too was freed from pain. Forgetting himself, Krsna, who assumed great prowess, attempted to cut off the head of Bana. Then Siva got up.

Siva said: —

Oh Lord, son of Devaki, what was ordained by me formerly has been accomplished by you who always follow my dictates. Do not cut off the head of Bana. Withdraw your weapon Sudarsana. At my bidding the discus shall always be rendered ineffective with regard to my people. Hence you withdraw from the battleground.

You are a great Yogin, the supreme soul and the exciter of men. Hence you ponder over this yourself. You are engaged in the welfare of all living beings. I have granted him a boon that he will not fear death. These words of mine shall remain true for ever. I am pleased with you.

Oh Visnu, sometime back he became haughty enough to say 'Give me battle' while he scratched his arms and forgot his goal. Then I cursed him that he will have his arms cut off. Oh Bana, at my bidding Visnu has cut off your arms. Now withdraw from the battlefield. Go back to your abode along with the married couple.

Sanatkumara said: —

Saying this and uniting them in friendship, Lord Siva returned to his abode along with his sons and Ganas. Krishna and Bana also withdrew. Everything was happy again.

Bana Attains the Position of Siva's Gana

Sanatkumara said: —

When Krsna left for Dvaraka with Aniruddha and his wife, Bana was distressed thinking of his previous ignorance. Then Nandin spoke to the grief stricken Bana whose limbs were smeared with blood and who repented repeatedly.

Nandisvara said: —

Oh Bana, devotee of Siva, do not repent. Siva is compassionate towards his devotees. Whatever has happened, has happened at his will. Consider this and remember Siva again and again. Fixing your mind in the primordial being, you celebrate his festival again and again.

Sanatkumara said: —

At the suggestion of Nandin, Bana immediately went to Siva's temple with a lofty mind and great courage. After going there he bowed to the Lord and lamented in great agitation. He eulogised him with various hymns. He shed his sweat and blood to propitiate Siva. He danced continuously. Then Siva appeared to him.

Siva said: —

Dear Bana, son of Bali, I am delighted by your dance. You choose the boon whatever is in your mind.

Sanatkumdra said: —

Oh sage, Bana asked for the healing of wounds, the skill in duels, everlasting position of Ganahood, the kingship for Usa's son at the city of Sonita, absence of enmity with the gods and Visnu in particular. He asked for absence of rebirth as a Daitya, special devotion to Siva without any aberration forever, friendship with the devotees of Siva and kindness to all living beings. Then he eulogised Siva.

Siva said: —

You will get everything.

Sanatkumara said: —

Then Lord Siva vanished. Through the grace of Siva, Bana attained the immortality of eternal time and becoming one of the attendants of Siva he rejoiced much.

Gajasura is Slain

Sanatkumara said: —

Oh Vyasa, listen to the story of how Siva killed Gajasura, the Lord of Danavas, by means of his trident.

Formerly when the Asura Mahisa was killed in battle by the goddess for the welfare of the gods, they became very happy. Oh great sage, his son the great hero Gajasura could not forget the slaying of his father by the goddess. He therefore went to the forest to undertake penance. Interestingly he performed penance meditating on Brahma. 'I shall not be killed by men or women overwhelmed by lust.' Thinking thus in his mind he directed his attention to austerities. He performed a severe penance in a valley on the Himalaya mountain.

Due to his penance, a fire originated from his head and scorched the three worlds. The gods scorched by the fire went to Brahma along with Indra and submitted to him.

The gods said: —

Oh Brahma, we are agitated on being scorched by the penance of Gajasura. We are unable to stay in heaven. Hence we seek refuge in you.

Sanatkumara said: —

Being thus requested, he went to Gajasura.

Brahma said: —

Oh Lord of Daityas, stand up, you have achieved perfection in penance. Oh dear one I have come to grant you a boon. Choose your boon as you wish.

Gajasura said: —

Oh Lord, if you are going to grant me a boon, let me be immune from death by men or women overwhelmed by lust. Let me be very powerful, valorous and invincible to the gods, the guardians of the worlds forever. Let me enjoy all prosperities.

Sanatkumara said: —

Thus requested by the Danava, Brahma granted him the rare boon. Securing the boon, Gajasura the son of Mahisa, returned to his abode with a happy mind. The great Asura conquered all the quarters and the three worlds. He made everyone subservient to him. He became the conqueror of the universe. He usurped the places of the guardians of the worlds and took away their glory. He sported in the palace of Lord Indra. He exercised a stern and fierce authority. The Danava, the son of Mahisasura harassed the excellent brahmins and the sages on the earth very much. Then Gajasura came to the capital city of Siva.

Oh sage, when the Lord of Asuras came there, there was a great tumult among the residents of Anandavana. When he arrived in the city, Indra and the other gods sought refuge in Siva. They eulogised him and mentioned everything.

The gods said: —

Oh great gods, the Asura has gone to your city. He is inflicting pain on your people. Oh storehouse of benignity, please slay him. Whichever quarter he approaches, the Danava is unbearably oppressive. 'I am not to be killed by men or women overwhelmed by lust', he shouts. Oh Lord of the gods, we have thus mentioned humbly the activities of that Danava. Please protect your devotees.

Sanatkumara said: —

Thus requested by the gods, Siva came there quickly with the desire of slaying him. On seeing that Siva had come roaring with the trident in his hand, Gajasura too roared. A wonderfully terrible and great battle was fought between them roaring heroically and hitting with various weapons and missiles. The brilliant Gajasura of great strength and valour pierced Siva, the slayer of the Danavas, with sharp arrows. Siva who assumed a terrible body, split with his terrible arrows, the arrows of the Daitya to small pieces like gingelly seeds, even before they reached him. Then, as Gajasura was charging towards him, Siva hit him with his trident. When the trident hit him, he was raised up like an umbrella. He then sang the glory of Siva.

Gajasura said: —

Oh great Lord, I am in every respect your devotee. Oh trident-bearing Lord, I know you as the Lord of heaven and destroyer of Kama. I desire to submit something, please listen to it. You are the only person deserving the worship of the worlds. You stand high above the universe. Everyone should consider a death like this which is conducive to glory in due course.

Lord Siva said: —

Oh Gajasura, Oh excellent Danava, I am delighted. Choose the boon favourable to you.

Gajasura said: —

Oh nude one, if you are delighted, wear this hide of mine sanctified by the fire of your trident. It is of your size, it is gentle to the touch, it has been kept as a stake in the battlefield, it is of divine nature and it is always pleasing. Let it ever emit an agreeable smell, let it be soft forever, let it be ever free from dirt, let it be your best ornament always. It shall not burn or shred to pieces. Oh nude one, if my hide is not meritorious how did it get into contact with your limbs in the battlefield? Oh Siva, if you are satisfied, please grant me another boon. Beginning from today, let your name be Krttivasas (one clad in elephant-hide).

Sanatkumara said: —

On hearing his words, Siva was pleased and replied to Gajasura, 'Let it be so'.

Lord Siva said: —

In this holy place, a means to the achievement of liberation, let your meritorious body become a phallic image yielding liberation to all. It will be the foremost of all phallic images yielding salvation, destroying great sins and named Krttivasesvara.

Sanatkumara said: —

After saying this Siva accepted the hide of Gajasura and wore it. When Gajasura, the Lord of the Danavas was killed, the gods returned to their original place and the universe attained normalcy.

Dundubhi Nirhrada is Slain

Sanatkumara said: —

Oh Vyasa, listen. I shall narrate the story of the moon-crested Lord Siva how he slew the Daitya Dundubhi Nirhrada.

When the Daitya Hiranyaksa, son of Diti, of great strength was killed by Visnu, Diti remained grief stricken for a long time. The wicked Daitya named Dundubhi Nirhrada, the uncle of Prahlada, the oppressor of the gods, consoled the dejected mother with the words.

After consoling Diti, the king of Daityas, an expert in using Maya began to think of the ways and means of conquering the gods easily. Thinking deeply in diverse ways the Daitya came to the conclusion that the brahmanas were the cause of the trouble.

The Daitya Dundubhi Nirhrada, the most wicked enemy of the gods, ran after the brahmins to kill them.

Dundubhi Nirhrada thought: —

Certainly the gods, including Indra, are supported by the brahmanas. The gods gain their strength from the brahmanas. If the brahmanas are destroyed the Vedas and the gods will perish. If the sacrifices are destroyed, the gods will lose their food. They will grow weaker and be easily conquered. I shall then confiscate the everlasting riches of the gods.

Where are these brahmanas in abundance? It is Varanasi indeed that is the place of many brahmanas. I shall finish that first and then go to other holy centres. Wherever these brahmanas live they shall be devoured by me.

Sanatkumara said: —

After thinking thus in accordance with the nature of his race, he went to Kasi and killed the brahmanas. When the excellent brahmanas went to the forest to fetch sacrificial twigs and the Darbha grass, the wicked Danava used to eat them there.

After that he used to lie hidden so that nobody could detect him. He was invisible in form. He wielded the art of deception. He could not be seen even by the gods. During the day he stood in the midst of sages engaged in meditation but observing the ingress and egress of people. But at night he took the form of a tiger and ate many of them. He used to eat unhesitatingly, never leaving a bone behind.

Once on the Shivaratri day, a certain devotee performed the worship of Siva and was engaged in meditation in his own hut. The Lord of Daityas Dundubhi assumed the form of a tiger and wanted to seize him. As the devotee was in meditation with a mind concentrated on Siva, the Daitya could not attack him.

Siva, the omnipresent Lord, knew his evil intention and decided to slay the Daitya. While the Daitya in the form of the tiger was about to snatch the devotee, Siva appeared before him. On seeing Siva coming out of the phallic image worshipped by the devotee, the Daitya in the form of a tiger increased in size.

The Danava glanced with a contemptuous look at Siva but the Lord caught him and pressed him under his armpit. The five-faced Lord hit the tiger on its head with his fist harder than thunderbolt. By the blow of the fist and the pressure at the armpit the tiger groaned aloud in great distress filling heaven and earth with the sound and died.

Agitated in their minds by the loud sound, the ascetics came there in the night itself following the track of the sound. On seeing the Lord there with the Lord of the beasts in his armpit they bowed to him. They eulogised him with many words.

The brahmins said: —

We are saved, Oh we are saved from this terrible obstacle. Oh Lord, please bless us. Oh preceptor of the universe, stay here alone. Let this place remain sacred always. Save us the dwellers in this holy centre from other mishaps too. Oh Lord of Parvati, offer fearlessness to your devotees.

Lord Siva said: —

If any one sees me here in this form with faith, I will undoubtedly remove his torments and mishaps. After hearing this story of mine and after remembering my phallic image in their heart, if a man enters the battlefield he will certainly win.

Sanatkumara said: —

In the meantime the gods came there along with Indra shouting slogans of victory jubilantly. After bowing to Siva with love, the gods joined their palms in reverence and eulogised Lord Siva.

The gods said: —

Oh Lord Siva, Lord of the gods, remover of the distress of your devotees, be victorious. We the gods have been saved by killing this demon. Oh fond of devotees, you shall protect them always. Oh Lord of the gods, wicked men shall be slain by you.

Sanatkumara said: —

On hearing these words of the gods, Lord Siva became delighted. After saying 'Yes,' he merged into the phallic image. The gods, thus surprised, returned to their respective abodes and rejoiced. The brahmins too in great delight returned the way they came.

Vidala and Utpala are Slain

Sanatkumara said: —

Oh Vyasa, listen to the story of the great Lord and how he killed his beloved Daitya whom he indicated by a sign. Formerly there were two great Daityas—Vidala and Utpala. They were great heroes, puffed up by the boon from Brahma that they could not be slain by a man.

The gods had been defeated in the battle by the two Daityas who considered the people of the three worlds as insignificant. Defeated by them, the gods sought refuge in Brahma. After bowing to him duly they submitted to him respectfully.

On hearing their account Brahma said, 'They will surely be slain by the goddess. Be bold. Remember Siva and Parvati respectfully. The supreme god will bring about welfare.' After saying this, Brahma kept quiet remembering Siva. The gods too returned to their respective abodes rejoicingly.

Then at the behest of Siva, the celestial sage Narada went to the abode of the Daityas and sang the glory of the beauty of Parvati. On hearing his words, the two Daityas were deluded by deception. Afflicted by the god of lust they desired to abduct the goddess. They thought to themselves where and when they would obtain Parvati.

Once Siva was engaged in sports. Parvati too was playing with a ball along with her friends in the presence of Siva. At times she looked up. At times she displayed the lightness of limbs. At times when she took deep breaths, bees hovered round her enticed by the fragrance. At times the bees made her eyes agitated. The lustre of her body spread all round through the partings of her gown. As the goddess mother of the universe was playing, she was seen by the Daityas who were going by the aerial path.

Desirous of abducting the goddess as they were tormented by the god of lust, they descended from the sky quickly after adapting the Sambari magic skill. The two wicked ones of fickle minds approached Parvati in the guise of Siva's attendants.

By the excessive tremulousness of their eyes they were recognized by Siva. The Lord shot a significant glance at Parvati, denoting that they were Daityas and not Ganas. They could assume any form.

Oh dear, she understood the sign of the eyes of her Lord Siva. Realising the significant glance, the goddess, hit both of them simultaneously with the ball. The powerful wicked Daityas, hit by the ball, whirled and whirled and fell on the ground.

After making the two Daityas fall like two ripe fruits from a tree. As they had attempted to do an evil action, the ball changed itself into the phallic image. That phallic image came to be known as Kandukesvara.

At the same time, Visnu, Brahma, other gods and the sages came there. Then all the gods received boons from Siva and at his bidding returned to their respective abodes delightedly. So were the residents of Kasi blessed with the boons.

On seeing Siva with Parvati, they bowed to him and eulogised him with devotion. Then Siva and Parvati too, went delightedly to their abode.

Brahma said: —

After narrating the story of the moon-crested Lord, Sanatkumara took leave of Vyasa. Thus the section called 'Yuddha' has been narrated to you, Oh excellent sage. Thus the whole of Rudrasamhita has been explained by me.